*The Economics of Cult*

CU00395140

Cultural policy is changing. Traditionally, cultural policies have been concerned with providing financial support for the arts, for cultural heritage and for institutions such as museums and galleries. In recent years, around the world, interest has grown in the creative industries as a source of innovation and economic dynamism. This book argues that an understanding of the nature of both the economic value and the cultural value created by the cultural sector is essential to good policy-making. The book is the first comprehensive account of the application of economic theory and analysis to the broad field of cultural policy. It deals with general principles of policy-making in the cultural arena as seen from an economic point of view, and goes on to examine a range of specific cultural policy areas, including the arts, heritage, the cultural industries, urban development, tourism, education, trade, cultural diversity, economic development, intellectual property and cultural statistics.

DAVID THROSBY is internationally known for his research and writing in the economics of art and culture. He is Professor of Economics at Macquarie University, Sydney, and has been a consultant to many government departments and private corporations, and to international agencies, including FAO, OECD, UNESCO, the World Bank, UNDP and UNCTAD. He is a member of the editorial boards of the *Journal of Cultural Economics*, the *International Journal of Cultural Policy*, *Poetics*, and the *Pacific Economic Bulletin*. He is a co-editor (with Victor Ginsburgh) of the *Handbook of the Economics of Art and Culture*.

# The Economics of Cultural Policy

DAVID THROSBY

CAMBRIDGE
UNIVERSITY PRESS

# CAMBRIDGE
## UNIVERSITY PRESS

University Printing House, Cambridge CB2 8BS, United Kingdom

One Liberty Plaza, 20th Floor, New York, NY 10006, USA

477 Williamstown Road, Port Melbourne, VIC 3207, Australia

314-321, 3rd Floor, Plot 3, Splendor Forum, Jasola District Centre, New Delhi-110025, India

79 Anson Road, #06-04/06, Singapore 079906

Cambridge University Press is part of the University of Cambridge.

It furthers the University's mission by disseminating knowledge in the pursuit of
education, learning and research at the highest international levels of excellence.

www.cambridge.org
Information on this title: www.cambridge.org/9780521687843

© David Throsby 2010

This publication is in copyright. Subject to statutory exception
and to the provisions of relevant collective licensing agreements,
no reproduction of any part may take place without the written
permission of Cambridge University Press.

First published 2010
4th printing 2015

*A catalogue record for this publication is available from the British Library*

*Library of Congress Cataloging in Publication data*
Throsby, C. D.
  The economics of cultural policy / David Throsby.
  p.  cm.
  Includes bibliographical references and index.
  ISBN 978-0-521-86825-9 – ISBN 978-0-521-68784-3 (pbk.)
  1. Cultural policy–Economic aspects.  2. Cultural industries.  I. Title.
  HM621.T57 2010
  306–dc22
  2010003264

ISBN  978-0-521-86825-9  Hardback
ISBN  978-0-521-68784-3  Paperback

Cambridge University Press has no responsibility for the persistence or
accuracy of URLs for external or third-party internet websites referred to in
this publication, and does not guarantee that any content on such websites is,
or will remain, accurate or appropriate.

# Contents

# *Preface*

Cultural policy is emerging as an increasingly significant component of government policy formation at both national and international levels. Aspects of cultural policy that currently figure in government policy agendas include: the prospects for the creative industries as dynamic sources of innovation, growth and structural change in the so-called new economy; the role of the arts and culture in employment creation and income generation in towns and cities, especially those affected by industrial decline; the appropriate means by which governments can support the creative and performing arts; legal and economic questions concerning the regulation of intellectual property in cultural goods and services; and the possibilities for public/private partnerships in the preservation of cultural heritage. At an international level, the problems of dealing with cultural goods and services in trade are becoming every day more prominent in various multilateral and bilateral trade negotiations, while at the same time the newly ratified United Nations (UN) convention on cultural diversity is having important implications for cultural policy in both the developed and developing world.

There is a growing scholarly interest in the field of cultural policy in several countries. As I point out in the concluding chapter to this book, much of this interest derives from the critical cultural studies tradition that is now strongly established in Europe, especially in the United Kingdom (UK). In addition there are several other streams in cultural policy studies that contribute at both a theoretical and an empirical level to the development of the field, including a significant amount of work dealing with issues in real-world policy administration. But in proportionate terms, relatively few of these studies derive from mainstream economic theory and analysis. Yet it can be argued that economics – standard macro- and micro-economics, public choice theory, institutional economics and other traditions within the discipline – has much to offer in an understanding of how the arts and culture are implicated in government policy formulation and implementation. Given that much public policy in the contemporary world – whether in education, health, social services, the environment or wherever – is being increasingly interpreted in economic terms, policy towards the arts and culture risks being marginalised and made irrelevant to the main game unless its relationships to economic policy-making can be understood and asserted.

Moreover there has been a distinct reorientation of cultural policy in its practical interpretation over the last few years. In the past, the cultural policies of governments at all levels and in many countries were focussed on the creative arts. In more recent times, the rise of the so-called creative economy and the growth of the cultural industries has shifted the policy emphasis towards the economic potential of the arts and culture sector. Rapid developments in information and communications technology have contributed significantly to this shift, as new means for the production, distribution and consumption of cultural goods and services come onstream. In these circumstances it is essential that policy analysis comprehends the economics of these trends – their causes, their consequences, and their transformative effect on traditional modes of cultural policy delivery.

The objective of this book is to fill a gap in the cultural policy literature by analysing the process of cultural policy-making from a broad economic perspective. There are both theoretical and practical aspects to this task. In the first place it is necessary to lay out the theoretical foundations on which an economic approach to the analysis of cultural policy is built. Thus throughout the book the relevant economic theory and analytical methods are described and discussed as a basis for consideration of particular policy applications. But in addition, at a practical level, it has to be shown how cultural policy takes shape in the many specific areas where it is applied – the arts, heritage, the cultural industries, regional development, copyright, international trade, etc. Thus the book has a dual readership in mind: firstly, policy analysts and researchers interested in an economic model of the cultural policy process that is theoretically sound and analytically workable, and, secondly, policy-makers themselves who are dealing with the everyday problems of managing the state's role in regard to the arts and culture in the contemporary market economy.

The book is not divided into sections, although the first three chapters as well as the concluding chapter stand somewhat apart from the rest in that they provide an overall overview of the state of contemporary cultural policy, and an account of how cultural policy can be interpreted as part of the broader processes of policy delivery by governments in the modern world. The bulk of the book (Chapters 4 to 14 inclusive) deals with the specific domains of policy concern one by one – the arts, the cultural industries, heritage, urban issues, tourism, international aspects, cultural diversity, education, development, intellectual property and cultural statistics.

In some respects this book is a sequel to my earlier work for Cambridge University Press, *Economics and Culture* (2001). The present volume carries forward some of the central ideas developed in that book. In particular, one of the main themes of *Economics and Culture* was to draw a distinction between economic and cultural value, and to argue that, although economics has much of importance to say about production, consumption and distribution in the arts and culture, a full understanding of the relationships between cultural and economic phenomena requires us to take a wider view. Hence the concept of cultural value was introduced as a necessary aspect of the value yielded in the production and consumption of cultural goods and services, alongside the sorts of value measurable with the tools of economic analysis. The same distinction is maintained in the present volume in the treatment of cultural policy. That is, I argue that an economic approach to cultural policy will necessarily account for both the economic and the cultural value involved in the policy processes being studied.

A number of people have contributed in various ways during the writing of this book. Like many researchers and writers, I owe a significant intellectual debt to my many colleagues and friends whose writings and whose discussions at seminars, conferences and workshops all around the world have helped to shape my ideas. As always I acknowledge the libraries in which I habitually work, which are both an indispensable source of materials and a haven for scholarly reflection; in particular, I am grateful for the facilities provided by the Macquarie University Library, the Fisher Library at the University of Sydney and the State Library of New South Wales. To the REACH gang in the Department of Economics at Macquarie University (Research in the Economics of Art, Culture and Heritage) I owe a great debt of gratitude for excellent research assistance at various times during the progress of this project – especially to Anita Zednik, Jan Zwar and Nick Vanderkooi. I also wish to express my special thanks to Laura Billington, whose editorial input and continuing commitment was an essential ingredient in bringing this book to completion. And finally thanks, as ever, to Robin.

David Throsby<br>
Sydney, June 2009

# Acknowledgments

Some parts of this book cover topics on which I have written in earlier papers. In several chapters I have adapted material from these earlier writings and I acknowledge with thanks the permission of the following publishers for the re-use, in edited or adapted form, of short extracts from the works listed: Il Mulino, for extracts from 'Change and challenge: two decades in the economics of art and culture', *Economia della Cultura* 4: 399–408 (2007); Korea Association for Cultural Economics, for extracts from 'Global convergence and the challenges to cultural policy', *Review of Cultural Economics*, 10(2): 3–14 (2007); Routledge/Taylor and Francis, for extracts from 'The concentric circles model of the cultural industries', *Cultural Trends*, 17(3): 147–164 (2008), and 'Modelling the cultural industries', *International Journal of Cultural Policy*, 14(3): 217–232 (2008); Springer Netherlands, for extracts from 'Determining the value of cultural goods: how much (or how little) does contingent valuation tell us?', *Journal of Cultural Economics*, 27(3–4): 275–285 (2003); Sage Publications Ltd, for extracts from 'Globalization and the cultural economy: a crisis of value?', in Helmut Anheier and Yudhishthir Raj Isar (eds.), *The Cultural Economy. Cultures and Globalization Series* Vol. II (2008); Palgrave-Macmillan, for extracts from 'Art, economics of', in Steven N. Durlauf and Lawrence E. Blume (eds.), *The New Palgrave Dictionary of Economics* (2008); Heldref Publications, for 'Assessing the impacts of a cultural industry', *Journal of Arts Management, Law & Society*, 34(3): 188–204 (2004); Elsevier/North-Holland and Ilde Rizzo, for extracts from 'Cultural heritage: economic analysis and public policy', in Victor Ginsburgh and David Throsby (eds.), *Handbook of the Economics of Art and Culture* (2006); the University of NSW Press, for extracts from 'The economics of the creative city: iconic architecture and the urban experience', in Robert Freestone, Bill Randolph and Caroline Butler-Bowdon (eds.), *Talking about Sydney: Population, Community and Culture in Contemporary Sydney* (2006); the Academy of the Social Sciences in Australia, for extracts from 'Creative Australia: the Arts and Culture in Australian Work and Leisure', Occasional Paper: Census Series Number 1 (2008); Ashgate Publishing Ltd, for extracts from 'Tourism, heritage and cultural sustainability: three golden rules', in Luigi Fusco Girard and Peter Nijkamp (eds.), *Cultural Tourism and Sustainable Local Development* (2009); the British Council, for extracts from 'Sweetness and light? Cultural diversity in the contemporary global economy', in Rosemary Bechler (ed.), *Counterpoint* (2004); Currency House, for extracts from 'Does Australia need a cultural policy?', *Platform Papers No. 7* (2006); and UNESCO, for extracts from the following documents: 'Vulnerability and Threat: Guidelines for the Implementation of Art. 8', and 'Culture in Sustainable Development: Guidelines for the Implementation of Art. 13' (comments on the Convention on the Protection and Promotion of the Diversity of Cultural Expressions) (2008); and 'The Evolution of Cultural Policy: Towards a New Cultural Policy Profile' (2009).

# Abbreviations

| | |
|---|---|
| ANZSIC | Australian and New Zealand Standard Industrial Classification |
| BBC | British Broadcasting Corporation |
| CBA | cost-benefit analysis |
| CPC | Central Product Classification |
| CVM | contingent valuation methodology |
| DCMS | Department for Culture, Media and Sport (UK) |
| FAO | Food and Agriculture Organisation of the United Nations |
| GATS | General Agreement on Trade in Services |
| GATT | General Agreement on Tariffs and Trade |
| GDP | gross domestic product |
| GNP | gross national product |
| IFPI | International Federation of Phonographic Industries |
| ISCO | International Standard Classification of Occupations |
| ISIC | International Standard Industrial Classification |
| MFN | Most Favoured Nation |
| NAICS | North American Industrial Classification System |
| NEA | National Endowment for the Arts (US) |
| NGO | non-governmental organisation |
| OHS | occupational health and safety |
| SNA | System of National Accounts |
| TRIPs | Trade Related Intellectual Property agreement |
| UIS | UNESCO Institute for Statistics |
| UNCTAD | United Nations Conference on Trade and Development |
| UNDP | United Nations Development Program |
| UNESCO | United Nations Educational, Scientific and Cultural Organisation |
| WCCD | World Commission on Culture and Development |
| WCED | World Commission on Environment and Development |
| WIPO | World Intellectual Property Organisation |

# 1 | *Introduction*

> Beginning is often the hardest part of all. Making those first
> marks on a blank canvas can be a daunting prospect, even for a
> professional painter.
> (Simon Jennings, *The New Artist's Manual: the Complete Guide
> to Painting and Drawing*, 2005[1])

## 1 The changing face of cultural policy

In 1967, UNESCO held a conference in Mexico City to discuss
cultural policy. One of the outcomes of this meeting was a series of
monographs produced over the course of the 1970s and early 1980s
in which member states of UNESCO, one by one, discussed what they
understood cultural policy to mean, and described the practice of cultural policy in their own country at that time. The resulting collection
of reports provides a fascinating insight into how government policy
towards culture was interpreted and implemented around the world
three or four decades ago.

Overwhelmingly the concern of cultural policy in those days was
with the creative arts – how they contribute to a civilised society, how
more people could be introduced to the benefits of artistic consumption, and how the arts content of education systems and the media
could be improved. The UK report, for example, discussed the Arts
Council of Great Britain, local authorities and the regional arts associations as the vehicles by which cultural policy was delivered; the BBC
and the press were mentioned, but only in terms of their contribution
to producing and reporting on the arts, not in a broader cultural context.[2] Policy towards heritage was also a significant component of the
cultural policy agenda for many countries, especially those in the developing world. The report for Bolivia was typical; it focussed on the post-
colonial assertion of Bolivian nationalism through its culture, especially
its intangible heritage of language, music, ritual and tradition.[3]

The UNESCO series of reports provides a vivid illustration of how greatly the landscape of cultural policy has changed in the intervening years. In particular, the 1970s cultural policy statements contained few if any references to the *economics* of culture, beyond an occasional reference to the administrative means for obtaining and deploying public funds for cultural purposes.[4] Now, in the opening years of the new millennium, economics is everywhere, and the ways in which cultural policy is interpreted and practised have been transformed. There are many factors that have contributed to this transformation, but they can be gathered together under two broad headings, one cultural, one economic.

Firstly, there has been an expansion in the scope of the term 'culture' in its application to cultural policy from a concern solely with the arts and heritage to a broader interpretation of culture as a way of life. Such an anthropological or sociological definition of culture as an expression of shared values and experiences is by no means new, even as a basis in principle for cultural policy, but putting the principle into practice is relatively recent, and indeed a widening of the ambit of cultural policy to encompass broader issues of social policy, for example, is still going on. Parallel with this has been a breaking down of the old equation of 'the arts' with 'high culture'; although pockets of resistance remain here and there, the distinction in pejorative terms between high and popular culture, or between and the high and popular arts, has now largely disappeared.[5] Instead cultural products and consumption practices are more commonly seen to lie along a spectrum, whose dimensions can be described using labels such as commercial/non-commercial, traditional/avant-garde, large-/small-scale, mass/specialised, majority/minority, and so on. So, as the usage of the term 'culture' has continued to expand beyond its high-art interpretation, the range of cultural activities of interest to policy has widened, and the coverage of cultural policy has extended from the arts and heritage to include policy towards film; the broadcast and print media; the wider cultural industries such as fashion, design and architecture; tourism; urban and regional development; international trade; diplomacy; and more.

The second major cause of the changes in cultural policy that we are witnessing at the present time is the radical transformation of the economic environment in which cultural goods are produced, distributed and consumed, brought about by what is loosely referred to as 'globalisation'. This term is widely used in the contemporary discourse to identify a series of related trends that can be observed in economic, social and geopolitical spheres. Essentially, globalisation can be defined as three phenomena: the breakdown of barriers to the movement of resources, especially capital and labour, between countries and regions; the emergence of a global marketplace for many commodities, with increased commercial opportunities for both national and transnational companies; and the internationalisation of communications, leading to, among other things, the free transmission of cultural symbols and messages around the world. There are both technological and economic causes underlying these phenomena; the digital revolution, the explosion in computational power available across a wide range of applications, the growth of the internet and the invention of new devices for communication and data transmission have together provided the technological impetus for globalisation, while its operations have been enabled by a widespread acceptance of neoliberal economic principles as the basis for national and international policy-making.

The effects of these trends on artists, creative workers, commercial and non-commercial firms producing and distributing cultural products, cultural agencies and institutions, and consumers, have been profound. To begin with, on the production side new communications technologies have fostered new forms of cultural expression and opened up new avenues for cultural exchange. At the cutting edge, artists working in new media are experimenting with innovative methods for making art and communicating it to consumers; these developments can be likened to R&D activities in industry, given that the eventual payoff (in both artistic and commercial terms) is uncertain but could be substantial. Manuel Castells has observed that this new technological environment can be described as cultural insofar as its dynamics are dependent on 'the culture of innovation, on the culture of risk, on the culture of expectations and, ultimately, on the culture of hope in the future'.[6]

Furthermore, new technologies have led to new ways for cultural producers to carry on their business operations, through improved information and marketing services, more efficient management systems, and so on. For example, museums and galleries are digitising their collections, performing groups are adopting electronic ticketing, newspapers are being made available on-line. At the same time, threats have emerged to traditional modes of cultural production and distribution, nowhere more evident than in the music industry, where illegal downloads from the internet continue to affect the revenue streams of performers, publishers and record companies.

The cultural impacts of globalisation have been looked upon with growing concern in many quarters. For example, fears have been widely expressed, especially in the developing world, that local forms of cultural expression and the assertion of distinctive national or regional cultural identities will be overwhelmed by the inexorable expansion of the global cultural marketplace. It is true that the adoption of new communications technologies means that cultural messages and symbols are being transmitted in volumes and at speeds that have never been witnessed before. In many cases the messages and symbols are associated with consumer products that, as they penetrate markets more and more widely scattered around the world, carry with them an inevitable sense of standardisation. It is not just the familiar images conveyed by global corporate branding, but also the more complex cultural content conveyed by television programmes or the songs of popular music performers that contribute to this feeling that we are living in an increasingly homogenised environment.

Nevertheless, the evidence on the cultural impact of globalisation is mixed, particularly because these are dynamic processes that are constantly evolving. If impact is measured by the observable spread of universally recognised cultural symbols as described above, certainly some homogenisation has occurred. But, the very threat of external cultural influences may actually sharpen the resolve of particular groups, be they local communities or nation states, to assert their own cultural distinctiveness. Indeed, there is little indication that cultural differentiation within or between countries is dying out. The celebration of specific cultural identities through art, music, literature, ritual, tradition, and in many other ways, is clearly alive and well in all parts of the world.

All of these developments have been reflected in one way or another in the financial environment in which cultural production takes place, particularly in the not-for-profit sector. Enterprises such as performing companies and public art galleries are facing greater competition for earned revenue, and sources of unearned revenue, such as donations and sponsorship, are harder to come by than they have been in the past. In circumstances where the neoliberal economic agenda of smaller government has taken hold, public budgets for support of culture are shrinking, without there necessarily being an expansion of private funding to compensate. Artists too are feeling the financial pinch, with surveys of their economic circumstances generally indicating that real incomes from creative work are static or declining over time.

A further factor that continues to influence the orientation of cultural policy is the changing nature of cultural consumption. Again it is the spread of new communications technologies that lies behind the transformation. New generations of consumers are using the internet, mobile telephony and digital media in ways that not only expand their range of cultural experience but also transform them from passive recipients of cultural messages into active co-creators of cultural content. The sense of empowerment brought about by these developments and the process of redefining cultural identities that they initiate are likely to continue as significant influences on the content of cultural policy in the future. In regard to more general trends in consumer demand for artistic and cultural goods and services, it is still unclear how factors such as rising real incomes, increases in leisure time and shifts in consumer tastes will affect demand for both traditional and new forms of cultural product in the years ahead.

## 2 The policy response

The trends discussed above have had a profound influence on the shape and direction of cultural policy at local, national and international levels. Increasingly, they have tended to push cultural policy towards becoming an arm of economic policy. To some extent this is not a new phenomenon – after all it was during the 1980s in countries such as the UK and Australia that advocates for the arts took to arguing the economic importance of the cultural sector as a means of justifying public funding.[7] But the co-option of an economic agenda for cultural policy in the present day is of a much more substantial kind. It derives from the emerging concept of the 'creative economy' – the idea that a creative sector can be identified within the larger macroeconomy which is a particular source of economic dynamism in the new information age. The idea has its origins in the proposition that creativity, whether in art, science, technology or commerce, is a key factor in generating economic success both for individual businesses and for whole economies.[8] Creativity, it is argued, is a prerequisite for innovation, and innovation is the driver of technological change, which in turn boosts economic growth. At its broadest, the creative economy includes a wide range of industries that extend well beyond the cultural sector, but an essential component – and the object of cultural policy – is the so-called cultural industries. In later chapters we shall be looking more closely at defining the cultural industries and examining their policy implications. For now, we focus simply on the importance of the cultural industries in shifting the orientation of cultural policy more strongly towards the economic aspects of culture.

The rhetoric of the creative economy is persuasive. Creativity is, after all, a far-reaching quality whose mysteries are scarcely understood, even by psychologists:[9] is it a characteristic of human beings, like intelligence, or is it a process by means of which novel problems are solved in novel ways? Artistic creativity, in particular, exerts a fascination that goes to the heart of human experience, both in the creation of art and in its reception by the viewer, the reader or the listener. To corral such an elusive phenomenon for an economic purpose is an intriguing leap that has the potential to bring the arts out of their self-referential exclusivity and to place them at the service of the economy. Once a logical sequence can be established, beginning with art and proceeding through artistic creativity, creativity in general, innovation, technological progress, competitive advantage, and leading in due course to growth in incomes, exports, employment and other indicators of economic success, government policy-makers tend to sit up and take notice. Since in many developed countries the cultural industries can indeed be shown to have grown faster than other sectors such as manufacturing and agriculture over the past decade or so when measured in terms of value of output or levels of employment, rhetoric is converted into fact, and the economic legitimacy of cultural policy is assured.[10]

A characterisation of the evolution of cultural policy over recent years as being its transformation into an arm of economic policy may appear somewhat far-fetched, seeming to subordinate the lofty purposes of culture to the sordid demands of the marketplace, a final realisation of the Adorno/Horkheimer nightmare of the commodification of culture.[11] Certainly for some observers the processes of cultural evolution driven by seemingly inexorable economic forces that we are witnessing in the contemporary world are a matter for despair, and if these trends are taken up by governments in their policy stance on matters to do with the arts and culture, their gloom becomes even deeper. But this book will argue that a concern for the economic aspects of cultural policy does not by any means imply a capitulation to an exclusively economic conceptualisation of art and culture. On the contrary, a fundamental proposition upon which the book's argument is based is that there is an essential distinction between the economic value and the cultural value of the activities and the goods and services with which we are concerned. Governments have multiple objectives, including the creation of cultural value in society alongside the generation of economic value in various forms in the economy. The distinctive characteristic of cultural policy lies in the sometimes overlooked fact that it actually deals with culture, an aspect of society and its functioning that transcends the purely economic.

Furthermore, the promulgation of a cultural-industries basis for cultural policy can be interpreted in another light, one which gains a place for culture on the national policy agenda that it might not otherwise achieve. To put it simply, the cultural industries might help to legitimise culture in the eyes of hard-headed economic policy-makers. Such policy-makers have tended to be uneasy with a cultural policy where the primary focus is on public assistance to the arts; typically they have believed that there is no special case for governments to support activities that should be commercially viable, and have probably been inclined to the view that existing arts funding is the outcome of regulatory capture by an articulate and self-serving arts lobby. These sceptics have remained unconvinced as to the existence of public-good benefits from the arts, and are doubtful that the community would be willing to pay for them, even if they did exist; hence a market failure justification for public intervention does not impress them. But the cultural industries are a different matter. Now the arts can be seen as part of a wider and more dynamic sphere of economic activity, with links through to the information and knowledge economies, fostering creativity, embracing new technologies and feeding innovation. Cultural policy in these circumstances is rescued from its primordial past and catapulted to the forefront of the modern forward-looking policy agenda, an essential component in any respectable economic policy-maker's development strategy. In this way the cultural industries agenda can be used as the Trojan Horse whereby culture is smuggled into the policy chamber where its voice can at least be heard.

## 3 Outline of the book

This volume deals with the application of theoretical and applied economics to the analysis of cultural policy. A definition of the latter term is provided by the premier journal in the field in the following terms:

Cultural policy is understood as the promotion or prohibition of cultural practices and values by governments, corporations, other institutions and individuals. Such policies may be explicit in that their objectives are openly described as cultural, or implicit, in that their cultural objectives are concealed or described in other terms.[12]

This definition includes a range of non-government actors in the exercise of cultural policy; however, although our discussion frequently touches on the interests and actions of firms, organisations and individuals outside of government, our primary concern throughout is with the exercise of *public* policy, whether at a local, regional, national or international level.

The first task of the book is essentially definitional. Chapters 2 and 3 outline respectively the scope of cultural policy and the elements of the policy process. In Chapter 2 we define cultural goods and services, and economic and cultural value, as fundamental concepts upon which our subsequent discussions will be based. The composition of the cultural sector is described, and the interpretation of production, distribution and consumption of the arts and culture as an economic process is explained. Finally in this chapter, we outline the range of public-sector ministries, departments and agencies with a potential interest in cultural policy; the extent of the list reflects clearly the broadening of cultural policy concern that we noted above.

Chapter 3 looks at the public-policy-making process as it is understood from an economic point of view. The first stage in policy development in any area is to establish the objectives that government action seeks to pursue. The standard set of *economic* objectives that governments typically regard as important can be stated clearly. However, defining the *artistic* and *cultural* objectives of cultural policy is more problematical, since they relate to concepts such as artistic excellence, diversity, cultural sustainability, and so on, which are difficult to identify and to measure. Nevertheless specifying them is essential, as on them depends the rest of the policy process. Once objectives are properly accounted for, attention turns to the means by which they are to be achieved; again we approach this question from an economic viewpoint, identifying the various areas such as fiscal policy, regulatory intervention and so on that governments use to put their policy programmes into effect. Finally in this chapter, the issue of monitoring and evaluation is raised, requiring the tracking of both economic and cultural outcomes in order to judge the success or otherwise of policy programmes or strategies.

The remainder of the volume is devoted to a consideration, chapter by chapter, of the specific areas of concern to public cultural policy, beginning in Chapter 4 with the creative arts. As noted above, this area has been the primary focus for cultural policy in the past and, notwithstanding the significant shifts in the orientation of cultural policy in more recent times that we have been discussing, it still remains a central component of the overall cultural policies of governments everywhere. But even though arts policy has stayed on the agenda, it has itself undergone change over time, affected by the drive for improved economic performance and greater accountability in public-sector policy delivery that has been seen in many countries in recent years. The critical policy issues have to do with justifying public funding, determining optimum levels of support, and deciding on the appropriate means and avenues for financial allocations. We discuss the two major economic approaches to providing assistance to individuals and organisations in the arts – direct funding provided by a Ministry of Culture or an Arts Council, and indirect support provided via the tax system.

The creative arts can be seen as an essential element of the cultural industries, the area to which we turn in Chapter 5. Matters of definition must be disposed of first (are they 'cultural' or 'creative' industries, and does it matter?). We then suggest various ways in which the economic contribution of the cultural industries can be identified, measured and analysed. Next, policy directions for the cultural industries are discussed, first in terms of the industries' economic contribution and then in regard to the cultural value they produce. Here, as throughout this book, we stress the importance of accounting for both economic value and cultural value when considering policy strategies.

As we noted earlier, policy towards cultural heritage has traditionally been a key feature of cultural policy statements and it remains today just as important as ever. Chapter 6 begins by identifying the three types of cultural heritage with which we are familiar: built, moveable and intangible. All are united in theoretical terms as items of cultural capital, a term used differently in economics from its accepted usage in sociology. A primary policy concern with heritage of whatever sort is to identify its value. We discuss in detail how the economic value of heritage is identified and assessed, and then do the same for cultural value. Policy issues applicable to heritage in general are considered next, including the appropriateness of sustainability as a paradigm for long-term heritage management, and the applicability of cost-benefit analysis for the appraisal of conservation investment projects. Then follows an account of policy matters specific to the three types of heritage in turn, and the chapter concludes with reference to the international conventions affecting heritage management, relating to heritage in both tangible and intangible forms.

Chapter 7 is devoted to the arts and culture in urban development. Although national governments take an interest in this field, it is primarily one of concern to regional and local administrations. Basic concepts relevant to the economic analysis of art and culture in the growth of cities include social, cultural and natural capital, sustainability and livability. After defining these concepts, we go on to consider three specific approaches to interpreting the role of the arts and culture in an urban context: the creative class, creative clusters, and the idea of a creative city. Of special interest is the importance of architecture in contributing to the cultural life of cities.

Given the extent to which urban economies in many parts of the world depend on the influx of tourists, a discussion of the arts in the economy of cities leads naturally to a discussion of cultural tourism, the topic taken up in Chapter 8. The economics of tourism as an area of applied economics deals with aspects such as: the contribution that tourism makes to the national, regional or local economy; impact studies of particular projects; and efforts to define sustainable tourism. Two interpretations of the term 'cultural tourism' are possible: one relates to the consumption of cultural experiences such as theatre or gallery visits by mass tourists, the other refers to the niche market occupied by the discriminating and specialised cultural tourist. The chapter discusses both types, and concludes with some policy observations.

Turning to the international arena, we consider culture in the world economy in Chapter 9. The major area of concern here is trade. The so-called cultural exception, whereby cultural goods and services seek to be considered differently from other commodities in trade negotiations, has been a prominent feature of trade discussions in recent years. We consider arguments both for and against the granting of special treatment towards cultural goods in trade. We also discuss other important cultural trade issues including the export of 'national treasures' and the repatriation of cultural property. Finally, this chapter examines non-trade issues in international cultural relations, including cultural exchanges, cultural diplomacy, and intercultural dialogue.

Chapter 10 deals with an issue that has grown in prominence in recent years, namely cultural diversity. In looking at the value attributable to cultural diversity, we draw a parallel with biodiversity, the importance of which is increasingly being recognised. A primary impetus towards recognition of cultural diversity has been, firstly, the *Universal Declaration on Cultural Diversity*, adopted by UNESCO in 2001, and the *Convention on the Protection and Promotion of the Diversity of Cultural Expressions*, which entered into force in 2007. The policy implications of this Convention are potentially far-reaching, and are becoming more widely appreciated as the process of implementing the Convention proceeds.

At the beginning of Chapter 11, the point is made that in some respects cultural policy and educational policy could be seen as almost synonymous, so pervasive are the interconnections between education and culture in society. The chapter discusses the economic interpretation of education as a contributor to human capital formation, and goes on to consider the two arenas in which arts education occurs: in schools where children learn about music, visual art, drama, literature, and so on; and in conservatoria, universities, art schools, colleges, etc., which are concerned with the education and training of artists. The chapter discusses educational policy in both of these contexts, and concludes with an examination of the determinants of arts consumption in the population at large as it is affected by consumers' educational backgrounds.

Developing countries have a particular interest in cultural policy. Chapter 12 outlines the role of culture in economic development, and discusses policy measures that seek to enhance both the economic and the cultural contribution that the arts and culture can make to the development process. A key concept here once again is sustainability;

we introduce the relatively new idea of culturally sustainable development and put forward some guidelines for its implementation.

One of the characteristics that can be used to define cultural goods and services is their actual or potential intellectual property content. The major area of intellectual property law and practice of relevance to creative products is copyright. Chapter 13 begins by explaining the basic economics of copyright, and shows how the assertion of artists' rights is most effectively handled by cooperative action through organisations such as copyright collecting societies. One of the most significant concerns in contemporary copyright administration is the effect of digital technologies; the transformation of the ways in which some cultural goods and services such as audio-visual products are distributed and consumed has made it possible for users to bypass copyright regulations, with adverse effects on the capacity of rightsholders to be properly rewarded for their creative effort. We discuss these issues and the policy measures that can be used to counter these problems.

An important stage during or after the implementation of any policy programme is the monitoring and evaluation function. In the cultural policy arena, this function requires cultural statistics of various sorts. Chapter 14 discusses the types of statistics that cultural policy analysts require, including data on the performance of the cultural industries, employment, prices, and so on. These data may be collected by government statistical agencies or gathered from independent surveys; in the latter respect we pay particular attention to the methodology for surveying professional artists. One difficulty encountered with statistical data relating to the cultural sector concerns the lack of comparability in data series across jurisdictions and across countries. An effort to lead to greater consistency in national statistical collections for culture is the new Framework for Cultural Statistics developed by the UNESCO Institute for Statistics. We discuss the structure of this framework and the prospects for its implementation.

The final chapter in the book draws some of the threads together. The legitimacy of cultural policy studies as an area of theoretical and applied research is discussed, and the validity of this volume's project of applying economic principles to this area is appraised. The conclusion is drawn that economics does indeed have something to contribute to an understanding of cultural policy. It is hoped that by the time the reader has reached the end of this volume, he or she will have found at least some reason to agree.

*Notes*

1 Quote is from Jennings (2005: 124).
2 See Green and Wilding (1970).
3 See Gumucio (1978). A poignant reminder of how political circumstances can change and how cultural intolerance can wreak disaster is
   provided by the report for Afghanistan (Rahel, 1978), which sets out
   a programme for heritage protection in that country, illustrated by a
   photograph of one of the Bamiyan Buddhas. These priceless cultural
   artefacts were destroyed by the Taliban in 2001.
4 This was despite the fact that at the original 1967 conference, UNESCO
   had argued for a recognition of the economic linkages between culture and development, pointing out that 'economic and social development should go hand in hand with cultural development' (UNESCO,
   1969: 10), and encouraging the application of economic models to the
   analysis of the production, distribution and consumption of the arts.
5 For an essay on art and popular culture in a cultural policy context, see
   O'Connor (2006).
6 See Castells (2001: 112).
7 Not a persuasive argument in economic terms; for an attempt to measure the economic impact of the arts at that time, see Myerscough
   (1988).
8 See, for example, Howkins (2001); UNCTAD (2008).
9 See further in Hayes and Stratton (2003: 70).
10 Of course the relationship between the cultural industries and cultural
   policy has been a long-standing matter for discussion within the cultural studies and political economy traditions (Garnham, 1990; Lewis
   and Miller, 2003; McGuigan, 2004; Hartley, 2005; Hesmondhalgh
   and Pratt, 2005; Pratt, 2005). However, the rapid technological change
   associated with globalisation that has occurred over the last decade or
   so has brought the cultural industries, and their role in cultural policy,
   into a new prominence; see also Bustamente (2004).
11 As envisaged in their disparaging description of the 'culture industries';
   see Adorno and Horkheimer (1947).
12 See the 'Aims and Scope' of the *International Journal of Cultural Policy*
   as set out on the inside front cover of any recent issue. For a discussion
   of 'implicit' cultural policy, see contributions to a special issue of the
   journal, published as volume 15, no. 1, 2009.

# 2 The scope of cultural policy

> ... having faith in the progress of humanity towards perfection,
> ... we grow to have a clearer sight of the ideas of right reason,
> and of the elements and helps of perfection, and come grad-
> ually to fill the framework of the State with them, to fashion its
> internal composition and all its laws and institutions conform-
> ably to them, and to make the State more and more the expres-
> sion, as we say, of our best self ...
>
> (Matthew Arnold, *Culture and Anarchy*, 1869[1])

## 1 Introduction

In days gone by, when cultural policy was concerned primarily or
solely with the creative arts, a definition of its scope was straightforward. The goods and services produced and consumed were easily recognisable – works of art and literature, music compositions,
theatre performances, and so on – and the individuals and organisations that might be targets for cultural policy occupied an identifiable
corner of the economic and social landscape – artists, performing
companies, music ensembles, etc., on the supply side, and the 'arts
audience' on the receiving end. The value of what was being done in
the name of art was taken for granted as the motivation for cultural
policies designed to nourish and improve society. Responsibility for
cultural policy within government rested quite naturally in a ministry
for the arts or culture or in an arts funding agency of some sort.

The expansion in the reach of cultural policy that we discussed in the
previous chapter has changed all that. No longer are the goods and services that comprise the output of the cultural sector confined to the arts;
rather, new definitions are required of cultural or creative goods and
services and the industries that produce them. The range of suppliers and
consumers of such commodities that are potentially the object of cultural policy measures has correspondingly extended well beyond the arts

14

sector, and the value of cultural activity is now subject to critical scrutiny, rather than being automatically assumed to be good. The widening reach of cultural policy is reflected also in the increasing number of government ministries and instrumentalities with an interest in this area.

This chapter charts these changes by looking at the ways in which the scope of cultural policy has expanded. We begin with the basic issue of identifying the products and the activities with which cultural policy is concerned, discussing contemporary approaches to defining cultural goods and services and measuring their value. We then go on to consider the composition of the cultural sector, the structure of cultural production, and the multiple areas of responsibility for cultural policy that have emerged in contemporary public administration.

## 2  Cultural goods and services

An economic analysis of cultural policy must begin with a fundamental question as to the nature of the goods and services that are likely to be of policy concern. If they are simply commercial commodities bought and sold on markets like any other products that circulate in the economy, the application of economic policy to their production, distribution, marketing, transport and consumption would be no different from economic policy-making in respect of any other commodity. If, however, cultural goods and services have distinctive qualities that set them apart from other products, they may have a claim to special policy attention.

To begin with, we draw attention to the somewhat confusing use of terminology that has emerged in this area, where the descriptions 'creative goods' and 'cultural goods' are used sometimes interchangeably and sometimes with different meanings. An obvious way to resolve this difficulty is to provide objective and unambiguous definitions of the adjectives 'creative' and 'cultural'. Such an approach requires definition of the corresponding nouns. In the case of *creativity*, there is no simple definition that encompasses all the various dimensions of this phenomenon. Nevertheless, the characteristics of creativity in different areas of human endeavour can at least be articulated. For example, it can be suggested that artistic creativity involves imagination and a capacity to generate original ideas and novel ways of interpreting the world, expressed in text, sound and image. This might be compared with scientific creativity, which relates to experimentation and problem-solving in other spheres of human activity.

In regard to *culture*, its definition can be simplified if it is accepted that it can be interpreted either in an anthropological sense, meaning shared values, customs, ways of life, etc., or in a functional sense, meaning activities such as the practice of the arts. Whichever of these notions of culture is accepted, the concept of cultural products can be articulated. There is some agreement now that cultural goods and services such as artworks, music performances, literature, film and television programmes, video games, and so on, share three distinguishing characteristics:

• they require some input of human creativity in their production;
• they are vehicles for symbolic messages to those who consume them, i.e., they are more than simply utilitarian, insofar as they serve in addition some larger communicative purpose; and
• they contain, at least potentially, some intellectual property that is attributable to the individual or group producing the good or service.

In addition, cultural goods have been described as experience goods, and as goods which are subject to rational addiction, meaning that increased present consumption will lead to increased future consumption, such that demand is cumulative.[2]

A further definition of cultural goods and services can also be proposed, deriving from a consideration of the type of value that they embody or generate, i.e., it can be suggested that they yield *cultural value* in addition to whatever commercial value they may possess, and that this cultural value may not be fully measurable in monetary terms. In other words, cultural goods and services are valued, both by those who make them and by those who consume them, for social and cultural reasons that are likely to complement or transcend a purely economic evaluation. These reasons might include spiritual concerns, aesthetic considerations, or the contribution of the goods and services to community understanding of cultural identity. If such cultural value can be identified, it may serve as an observable characteristic to distinguish cultural from other types of commodities.[3]

Whichever of the above definitions is accepted, *cultural* goods and services can be seen as a sub-set of a wider category of goods that can be called *creative* goods and services. The latter are simply products that require some reasonably significant level of creativity in their manufacture, without necessarily satisfying other criteria that would enable them to be labelled 'cultural'. Thus the category 'creative goods' extends beyond cultural goods as defined above to include products such as advertising and software; these latter goods and services can be seen as essentially commercial products, but they do involve some level of creativity in their production. Since the subject of this volume is cultural policy, we shall henceforward confine ourselves to a consideration of *cultural* goods and services.

## 3  Value and valuation

A basic concept that underlies consideration of policy in any area of public concern is that of value. The consumption behaviour of individuals is motivated by the value they attach to the goods and services they consume, the production of value is the *modus operandi* of business firms, and value to society at large guides (or should guide) the decisions of government. At its most fundamental, value can be thought of as the worth, to an individual or a group, of a good, a service, an activity or an experience, with an implied possibility of a ranking of value (better to worse, or higher to lower value) according to given criteria. The process by which value is assigned to something is referred to as *valuation* or *evaluation*, described by Steven Connor as the process of 'estimating, ascribing, modifying, affirming and even denying value'.[4] We should also note the occasional use of the word *valorization* to mean a process by which value is imparted to some object as a result of deliberative action or external event, such as the increase in value accorded to sites of cultural heritage when they are added to the World Heritage List.

The expansion in the scope of cultural policy to which we have been referring implies a corresponding expansion in the relevant concepts of value that are significant in policy-making. In earlier times, when support for the arts was the main policy concern, the appropriate interpretation of value was one related to artistic or cultural criteria. Now, with the shift towards an economic orientation for cultural policy, notions of economic value must be introduced into the picture, and indeed reference to the economic consequences of alternative strategies might nowadays play a dominant role in many cultural policy decisions. It is necessary therefore to specify the value concepts upon which the expanded realm of cultural policy should be founded. Accordingly, throughout this book a distinction is maintained, when considering the economics of cultural policy, between the economic value and the cultural value yielded by the goods, services, activities, industries, policy interventions, and so on, with which we are concerned – in short, we argue that this duality of value applies to all the phenomena of relevance to the cultural policy field.[5]

To clarify how the twin concepts of economic value and cultural value can be made operational for cultural policy purposes, we need to describe their definition and the methods for their assessment. Looking first at economic value, we can observe that within the neo-classical paradigm, the Benthamite concept of utility is assumed to underlie consumers' formation of value, reflected in due course for particular goods and services in equilibrium prices that emerge in competitive markets and in people's stated willingness to pay for non-market effects. However it arises, value in the economic sphere is ultimately expressible in financial terms. In contrast to this well-defined concept of economic value, the interpretation of cultural value in relation to art objects and other cultural phenomena is by no means clear-cut. It has long been a source of controversy within philosophy, aesthetics and art history; indeed a confrontation between absolute and relative theories of value in the postmodern world has provided cultural theory with a crisis of value that shows no signs of being resolved. Whether there is a right or a wrong in this debate is of less relevance for our discussion than the undeniable fact that cultural value is complex, multifaceted, unstable, and lacks an agreed unit of account.

The distinction between economic value and cultural value creates a dilemma for the process of valuation. On the one hand the neatly circumscribed principles of economic evaluation lead to what appear to be unambiguous estimates of the economic value of cultural goods and services, whilst on the other hand cultural value seems to resist precise, objective and replicable means of assessment. The two interpretations pull in different directions, creating uncertainties surrounding a core question in cultural policy: what values should count in decision-making in relation to the production, distribution and consumption of cultural commodities?

Nevertheless, the existence of a duality of value and its attendant problems of valuation should not deflect the cultural policy analyst from the task of assessing value as fully and accurately as possible. In particular, considerable progress has been made at both theoretical and empirical levels in assessing the *economic* value of cultural goods and services, using a range of techniques familiar to applied economists. Let us consider briefly the basis upon which economic analysis is applied to cultural goods and services in order to assess their economic value.

Valuing cultural goods and services in economic terms requires a recognition of the fact that such goods fall into the category of *mixed goods*, i.e., goods that have both private-good and public-good characteristics. Private goods and services are those whose benefits accrue entirely to private agents (indiviuals or firms); in other words such agents can appropriate the benefits for themselves by acquiring property rights over the good or service involved. People buying a book or attending a play, for example, enjoy the book or the performance as private individuals, and the valuation of their *use benefit* is reflected in the price paid for the book or the theatre ticket.[6] Public goods, on the other hand, are those whose benefits accrue to everyone in a given community; economists describe them as *non-excludable* (once they are produced they are available to everyone and no one can be excluded from consuming them) and *non-rival* (one person's consumption does not diminish the amount available to others). Public goods are classified as *non-market goods* because there is no market on which the rights to them can be exchanged; their benefits arise outside of conventional market processes. Paradigm cases of public goods include the services of national defence and a free-to-air broadcast television signal.

Why might at least some cultural goods and services have these public-good properties in addition to their functioning as private goods? We can answer this question in relation to the arts by looking at the ways in which people in society might value the arts in general, as distinct from their valuation of specific art commodities or experiences that form part of their own private consumption. Three sources of non-market benefits for the arts can be identified: an *existence* value (people value the arts simply because they exist); an *option* value (people wish to retain the option that they may wish to consume the arts at some time in the future); and a *bequest* value (people think it is important to pass the arts on to future generations). All of these sources of value need to be taken into account when assessing the economic value of a cultural good or service. They can be measured by finding out how much people are willing to pay for these benefits, for example by donating to a specific fund, or through an ear-marked tax increase. Well-developed methodologies exist for estimating willingness to pay, including contingent valuation methods and choice modelling. We shall return to these matters in later chapters. For now it is important simply to understand that a full assessment of the economic value of culture must account both for the direct use value as revealed in the markets for cultural goods and services, and the non-use value as estimated by alternative analytical procedures.

To a neoclassical economist, a full assessment of the market and/or non-market value of any good or service, including cultural goods, would be provided by measuring actual payment and/or potential willingness to pay, the reasoning being that a person could not be regarded as attaching value to any good or service that he or she was not prepared to pay for. However, stepping outside the framework of neoclassical economics raises some broader issues in considering the value of cultural goods and services. We can ask: are there collective benefits of culture that cannot be factored out to individuals and yet are important for decision-making? In particular, there may be concern that the standard economic model cannot entirely encompass those elements of a cultural good that gives rise to what is understood to be its cultural significance. Such considerations lead us into an alternative discourse which entertains the concept of cultural value that exists in addition to whatever economic value the good might possess. Cultural value in this context is a multifaceted concept reflecting qualities such as the aesthetic, symbolic, spiritual or historical values attaching to a particular item. Of course such qualities may affect individual valuations of the item in question and, to the extent that they did so, would be reflected in any economic analysis of the item's value. But there is also a sense in which some such values can only be fully realised in collective terms, and cannot sensibly be represented in individual monetary valuations. Take, for example, the notion of identity. We say that a nation's culture is important because it expresses the people's identity – it tells their stories, it helps define who they are. It is difficult to translate this value into willingness to pay; indeed it is hard to see how the value of identity can be expressed in financial terms at all. Yet identity is something that is valuable to society at large and clearly affects decision-making in the cultural policy arena.

Identifying cultural value is one thing, measuring it is another; ascribing aesthetic and other non-monetary values to artworks, artefacts, and so on, has long been a critical question for a number of disciplines interested in art, culture and society. If we were to adopt the mindset of the neoclassical economist, we might suggest that the cultural worth of an artistic good, for example, could be interpreted as being formed by a negotiated process akin to a simple market exchange. When a cultural good such as a painting or a novel is made available to the public, consumers absorb, interpret and evaluate the ideas contained in the work, discussing and exchanging their assessments with others. In the end, if a consensus is reached, the assessed artistic value of the work could be interpreted as something like a cultural price – an exchange value reached by negotiation amongst parties to a market transaction, where the 'market' is that for the cultural content of the work. Indeed it can be argued that creative artists in fact supply a dual market – a physical market for the good, which determines its economic price, and a market for ideas, which determines the good's cultural price. In the goods market, there is a single price at any one time, because of the private-good nature of the physical work; in the ideas market, there are always multiple valuations, as befits the pure public-good properties of artistic ideas. Prices in both markets are not independent of each other, and are subject to change over time as reassessments of the work's economic and cultural worth occur.

Such a theory may have intellectual appeal but it provides little comfort for the empirical analyst, and something more practical will be required if the notion of cultural value is to be made operational so that it can be incorporated into actual decision-making in the cultural policy arena. There are several lines of attack here. One possibility is to deconstruct the idea of cultural value into several components and to seek numerical or other scales to represent judgements based on defined criteria.[7] To illustrate, following Throsby (2001: 28–29), it can be suggested that the cultural value of an artwork, for example, could be represented in terms of the work's aesthetic, spiritual, social, symbolic, historical and authenticity qualities, all of which could be assessed by a given observer, and aggregated over a group of observers to reach some consensus judgement against each criterion.[8] The assessment in a case like this could be made in terms of ordinal or qualitative scales measuring the strength or importance of each attribute as exhibited by the item in question. If such judgements can be expressed as, or converted into, cardinal scores, they have the advantage that they can be combined, using any desired weighting system to reflect the assumed relative importance of the individual criteria. Such an approach is clearly no more than an ad hoc means of giving formal expression to judgements that would otherwise be left simply to informal processes. Nevertheless, these methods might be a workable way of providing, for specific policy options, some sort of aggregated quantitative representation of the cultural value of alternative strategies.

Whose judgements should count in such an assessment? In areas of public policy-making where particular expertise is required in order to reach an informed decision, the opinions of people who know are generally sought; for example, in allocating grants for medical or scientific research, governments usually rely on the advice of experts. The same can be argued to be the case in the cultural field. If decisions are required on the cultural value of paintings or heritage buildings or archaeological finds, the views of art critics, architectural historians and archaeologists respectively must be taken seriously. Thus in a practical policy context, a group of experts in a particular cultural arena could be asked to come up with a consensus judgement of the cultural worth of particular activities that were the object of some policy strategy. Alternatively, adopting a more 'democratic' approach, appeal could be made to public opinion on various policy measures using survey techniques or other means of distilling a popular view. In either case the intention is to transcend the variability of individual judgements by amalgamating them into some definable consensus.

We return to the issue of measuring economic and cultural value in Chapter 6, in our discussion of cultural heritage.

## 4  Composition of the cultural sector

In line with the widening ambit of cultural policy and its extension beyond a concern simply for the arts, the range of stakeholders who have an interest in cultural policy – as producers, distributors, consumers, or as policy-makers – has likewise expanded. Such stakeholders inhabit the 'cultural sector', a term that can be used to describe the collection of organisations and individuals that are directly involved in the production, distribution or consumption of the arts and culture in the economy and in society. We can identify the various groups of stakeholders that comprise the cultural sector as follows:

- *Cultural workers*: People working in cultural production include the primary producers of cultural material (artists and other creative professionals) and those non-creative workers whose employment lies within the sphere of cultural production, such as support staff in arts organisations. Also included are teachers of music, drama, dance, etc., and other artistic and cultural educators and trainers.
- *Commercial (for-profit) firms*: This category includes large numbers of small- to medium-sized enterprises that produce cultural goods and services of various sorts, and a smaller number of large corporations that operate at a national or transnational scale. Although established on a commercial basis, the motivations of firms in the small-to-medium group are likely to have a significant cultural emphasis, whereas large-scale corporate enterprises in the cultural sector are generally likely to be driven more strongly by financial motives.
- *Not-for-profit firms*: Incorporation of private-sector firms on a not-for-profit basis is prevalent in theatre, opera, dance and music, and occurs occasionally in other areas of the arts, for example in artists' cooperatives and collectives. In all these organisations it is likely to be artistic rather than financial objectives that are paramount. This category also includes those organisations in the cultural sector such as professional societies, unions, industry organisations and other NGOs that are operated as non-profit service-providers to the arts and culture rather than as profit-seeking companies.
- *Public cultural institutions*: All levels of government from national to local are likely to own and operate cultural institutions of various sorts, including museums and galleries, libraries, archives, heritage sites, performing arts companies and venues, and public broadcasting companies.
- *Education and training institutions*: Schools, colleges and other facilities providing education, training and skills development in the arts and cultural field fall into this group. Such institutions include art schools, conservatoria, drama schools, and so on. They may be publicly or privately owned and operated. An interest in the arts and culture also extends to the general education system, particularly via the exposure of schoolchildren to the arts as part of their normal curriculum.
- *Government agencies and ministries*: A range of public-sector instrumentalities exist with direct or indirect responsibilities in the cultural field. We consider the make-up of this group in more detail below.

- *International organisations*: Cultural policy-making at the international level cuts across a number of UN and related agencies. Primary responsibility rests, of course, with UNESCO, but there is a cultural component to the work of many other players at the international level, both within and outside of the 'UN family'. These include UNDP, UNCTAD, FAO, WIPO, the OECD and the World Bank, as well as a number of international NGOs in the cultural field.
- *Consumers and consumer organisations*: This category comprises a very large group indeed, since virtually everyone is a cultural consumer of one sort or another. Looked at from this viewpoint, the reach of cultural policy is especially wide-ranging; since almost everyone watches television, for example, a policy measure affecting the cultural content of television broadcasts will touch the entire community. Cultural consumption is frequently analysed using Richard Peterson's distinction between 'omnivores' (people who engage in a wide range of cultural consumption) and 'univores' (those who concentrate on one cultural form).[9]

## 5  Production, distribution, consumption

The expansion in the range of stakeholders who have an interest in cultural policy in the contemporary world, as described in the previous section, means that the relationships of interest to the cultural policy-maker have correspondingly widened in scope, from a concern solely with relatively simple processes of production and consumption of the arts to a wider view of the more complex patterns of production, distribution and uptake of cultural goods and services in the economy and society at large. In this section we consider two complementary approaches to depicting the relationships between stakeholders in the cultural production sector: the concept of the value chain and the concentric circles model.

### The value chain for cultural goods and services

In its simplest form, the analytical model of the cultural production chain is one where the initial creative ideas are combined with other inputs to produce a creative good or service, which may then pass

through further value-adding stages until it enters marketing and distribution channels, and eventually reaches the final consumer. For
some cultural goods this process is very simple – a visual artist selling
her paintings direct to the public from a street stall, for example, represents a value chain with only a single link. For other goods, however,
the process can become quite complex, as the creative idea is transformed or reformatted at successive stages. For example, a musical
idea might begin with a composer writing a song and passing it on to
a publisher who transforms it into a tangible printed form. From there
the idea might be realised as a live performance before an audience,
with the performance subsequently being recorded and marketed by
a record company. The record will pass through a sequence of wholesale and retail value-adding until bought by a consumer, or it may be
uploaded onto the internet and subsequently accessed by consumers
who may or may not pay a price for on-line delivery. Subsequently the
song may be re-packaged as background music for a film, with further value added along the way. Thus the overall chain can become
quite attenuated, one effect of which is usually to diminish the relative
share of total revenue accruing to the creator of the original idea, in
this instance the composer of the song.

The apparent linearity of the value chain may be replaced, for
some cultural products, by something more akin to a value network,
where multiple inputs, feedback loops, and a pervasive 'value-creating
ecology' replaces a simple stage-wise process.[10] In film-making, for
example, a complex multi-layered process is involved in bringing
together the many creative and non-creative inputs required to produce the finished product, which may even then be subject to further
reiterations and re-workings. Identifying the value added by the various players in these sorts of circumstances can become a very complicated task.

From a policy point of view, depicting the cultural production
process as a value chain allows an analysis of the effects of policy intervention at various points in the chain. For example, in
assessing the impacts of existing policy measures, or in determining the optimal point at which to apply prospective measures, the
policy analyst can use the value-chain concept to clarify where the
effects of intervention have been or will be felt, and who are the
affected stakeholders upstream or downstream from the point of
intervention.

## *The concentric circles model of the cultural sector*

In the contemporary policy environment, an important focus of cultural policy is on the growth of the cultural industries, so it is necessary to understand how these industries can be conceptualised and how they relate to one another and to consumers. We shall be considering the cultural industries in detail in Chapter 5; for now all that is required is a brief and intuitive overview of how the distinction between economic value and cultural value can be used to inform an approach to modelling the cultural industries.

A model of the cultural industries that is based on this value distinction is the so-called 'concentric circles model',[11] which asserts that it is the cultural value, or cultural content, of the goods and services produced that gives the cultural industries their most distinguishing characteristic. Different goods have different degrees of cultural content relative to their commercial value; the model proposes that the more pronounced the cultural content of a particular good or service, the stronger is the claim of the industry producing it to be counted as a cultural industry. Thus are the concentric circles delineated: at the centre are core industries in which the proportion of cultural-to-commercial content is judged to be highest according to given criteria, with layers extending outwards from the centre as the cultural content falls relative to the commercial value of the commodities or services produced. On this basis a series of layers or circles can be proposed, with the core creative arts (music, performing arts, visual arts, etc.) at the centre, surrounded by other core industries such as film, museums and galleries. The next layer is the wider cultural industries of the media, publishing, and so on, and finally there are cultural industries where the commercial content of output is highest, such as fashion, advertising and design.

The model proposes that creative ideas and influences originating in the core diffuse outwards through the concentric circles. How does this occur? At one level it may arise through the sorts of generalised communication and exchange processes that govern the circulation of knowledge and information in the economy and society at large; for example, the plot of a novel or play may suggest ideas for a video or computer game, or a painter's work may inspire a fashion creation. Alternatively, the diffusion of ideas may arise through the fact that the creative people who generate them actually work in different industries, providing direct input to the production of cultural content in industries further from the core or outside the cultural industries altogether; for example, a visual artist may have a creative practice producing original artworks, but may also work in the design industry, or an actor may appear on stage in the live theatre, as well as making television commercials in the advertising industry. However it happens, it is the creative ideas that generate the cultural content in the output of these industries.

As an interpretation of the structure of cultural production, the concentric circles model can be seen as a static snapshot at a given point in time, in contrast to a dynamic form of analysis such as the value chain model discussed above. In the concentric circles model, downstream functions such as distribution are represented as distinct industries in their own right, incorporating original creative ideas produced in the core into their production processes as intermediate inputs. For example, television scriptwriters, located at the core of the model, sell their work to broadcasters located in the 'wider cultural industries' circle. At a given point in time the output of both industries – the scriptwriting industry and the television industry – can be observed and, under appropriate assumptions, the cultural content of their output assessed.[12]

There are several implications for cultural policy arising from use of the concentric circles model as a means of representing the structure of the cultural industries. Firstly the model provides a basis for formulating statistical classification systems for the cultural production sector, enabling the orderly collection of data on output, value added, employment, etc., which are relevant for policy purposes. Secondly, the concentric circles model is readily adapted to fit formal analytical methods, such as input-output analysis or computable general equilibrium models, which may be used to investigate inter-industry relationships within the cultural sector or between the cultural industries and other parts of the economy. Finally, interpreting the cultural industries as a radiating system with the pure creative arts at the centre provides a direct means of representing the core role of the arts in motivating and sustaining the entire cultural sector. In the Introduction to this book it was asserted that adoption of a cultural-industries approach to a consideration of cultural policy did not necessarily imply a sell-out to economics, nor a subjugation of the lofty ideals of the arts to the mechanical forces of the marketplace. The concentric circles model makes it explicit why cultural policy need not marginalise the arts or consign them to some peripheral or irrelevant status. On the contrary, the model actually points towards the need for a strong, dynamic and sustainable arts sector as an essential source of the creativity that drives the cultural industries and that can animate innovation and development in other parts of the economy.

## 6  Cultural policy in government administration

We have been arguing that cultural policy is nowadays not a single entity but involves multiple components that ramify throughout the structure of public administration in line with the expanding concept of cultural policy in the contemporary world. The areas of government responsibility that are likely to have some involvement with cultural policy include the following:

- *Arts/culture ministry*: Notwithstanding the shift in cultural policy away from a sole concern with the arts, there is no question that ministries or departments with designated responsibility for arts and cultural heritage remain as the principal locus for the delivery of cultural policy in most administrative systems. This point is reinforced by the core role envisaged for the creative arts in the cultural industries model outlined above.
- *Finance/treasury*: Cultural policy in all areas is likely to require significant commitments of public expenditure. Participation by the government departments and ministers with responsibility for financial provision is likely therefore to be critical in cultural policy formulation and implementation.
- *Industry development*: The cultural industries' potential role in contributing to incomes, economic growth and employment creation makes them an obvious target for industry development strategies, assessed at national, regional or local level.
- *Labour*: More specific policies affecting the labour market for cultural workers will be of concern to employment ministries, including industrial relations, occupational health and safety, human resource management, and so on.
- *Trade*: International trade in cultural goods and services can be both a major stimulant to exports and an irritant in trade negotiations,

as we shall see in Chapter 9. Trade ministries have an important role to play in cultural policy formulation because of this.

- *Education*: As we shall see in detail in Chapter 11, there are two aspects to the involvement of education in cultural policy. The first concerns the role of arts education in schools, where exposure to active participation in music-making, visual art, dance, creative writing, etc., not only enriches children's cultural lives, but also enhances their learning abilities in other areas. The second relates to the vocational training and skill development of creative workers to furnish the need for specialised creative input in the cultural industries across the board.
- *Urban/regional development*: The concept of the creative city, to be discussed in Chapter 7, has become a powerful talisman for urban planners. Cultural policy has much to contribute towards re-vitalising depressed urban areas, improving livability, and stimulating urban and regional economic growth.
- *Environment*: In a world adapting to climate change, the creative industries have a particular role to play, not just through exemplary environmental practice in their own operations, but also through the contribution that creative ideas in design, architecture, etc., can make to the development of carbon-reducing technologies in other industries.
- *Information technology and the media*: In some countries, policy in the communications area is driven solely by economic considerations to do with innovation, productivity and media ownership. Yet IT and media are important in the transmission of cultural content, and hence are implicated in cultural policy considerations.
- *Legal affairs*: The major way in which the legal services of government are involved with cultural policy is through the formulation and enforcement of intellectual property law. Copyright is a significant component of the regulatory framework in which the production and distribution of cultural product occurs, as we shall see further in Chapter 13.
- *Social welfare*: There is an important role for cultural policy in the implementation of strategies concerned with cultural pluralism and the promotion of social cohesion in communities. These aspects are nowadays gathered together under the heading of cultural diversity, to be discussed in more detail in Chapter 10.

## 7 Conclusions

This chapter has dealt with the expanding scope of cultural policy in the contemporary world. It has been argued that cultural goods and services do indeed occupy a distinctive place in the array of commodities produced in the present-day economy that sets them apart as an object of policy attention. The distinctiveness arises particularly from the fact that cultural goods and services engage creativity in their production, and give rise to both economic and cultural value. The latter quality serves to connect cultural policy to the fundamental nature of culture as a characteristic of civilised human existence.

We have also pointed to the greatly increased range of stakeholders who have an interest in cultural policy, once such policy shakes off the restrictions imposed by its being confined simply to arts policy and embraces wider questions concerning the role of art and culture in contemporary society. Similarly, extending the scope for cultural policy entails taking a broader view of the processes of production, distribution and consumption of cultural goods and services; the value chain concept and the concentric circles model of the cultural industries are both useful here as means of systematising the analysis of cultural policy and its effects. In particular, the latter model provides a basis for interpreting the place of the creative arts in this widened cultural policy domain.

Finally, we have indicated the substantial increase in the number of government ministries, departments and administrative units that have an interest in some aspect of cultural policy, once its reach is extended beyond a concern merely for the arts. Such multi-dimensionality to cultural policy makes the whole policy process more complicated, as will be discussed in the following chapter. Underlying it all, however, remains the essential task of recognising the twin sources of value, economic and cultural, as the basis for delivering policy outcomes by the public sector. The art of policy-making in this area is in finding the right balance between the two.

*Notes*

1  Quote is from Arnold (1869 [1935]: 204).
2  A characteristic they share with certain other goods such as addictive drugs; see further in Throsby (2006: 7).

3 Note, however, that although there may be broad agreement that cultural value can be looked to as a signifier of a cultural good, there are differing interpretations of how it should be assessed. For example, adopting an extended view of popular culture widens considerably the range of products to which cultural value might be attached, to the point where, ultimately, everything has cultural value and the concept becomes meaningless.

4 Connor (1992: 8).

5 This duality between economic value and cultural value is the unifying theme for a collection of essays on value in economics, culture and art by a multidisciplinary group involving economists, art historians, anthropologists and cultural theorists; see Hutter and Throsby (2008).

6 In fact the benefit they receive may be worth more than the price paid, if the amount they were prepared to pay for the book or the ticket exceeded the market price; this excess is known as *consumer's surplus*, and strictly speaking should be evaluated in any study of the economic value of a particular private good or service.

7 See, for example, Nijkamp (1995); Choi, et al., (2007).

8 An example of an empirical exercise that attempts to assess the cultural and economic value of artworks is reported in Throsby and Zednik (2008).

9 See Peterson (1992); for an empirical study, see Chan and Goldthorpe (2005).

10 See Hearn, et al., (2007); value networks may be particularly relevant in a digital environment (Keeble and Cavanagh, 2008).

11 For a more detailed treatment of this model, see Chapter 5.

12 Note that the production and distribution of some cultural goods involves many more distinct stages, and hence different industries, than this simple example suggests. For instance, the production and distribution of music involves the live performance industry, the music publishing industry, the recording industry, the broadcasting industry, etc., all of which are represented in the various layers of the concentric circles model.

# 3 | *The policy process*

SIR HUMPHREY APPLEBY: This country is governed by ministers making decisions from the alternative proposals which we [civil servants] offer them. If they had all the facts, they would see many other possibilities, some of which would not be in the public interest ... So long as we formulate the proposals, we can guide them towards a correct decision ... In order to guide the Minister towards the common ground, key words should be inserted with a proposal to make it attractive. Ministers will generally accept proposals which contain the words *simple*, *quick*, *popular* and *cheap*. Ministers will generally throw out proposals which contain the words *complicated*, *lengthy*, *expensive*, and *controversial*. Above all, if you wish to describe a proposal in a way that guarantees that a Minister will reject it, describe it as *courageous*.

(Jonathan Lynn and Antony Jay, *Yes Minister*, 1984[1])

## 1 Introduction

There are standard approaches to systematising the policy process in any area of public administration that are well understood in theoretical terms and widely adopted in practice, at all levels of government from local to national. The sequence of stages can be summarised as the following six steps:

- specification of *objectives* of policy agendas, strategies or measures;
- allocation of *responsibilities* to the appropriate areas of the administrative machinery;
- policy *coordination* between areas of administration in pursuit of 'whole-of-government' or 'joined-up-government' efficiency standards;
- choice of the policy *instrument or instruments* best fitted to achieve the desired outcomes;
- *implementation* of policy measures; and

- *monitoring and evaluation* of the effects of policy action, and feed-back to inform future policy development.

In this chapter we discuss the processes of policy-making as they relate to cultural policy generally, as a prelude to more detailed consideration of specific areas in subsequent chapters. An under-lying premise is the fact that much of public policy is nowadays interpreted in economic terms, reflecting the dominance of an eco-nomic way of thinking in guiding the behaviour of governments in the contemporary world. We see evidence of this all around us. For example, areas thought of in earlier times as being part of a social welfare system are now more often seen as aspects of economic policy. Health policy provides a good illustration; this is an area that nowadays is increasingly constructed in terms of contractual arrangements between the state and the people, where the worth of alternative strategies for providing medical and hospital care is assessed in terms of their financial benefits and costs. The same sorts of influences are at work in the cultural policy arena. Thus our discussion of the cultural policy process in the present chapter begins with a consideration of how culture fits into the *economic* policy objectives of governments.

But despite its dominance, economics is not the only game in town, and governments clearly acknowledge that they have a responsibility for the social and cultural well-being of society that extends beyond purely financial concerns. Most political leaders, if set the task of articulating a mission statement for the government they represent, would almost certainly include within it a grandiloquent reference to the importance of culture in the life of the nation, and would rec-ognise a collective responsibility to pay attention to this area. Hence we must also consider the purely *cultural* intentions of cultural pol-icy. Indeed it hardly needs pointing out that it is precisely its cultural content, however culture is defined, that serves to set cultural policy apart from other areas of government concern and that endows cul-tural policy with its distinctive significance.

In the following sections we discuss the distinction between the economic and cultural objectives of cultural policy, the major instru-ments whereby policy is implemented, and the problems of monitoring and evaluation of cultural policy when both economic and cultural outcomes are regarded as important.

## 2 Economic objectives of cultural policy

National governments are generally understood to have a series of objectives in managing the national economy, including the promotion of market efficiency, achievement of an equitable distribution of income and wealth, encouragement of economic growth, and the maintenance of full employment, price stability and external balance. The weight given to these different objectives is a political matter and the relative importance accorded the specific goals varies over time and between countries. Furthermore, it is rare that they can all be achieved simultaneously, and difficult trade-offs frequently arise. Policy-making in these circumstances is not helped by the fact that economists' capacity to forecast the future directions of the economy or to predict the outcomes of alternative policy measures is limited, to say the least. Thus policy choices often have to be made on the basis of faith and hope rather than the certainty of achieving particular desired results.

How do the various economic objectives of government as listed above relate to cultural policy formation? Let us consider each objective in turn.

### *Efficiency*

The promotion of economic efficiency has become a major focus of policy concern for governments managing free-market economies in the contemporary world. The neoliberal economic ideology upon which such economies are founded relies on the proposition that free markets are the appropriate mechanism for the allocation of resources in the economy, and that the public interest is best served by governments that confine their intervention to ensuring that markets work as freely and as efficiently as possible. This ideology is deemed to apply both to goods markets, hence proscribing any form of industry protection, and to input markets, thus forbidding interference in areas such as the setting of minimum wages.[2]

Nevertheless, despite the minimalist role for government intervention envisaged in the standard model of the operation of the macro-economy, it is conceded that markets do in some circumstances fail. The first and most important source of market failure is the occurrence of public goods, as defined in the previous chapter. We noted there that the arts and culture can be argued to have public-good characteristics through their contribution to providing diffused community benefits that are not able to be captured in market processes. If this is so, the overall output of arts and culture will, according to the competitive model of supply and demand, be less than the social optimum, providing an in-principle justification for government intervention to boost supply. Such intervention could take many forms, the most immediately apparent of which is the provision of subsidy to cultural producers to enable their output to increase. However, as economists are quick to point out, intervention may have associated costs, and will only be warranted if it can be shown that at the margin such costs do not exceed the benefits produced.

It is a curious irony that in the long-running debate about the justification for public support for the arts,[3] advocates from the arts community have often failed to appreciate how persuasive the public-good case can be in their disputes with economic sceptics. Most neoclassical economists are likely, if pressed, to admit that market failure does occasionally occur, and will entertain at least in principle the validity of the case for arts assistance made on these grounds, provided of course that the case is supported by credible empirical evidence as to benefits and costs.

Market failure occurring through the existence of non-market effects also arises because of particular characteristics associated with some specific areas of the arts and culture, for example in the benefits provided by cultural heritage. In addition to supplying a generalised public good, heritage may also give rise to what are called beneficial externalities. Externalities are close relatives of public goods, and arise as both positive and negative spillovers in production or consumption; they are the unintended side-effects of activities the main purpose of which lies elsewhere. Positive externalities may arise in the area of cultural heritage if, for example, the beauty of heritage buildings located in city streets is enjoyed by passers-by. These beneficiaries cannot be made to pay for the pleasure they receive, and so the owners of the buildings must themselves bear the full costs of maintaining their properties in good condition. In principle, the existence of such external benefits may warrant some collective assistance to property owners to ensure the continued provision of this benefit.[4]

A further area of market failure resulting from the existence of non-market effects arises through the public-good nature of artistic ideas embodied in creative works of literature, visual art and music. The expression of such ideas may in some circumstances be appropriated by individuals or firms without authorisation by, or payment to, the original creator. The transmission of music through radio broadcasts or the internet is an example; users may be able to record the broadcast or download the music file free of charge, and the songwriter or performer receives no reward. Copyright law exists to define property rights in these circumstances and to provide a market in which rights can be exchanged. Government regulation in this area can be seen as a response to market failure that is aimed at restoring economic efficiency, by establishing a market where one did not exist before.[5]

Economists also point to the fact that competitive markets are subverted and inefficiencies arise if increasing returns to scale or declining average costs exist in production. Firms subject to high fixed costs need to produce substantial levels of output so that their average costs per unit of output will be low enough to make production worthwhile. In these circumstances only a relatively small number of firms in the industry will be capable of reaching an economically efficient scale of production; this phenomenon is evident, for example, in the newspaper or television industries. Firms in such industries, if left to their own devices, may attain such market dominance that they can make excess profits at the expense of consumers. Competition may also fail for other reasons, for example when industries become increasingly concentrated because of mergers or the unrestrained takeover of smaller firms by larger ones. These considerations provide the rationale for government policies of regulating natural monopoly and promoting competition in the economy. They also constitute the basis for the so-called infant-industry argument for protection, which is designed to shield emerging industries from competitive pressures to allow them to grow to a sufficient size to be able to stand on their own feet. In the cultural industries arena, such arguments have been used in the audio-visual area to provide an economic basis for the protection of film-making in small domestic markets, and for stimulating the growth of emerging high-technology industries producing cultural product such as computer games.

A final source of market failure where government intervention to promote economic efficiency may be warranted arises if one side of a market, usually the buyer's side, is not fully informed about the goods or services being traded. The achievement of efficiency in the standard exchange model is based on an assumption that market participants have full information, and if this assumption is not upheld, government action to improve the availability of information may be justified, for instance through various consumer protection measures. In the arts, such arguments may be used to rationalise public assistance to advertising or marketing of artistic activities, and more broadly as an argument for arts education to improve people's capacity to make informed choices in regard to their present or future cultural consumption.

## Equity

Economic theory acknowledges the fact that the pursuit of efficiency does not necessarily lead to an allocation of resources in the economy that anyone would regard as fair. Indeed there can be many 'efficient' patterns of resource allocation, and judgements as to which one would be fairest are likely to vary amongst different observers. Economists are wary of venturing too far into questions of the equitable distribution of income and wealth, on the grounds that such questions involve value judgements that are the prerogative of individuals, and as such cannot be presumed or imposed by anyone else. Nevertheless most governments do accept the ethical proposition that poverty alleviation in society is an appropriate objective of public policy,[6] and accordingly adopt fiscal and regulatory measures to go some way towards redistributing income and wealth from rich to poor, for example through progressive taxation or through the provision of social goods like education and health services for lower-income households.

In the simplest models of macroeconomic management, the tasks of promoting economic efficiency and achieving equity are seen as separate and indeed sequential. That is, the first task of government is to ensure that the nation's resources are being utilised in an efficient manner and then, if the resulting allocation is deemed unfair, to seek alternative efficient allocations which better serve equity objectives, until one is found that is agreed to be acceptable (or even optimal) in equity terms. The implication of such a staged process is that governments should not be concerned if a particular efficiency measure has untoward distributional effects – these will be taken care of in the final redistribution that will complete the policy process.

Such arguments have been used in debate about the impact of subsidies to the arts. If it is true that opera, for example, is consumed
predominantly by the rich, subsidies provided by government to opera
companies which have the effect of lowering prices of admission will
be regressive in their incidence. Since the subsidies are financed out
of general taxation it is unfair, so the argument goes, that poor taxpayers should be called upon to finance the pleasures of the well-off.
The counter-argument is that the subsidy is provided for the purpose
of promoting economic efficiency – opera is subject to high set-up
costs, and possibly generates some public-good benefits, hence some
encouragement to increasing the output of opera may be warranted
if the marginal value of the benefits attained exceeds their marginal
cost. The contribution to the subsidy that the non-opera-going poor
make through their taxes will be appropriately offset by the benefits
they receive through the general redistributive mechanisms in place in
the economic system.

While such an argument is plausible in principle, its application in
practice leaves many critics of arts subsidies unconvinced. Even opera
companies' well-intentioned efforts to spread access to their performances to wider socio-economic strata fail to impress. Yet it remains a
troubling fact that many government policies have untoward distributional consequences, possibly involving substantially larger transfers
than are implicated in subsidies to the arts. Thus questions arising in
regard to the equity effects of arts subsidies need to be raised in the
wider context of the extent and effectiveness of a government's redistributive policy agenda overall.

## Growth

Government objectives of promoting economic growth are directly
relevant to policy towards the cultural industries, since, within the
creative economy rubric, these industries are seen as a sector contributing significantly to economic dynamism. In the UK, for example,
output of what is referred to in that country as the creative industries
sector (comprised largely of industries that fit the cultural-industries
definition of the previous chapter) grew at a rate of 5 per cent per
annum over the period 1997–2004 when measured as value added,
compared to 3 per cent for the rest of the economy.[7] In developing countries, too, the cultural industries have been singled out for

special attention in government growth strategies; for example, South Korean policy has encouraged the expansion of the audio-visual and new media industries, and the growth performance of these industries in recent years has been impressive.[8]

The role of the cultural industries in contributing to economic growth has also been witnessed in a variety of urban settings, from established cities such as New York and London, the cultural facilities of which act as a magnet to inbound tourism and stimulate economic activity as a result, to newly emerging mega-cities in the developing world such as Shanghai. In the latter case, the city's municipal government has stated explicitly that the development of creative industries, including performing and visual arts, television, architecture and fashion, is one of its priorities during the Eleventh Five Year Plan from 2006–2010; these industries now account for around 6 per cent of the city's gross regional product.[9] In a wider urban context, culture figures prominently in the rhetoric of 'creative cities', an agenda that has as much to do with the economic functioning of the urban complex as it does with fostering cultural participation or creating livable environments for the city's inhabitants.[10]

## Full employment

As traditional manufacturing industries decline and as labour-saving technologies are increasingly adopted throughout the economy, workers are made redundant; in these circumstances the maintenance of full employment becomes a particularly important task for governments. In the arts and culture area it is again the cultural industries that are implicated in the pursuit of this objective of economic policy. This is hardly surprising, in view of the significant growth rates of the cultural industries in a number of countries as noted above; these growth rates have been reflected in substantial increases over time in levels of employment in both creative and non-creative occupations. For example, taking the cultural sector of Europe as a whole, the average number of employed persons grew by between 3 to 5 per cent from 1995 to 2000, with significantly higher growth rates in some countries.[11]

As a basis for an effective employment policy, the cultural industries offer governments a particularly attractive target for investment, since the labour content of cultural output is typically higher than in other sectors. In the production of the creative arts, for example, the ratio of labour to capital in the inputs to production processes in theatre, film-making, visual arts, and so on, is typically greater than in other industries, suggesting a more significant marginal contribution to employment to be obtained from the marginal unit of capital invested in these industries compared to elsewhere. It is also argued that the types of jobs created in the cultural sector are greener, more enjoyable and deliver greater non-pecuniary rewards to workers than is the case for jobs in other sectors such as manufacturing.

As in the case of growth policy discussed above, employment policy in the cultural sector has found particular application in urban development. Cultural activities of various sorts have been used as a circuit-breaker to deal with problems of urban youth unemployment and social isolation. Arts projects in some cities have been used to revitalise depressed areas and restore a sense of civic pride.[12]

## Price stability

The objective of controlling inflation is an important aspect of both the fiscal and the monetary policy of governments in their efforts to manage the contemporary market economy. The implications for cultural policy are unlikely at first glance to be particularly significant, since cultural goods and services comprise a relatively small component of household expenditure, and movements in their prices do not have a noticeable impact on overall changes in the price level. However, this is not to say that cost inflation is irrelevant to the operations of cultural enterprises[13] or to consumers of cultural products; rather it is to say that in pursuing the objective of controlling the level of inflation in the macroeconomy, governments are likely to look elsewhere.

Nevertheless, the actions of governments in implementing measures to stabilise prices may have indirect implications for cultural policy if such actions take effect through, for example, restrictions on public outlays designed to reduce budget deficits. In such circumstances all avenues of government expenditure are likely to be on the table as candidates to be cut, but some politicians may well see cultural programmes as being easier in political terms to prune or to abolish altogether than are other areas of expenditure such as education, health or national security.

## External balance

Cultural goods and services enter the external account on both sides of the ledger, with the proportions varying substantially between countries. Some countries, such as the United States, are net exporters of cultural goods and services; others, such as many developing countries, are net importers. Assessment is problematical because although physical trade in cultural product can be traced reasonably accurately, it is far more difficult to provide a comprehensive account of financial flows between countries in the form of royalties and other payments arising from the buying and selling of rights to cultural material such as television programmes. Without such transactions included, estimates of total cultural exports and imports remain incomplete.

What data do exist show considerable expansion over recent years in trade in tangible products derived from a range of cultural industries, including design, publishing, visual and performing arts and new media. Indeed UNCTAD has argued that the creative industries constitute a new dynamic sector in world trade with particular potential to contribute to the foreign exchange earnings of developing countries; China, for example, is by far the largest exporter of tangible creative goods, with a market share in this area of about 20 per cent in 2005, and an annual growth rate of about 18 per cent over the period 2000–2005.[14]

In these circumstances the economic objectives of government in regard to the balance of trade may be importantly served by cultural policy, both through export promotion and through import substitution via the encouragement of local cultural production. The latter possibility is especially relevant in the area of television production, where local content quotas may be imposed in order to provide space for the domestic industry in the face of external competition. When this happens, economic and cultural policy objectives become entwined, as we shall see further in Chapter 9.

## 3 Artistic and cultural objectives of cultural policy

At the beginning of this chapter we noted that in addition to the economic objectives of public policy, governments also recognise a responsibility towards the arts and culture relating to the intrinsic importance of culture to the lives of the people. How can these cultural objectives be specified in a manner that distinguishes them from a purely economic agenda? As we have already pointed out, a guiding theme of this volume lies in the distinction between economic value and cultural value. Such a distinction enables the economic and cultural objectives of cultural policy to be separated, with the latter formulated as the task of enhancing the output and reception of cultural value in the economy and in society.

Four sources of cultural value can be identified: arts production and consumption; cultural identity and symbolism; cultural diversity; and cultural preservation and continuity. Let us consider these four in turn.

## Producing and consuming the creative arts

The creative arts have traditionally been the principal focus for governments in spelling out their cultural objectives, with the result that arts policy, as noted in Chapter 1, has been the primary element, or even the only element, in many cultural policy statements. The objectives of arts policy will be considered in more detail in Chapter 4; for now we can summarise these objectives as specified by most funding agencies in terms of the following three dimensions:

- *Excellence*: If the cultural value of art is to be judged independently of whatever commercial value it might possess, the emphasis will be on artistic quality, judged against appropriate standards as set by professional practice in the relevant artform. Of course the word 'excellence' means different things to different people, so translating this notion into an agreed objective of cultural policy may not be an easy matter. The usual procedure when appealing to this objective as a guide in making funding decisions is to rely on the judgement of informed practitioners in the arts, whose consensus opinions on what constitutes excellence are taken as decisive.[15]
- *Innovation*: The cultural value of extending an artform in new directions is widely recognised and provides a basis for an objective of fostering innovation in creative work as a further aspect of arts policy. Supporting innovation in this sense can be seen as similar to research and development expenditures in science, which are motivated by the same sort of exploratory purpose. Research and development at the frontiers of artistic practice is a risky business with an uncertain payoff, but every now and then, just as in science and

technology, success is achieved. In such cases the yield in terms of cultural value might be substantial, and there could be associated economic gains as well.

- *Access*: It can be argued that the cultural value of art becomes a reality only when it is experienced by someone. Thus the cultural objectives of arts policy almost always include a goal of widening access to artistic consumption in the community. This element of policy is clearly related to the broader equity objectives of government as discussed above, incorporating notions of fairness in access to cultural participation and enjoyment. There is sometimes also a paternalistic flavour to such objectives, reflecting a view, traceable to the nineteenth century, of the arts as a means to improve and civilise the ignorant masses.

## Defining cultural identity

The recognition and celebration of national, regional or local identity is an important objective of cultural policy at each of these levels of government. This objective can be articulated in terms of the cultural value accruing to individuals through the understanding of who they are. As noted in Chapter 2, this is one type of cultural value that clearly stands outside the limits of economic assessment; it makes little sense to ask people to express their valuation of their cultural identity in terms of willingness to pay.

The value of cultural identity contributes to cultural policy objectives via a number of avenues. Importantly, it becomes an aspect of arts policy when support is directed towards artistic work in any medium that expresses something specifically about the country or region in which it is located or produced. Similarly in media policy, local content restrictions are an embodiment of the cultural objective of providing opportunities for domestic voices to be heard. Identity also plays an important role in the formulation of the objectives of heritage policy; both tangible and intangible cultural heritage make strong contributions to an understanding of the cultural identity of the communities to which they relate.

## Celebrating diversity

The cultural life of the people, whether experienced through artistic creation or consumption, or more broadly through shared traditions, rituals and social engagement, is a source of cultural value, or social value, or both – the precise terminology is less important than the recognition that such collectively experienced value derived from the arts and culture can be a significant contributor to social cohesion, and as such its enhancement is an important objective of cultural policy. These social aspects of cultural policy can be interpreted within the current debate on cultural diversity, a debate that has been given particular focus through the entry into force in 2007 of the UNESCO *Convention on the Protection and Promotion of the Diversity of Cultural Expressions*. We shall discuss these issues in greater detail in Chapter 10; for now it suffices to point to the wide-ranging role of diversity in the formulation of cultural policy objectives, a role that extends across a variety of social aspects of the arts and culture, from the instrumental functions of the arts in building social capital to issues of cultural pluralism and ethnic diversity in urban communities.

## *Ensuring continuity*

It is well known that an individualistic model of human behaviour, one which portrays people's interests as being focussed solely on themselves to the exclusion of anyone else, is likely to under-represent the concerns that people feel for others. One aspect of this interpersonal dimension to human nature is demonstrated by the fact that individuals feel a connection with both past and future generations; in other words, the continuity of human existence is important to them. There are several aspects of the cultural objectives of cultural policy that relate to this issue:

- *Heritage*: The cultural value of heritage is inherently bound up with the sense that the existing stock of tangible and intangible cultural capital represents both a link with the past – an inheritance that tells us a great deal about ourselves and where we have come from – and a link with the future – surveys of public attitudes to heritage reveal a widespread acceptance of a responsibility to pass on our valued cultural resources to our children, our grandchildren, and beyond. This 'bequest value' does have an observable economic component, measurable as a willingness to pay for heritage conservation, but there is likely to be a significant non-financial component as well – an ethical belief in the importance of continuity. The generation of this sort of cultural value provides one element in the objectives of heritage policy, as we shall see in Chapter 6.

• *Education*: An aspect of continuity is reflected also in the transmission of knowledge and skills from one generation to the next, one of the tasks of education and training. Aside from its purely economic objectives directed at improving human capital and increasing productivity, education policy also has significant cultural objectives. Education in the arts for schoolchildren raises cultural awareness and assists in taste formation, and also lays the foundation for a potentially more diversified and rewarding cultural life for the individual in later years. The educational objectives of cultural policy are also expressed in the area of vocational education, i.e., the training of artists and creative workers of all sorts. It can be argued that pursuit of the cultural goals of arts policy will be facilitated if a well-educated cohort of artists is available to contribute through their professional practice to the continuity of the artform in which they are working.[16]

## 4 Instruments

Once objectives are determined, the implementation of policy is effected through the use of various policy instruments available to government. The choice of instrument to achieve given ends is by no means a straightforward matter – the so-called assignment problem, referring to the allocation of instruments to tasks, requires an understanding not just of the effects of specific measures on target variables such as the rate of unemployment or the money supply, but also an appreciation of the complex ways in which variables in the economic system are interrelated, such that change in one may flow on to changes in others.

Instruments may be classified in several different ways. One approach is to relate policy tools to the government agency most responsible for putting them into effect – the Treasury for fiscal policy, the Central Bank for monetary policy, and so on. Another is to focus on the broad targets of policy, such as public revenues and expenditures, government debt, prices and incomes, etc. Our task for present purposes is simply to separate out the major types of instruments that governments can use to pursue the economic and cultural objectives of cultural policy as outlined above. Accordingly, five groups of policy tools are specified under the following headings: fiscal measures; regulatory measures; industry assistance measures; labour market intervention; and trade policy. These categories are neither watertight nor fully comprehensive, and there is considerable overlap between them. Nevertheless they do provide a systematic basis for discussion.

We consider the essential components of each group of instruments in turn, leaving a more detailed consideration of specific measures to the relevant chapters later in the volume.

## Fiscal policy

Fiscal policy refers to measures that are put into effect through government expenditure and/or through raising of public revenue through the tax system. Since much of cultural policy in pursuit of both economic and cultural objectives requires a commitment of resources by government, it is not surprising that fiscal policy measures are amongst the most important cultural policy tools. They may be exercised in a number of different ways:

• *Direct provision of cultural goods and services*: Governments may choose to make cultural provision through public ownership and operation of cultural facilities of various sorts, such as museums, art galleries, libraries, performing arts venues, public-service broadcasting stations, and so on. The fiscal allocations to provide these goods and services relate to both the capital requirements and the operating expenditures of the enterprises and institutions concerned. In many cases, publicly owned and operated organisations are able to supplement their government funding by raising revenue from other sources, including the organisations' capacity to generate income from the sale of the goods and/or services they produce. There are many variations in the corporate and administrative structures of public cultural institutions: some are effectively government departments, some are set up as statutory corporations, some function as quasi-private-sector firms but with majority public ownership, and so on. All, however, are united in their ultimate dependence on the fiscal policy decisions of the government for their financial well-being.

• *Subsidies and grants to cultural producers*: Traditionally, a primary avenue for the implementation of arts policy has been, and continues to be, through the provision of grants or other forms of financial assistance to individual artists and arts organisations. The justification for deploying fiscal policy in this way might be expressed in terms of rectifying market failure, as described earlier, or as a means of pursuing the purely artistic or cultural objectives discussed above. Either way, the level and quality of output of artistic goods and services is the target, and the subsidy is seen as the most appropriate instrument. When organisations are assisted via grants from the public purse, it is generally a requirement that they be incorporated on a not-for-profit basis; the payment of public subsidy to commercial firms may in some circumstances be warranted, but such an occurrence in the arts is unusual. A variety of mechanisms exists for the distribution of subsidies to the arts, as we shall see further in Chapter 4.

- *Tax concessions*: Cultural policy can also be implemented through the tax system: individual artists may be afforded income tax relief; arts organisations may avoid corporate income taxes if they operate as not-for-profit enterprises; and such organisations may have some or all of their indirect tax liabilities waived through exemption from property taxes, payroll taxes, value-added tax, export duties and other financial impositions. Furthermore, artists and arts organisations in many countries receive income in cash or in kind from individual and corporate donors, philanthropic trusts and cultural foundations of various sorts, all of whom or which are motivated to give as a result of government tax concessions; these donors are allowed to offset their cultural gifts as a deduction or rebate against their income tax. The fiscal policy aspect of this form of support for the arts arises through the setting of concessional tax rates, and the cost to government is measured in terms of revenue forgone on the income side of the public-sector budget.

- *Assistance to consumers*: It is not only artistic producers who may be the beneficiaries of fiscal measures to support the arts. Schemes are occasionally proposed to channel assistance directly into the hands of consumers, for example through provisions of vouchers for free or reduced-price admission to selected arts events. Another method by which governments can promote arts consumption is via the provision of information and marketing services to improve consumer awareness and encourage cultural participation.

## Regulatory policy

Governments have an important responsibility to set up and manage the regulatory framework within which the economy operates. Much of this is taken for granted in everyday life – the infrastructure of the legal system, for example, or the prudential requirements that are supposed to control the nation's banks and finance houses. Individuals and organisations in the cultural sector are as much a beneficiary of these sorts of infrastructure as anyone else, with some aspects being of particular relevance to specific areas of cultural production, such as the importance of a workable contracts system to the film industry.

Apart from these general aspects of the regulatory environment, there are several specific areas in cultural policy where the instrument of regulation plays a distinctive role:

- *Intellectual property law*: Perhaps the most important form of regulation affecting cultural producers is that designed to protect their property rights over creative work. As we shall see further in Chapter 13, copyright has the purpose both of ensuring public access to creative material and of enabling creators to be rewarded for their effort. Copyright legislation enacted by government provides the framework within which rights can be defined, revenue can be collected and distributed, and compliance can be enforced. International conventions exist which govern the intellectual property relationships between countries. In some countries, copyright is extended to include additional forms of protection, such as a *droit de suite* or resale royalty applying to repeat sales of visual artworks.
- *Cultural rights*: A related area concerns the definition and assertion of cultural rights. Such rights may take several forms. A variant of copyright is the moral right that an artist may be permitted to exercise over the way his or her work is represented or used. Such a right can relate to attribution, whereby an artist's claim to authorship must be acknowledged, or to integrity, a requirement that a work cannot be altered, dismembered, destroyed or relocated without the permission of the artist. Moral rights require specific legislation, and have been invoked particularly in the areas of film, visual art and sculpture.[17] Another form of cultural right is that accorded indigenous people to pursue traditional cultural practices on their own land or in their own communities. Such rights may relate to language, ritual, etc., or to the granting of the right to gather food

through hunting, fishing, and so on, in ways that might otherwise be proscribed. Under this heading we can also draw attention to concerns in some countries with codifying the rights of professional artists. Such rights might include those already discussed above, but may also extend to definition of professional status, i.e., the right of an artist to be recognised and treated as a professional in industrial matters or in dealing with the tax or social welfare system. Finally, cultural rights also extend to freedom of speech and freedom of expression. In the cultural policy arena these issues arise, of course, in the debate about artistic censorship. For example, the so-called culture wars in the United States in the 1980s and 1990s were an example of the confrontation between artists and their supporters on the one hand, and the conservative right on the other, about artworks that were considered by the latter to be obscene or anti-religious.[18] Similar disputes have arisen in other countries from time to time. The extent of regulatory intervention to limit freedom of artistic expression varies markedly in different countries and at different times around the world.

- *Media policy*: Regulation is an important instrument in efforts by government to manage the print and broadcast media. Regulatory measures are deployed in some countries to prevent too great a concentration of media ownership in too few hands. They are also used to control the type of material that is distributed to the public, especially via free-to-air television. For example, most countries impose minimum requirements for certain types of programmes such as children's programmes or news broadcasts. Some governments also specify quotas for the transmission of domestically produced material such as drama, in an effort to prevent saturation by imported product. These trade-related aspects of cultural policy will be discussed further in later chapters.
- *Heritage policy*: Regulation is one of the principal instruments used in the protection of cultural heritage, as we shall see in Chapter 6. The listing of historic buildings, for example, is a regulatory device designed to safeguard such buildings from demolition, to control the extent to which they can be modified, and to encourage their conservation. Treaties such as the World Heritage Convention are examples of international regulatory arrangements which provide incentives to governments to act responsibly towards globally significant heritage sites in their care.

*Industry policy*

Governments use industry policy as a means of encouraging the establishment and expansion of industrial sectors that are believed to be of importance to current and future employment and economic growth. This may involve the dismantling of tariff protection that is shielding industries from the rigours of international competition, or it may be focussed on cultivating the development of one or two specific industries regarded as potential 'winners', through the provision of tax incentives, investment allowances, etc. At the regional or local level, industry policy may be a preferred instrument to attract the relocation of businesses that will provide a boost to regional economic growth. In situations where particular industries are targeted, the expectation is that industrial expansion will not only yield direct economic benefits but will also generate positive externalities that will spill over to other businesses through faster diffusion of technology and skills, complementarities in investment, and so on.

Industry policy is of particular relevance, of course, to the cultural industries if they are thought to offer good prospects for contributing to employment and output growth, and/or if they are seen as a source of the sorts of beneficial externalities mentioned above. The design industries are sometimes targeted for these reasons, as are those industries developing digital technologies in the provision of cultural content in areas such as gaming. The instruments that governments can use in pursuit of industry policy towards the cultural sector include the following:

• *Business start-ups*: Given the predominance of small-to-medium enterprises (SMEs) in the cultural industries of most countries, it is often through small-business programmes that industry assistance is most effectively provided. Such assistance might include business incubators, the provision of finance, skills development in business management and entrepreneurship, and so on.
• *Industry development strategies*: Sometimes governments put together an industry development scheme composed of various elements and identify it as a specific national strategy. For example, a National Tourism Strategy might involve coordination of planning arrangements for the tourism industry, targeted marketing campaigns, assistance to certain operators, and so on; cultural tourism could be a beneficiary of such a strategy.

- *Creative clusters*: The clustering of creative businesses is an observable phenomenon, where networking and reciprocal externalities provide benefits to the businesses involved. Such clustering may occur spontaneously, but it may also be initiated or encouraged by industry policy, for example through the establishment of cultural industry parks. Such interventions may also be important in terms of their employment effects, through the pooling of labour and skills in particular areas of cultural production.

We will return to a more detailed discussion of policy for the cultural industries in Chapter 5.

## Labour market policy

We have stressed at many points in this discussion the importance of employment for cultural policy. Many of the policy instruments that we have considered above will have positive employment effects that are either deliberately intended or incidental to the pursuit of other objectives. But there is also scope for use of specific labour market instruments in the implementation of cultural policy by governments concerned with the welfare of artists and other creative workers. Such instruments include:

- *Labour market interventions*: In addition to providing grants and other measures to help individual artists, as noted above, governments can also assist practitioners through minimum wage legislation for cultural workers, schemes to provide financial support via the dole, superannuation and pension arrangements for artists, and so on.
- *Occupational health and safety*: In some areas of cultural production, artists and other creative workers are exposed to risk of injury or to unsafe working practices, necessitating the formulation of appropriate OHS protection measures. This arises especially in fields such as dance, circus, theatre, music, sculpture, and some areas of the crafts.
- *Vocational training and skills development*: In many areas governments acknowledge the need to provide assistance for vocational training in order to ensure a continued supply of skilled workers to the labour market in particular industries; the cultural industries may be targeted for such support as part of a government programme for industry expansion.

## Trade policy

A number of the policy instruments discussed above have implications for international trade. Subsidies to domestic film producers, for example, may enable them to sell their product more effectively into export markets, whilst regulations mandating minimum local content in television broadcasts will almost certainly result in reduced imports of foreign programmes. Thus cultural trade is an area of concern to governments that spreads quite widely through the economic system. In its more specific sense, however, cultural trade policy can be taken to refer to that part of a government's overall dealings with international trade that relates directly to the import and export of cultural goods and services, matters that fall to the responsibility of the trade minister and the associated bureaucratic machinery. Domestic trade policy is significantly constrained by obligations that are imposed on countries by their participation in multilateral trading arrangements under the auspices of the World Trade Organisation, and by any bilateral trade agreements entered into. Subject to these limitations, the main instruments of trade policy of relevance to culture are summarised below, prior to a fuller consideration in Chapter 9:

- *Export promotion*: Although direct export subsidies may not be permissible, governments can promote international sales of cultural product in other ways, for example by facilitating touring overseas by national performing companies. Such endeavours are likely to spring more from cultural than from economic motives – the promotion of the nation's cultural image abroad, for example. Nevertheless, raising the profile of a country's culture in foreign lands may also be an element in a wider trade agenda, in pursuit of the old adage 'where culture leads, trade follows'. Thus sending a symphony orchestra or a dance troupe or an art exhibition to a potential trading partner may increase mutual understanding between countries and facilitate trade deals in commodities far removed from the arts and culture.
- *Import controls*: The standard instruments for intervention on the import side are tariffs and quantitative restrictions such as import quotas. In a world trading system predicated on the doctrine of free trade, such impediments are frowned upon and the expectation is

that where they exist they will be reduced or removed. Nevertheless, exceptions have been made for cultural goods and services, based essentially on the proposition that it is the cultural value of the goods and services involved that gives them the right to be treated differently from ordinary commercial merchandise.

## 5 Monitoring and evaluation

Once any policy strategy or specific policy measure has been implemented, it is important to governments to know whether the desired objective has been achieved. Information on the success or otherwise of various policies allows an assessment of their efficiency and effectiveness, and provides valuable feedback to help improve policy performance in the future. The two principal steps involved in measuring policy processes and outcomes are monitoring and evaluation. These steps may occur sequentially or in parallel, and may be one-off or continuing, depending on the nature of the policies under review.

In regard to the monitoring and evaluation of cultural policy, we can separate out the business of tracking economic outcomes and that of tracking cultural outcomes.

### *Tracking economic outcomes*

Monitoring the economic consequences of policy implementation should in principle be reasonably straightforward, since there are readily available and universally acceptable metrics according to which outcomes can be measured, such as monetary values of output, levels of employment, numbers of consumers, and so on. The variables to be monitored will depend on the type of policy being implemented, and are likely to include:

- observable levels of output, such as number of artworks sold, number of attendances at art events, number of visitors to museums, etc.;
- measures of the value of output, such as gross value of production, value added, etc.;
- levels of exports/imports of cultural product;
- rates of growth according to various economic indicators;
- price levels for cultural goods and services; and
- income levels of creative workers.

Governments rely on various sources of data in monitoring these types of variables, including, importantly, their own statistical agencies. In addition, special-purpose exercises may be undertaken to gather data on the impacts of specific policy measures.[19]

As we have noted earlier, observable market-related outcomes comprise one aspect of the economic value yielded by cultural policy. The other major component of this economic value derives from the non-market effects of policy measures, those generalised benefits accruing to people at large that are not captured through market-based exchange. When such benefits arise in the form of public goods or positive externalities, their value is measurable using assessment techniques such as hedonic price analysis or contingent valuation methods, to be discussed in Chapter 6 in the context of their application to cultural heritage. However, the implementation of non-market valuation methodologies is something that must generally be undertaken on a project-by-project basis, and the data are by no means easy or straightforward to collect. Thus the use of these approaches in the monitoring and evaluation of cultural policy, both at an aggregate level or in regard to specific policy measures, is unusual. To the extent that non-market effects are important in particular situations, any economic evaluation that ignores them is likely to be incomplete.

## Tracking cultural outcomes

Monitoring and evaluation of the cultural outcomes of cultural policy is much more difficult than the tracking of economic effects, for two obvious reasons: firstly, there is no acceptable unit of account by which cultural value can be measured, and secondly, evaluation of cultural impacts must rely to a significant extent on subjective judgements. Nevertheless, efforts to assess how successfully cultural goals have been pursued can be made more systematic if a distinction is drawn between those aspects that can be objectively described and those which will inevitably entail some subjective elements:

- *Objective evaluation*: A number of quantitative and qualitative indicators of culturally relevant outcomes can be proposed that do not rely on subjective assessments. For example, a cultural objective of increasing locally produced innovative arts output can be tracked by reference to the number of exhibitions of cutting edge contemporary art resulting from a particular grants programme, or by counting the number of new plays commissioned by a sub-sidised theatre company. Likewise if a cultural goal of arts policy is to widen access to artistic experience amongst a cohort of young consumers, the extent to which the goal is achieved can be measured from detailed statistics on arts consumption by different socio-demographic groups. Similarly, media policy objectives motivated by cultural rather than economic intentions that are pursued, for example, through local content regulation, can be readily tracked via objective data on the content of television programming, and the success of this policy in raising the consumption of domestically produced material is observable in audience ratings.

- *Subjective evaluation*: Since much of the assessment of cultural value depends on the subjective opinions of the individuals who are doing the assessing, any evaluation of the success of particular policies in achieving cultural objectives is likely to vary from person to person. Judgements relating to aesthetics, for example, are especially prone to the vagaries of individual taste. Similarly, a goal of promoting excellence in artistic output is likely to be difficult to pin down because of disagreements on how the concept of excellence should be interpreted. Nevertheless, as discussed in the previous chapter, some progress can be made in monitoring and evaluation of subjectively judged outcomes by reference to aggregated opinions, whether those of individuals whose judgements are regarded as relevant or those of the public at large.

## 6 Conclusions

The cultural policy process that has been the subject of this chapter follows a sequence that is common to most areas of government administration. Put in simple terms, the sequence begins with the articulation of objectives, proceeds through the choice of instruments and the business of their application, and culminates in the achievement or otherwise of desired outcomes that can be monitored such that lessons for further policy development can be drawn. We have argued that the characteristic that distinguishes cultural policy from other areas of government responsibility is, not surprisingly, its cultural content, a distinction that is represented in our formulation by the explicit separation of economic value and cultural value as the double-bottom-line of any policy strategy. We have indicated the ways in which both the economic and the cultural objectives of cultural policy can be articulated, such that a common set of policy instruments can be deployed to pursue them. The process of monitoring and evaluation of outcomes requires careful assessment, to the extent possible, of both the economic and the cultural value generated.

However, there remains an unresolved and overarching issue that is required to bring the double-bottom-line to a single policy conclusion: how is the weighting to be determined between economic value and cultural value in prospective policy judgements? In different areas of cultural policy there is often an observable tendency to emphasise one source of value over the other – arts policy, for example, generally places cultural aspects uppermost in the policy framework, whilst more recent interventions in favour of the cultural industries have had clear economic motives in mind. Nevertheless, in the end some trade-off between the two sources of value is likely to be inevitable, and at this point the economist is inclined to shrug his or her shoulders and say that making such a trade-off is a political matter. Whilst it is true that major policy decisions must ultimately be made in the political arena, the policy analyst can at least shine some light on the policy process. The intention of this chapter has been to point out two ways in which that illumination occurs: firstly through the provision of a systematic framework for analysing the cultural policy process, and secondly by an insistence on the significance of both economic value and cultural value as representing the dual purpose of government policy towards the cultural sector.

*Notes*

1 Quote is from Lynn and Jay (1984: 141).
2 Until recently, the neoliberal ideology was applied to financial markets as well, but the credit crisis of 2008, which saw unprecedented interventions by governments in free-market economies around the world, has marked a significant departure from the laissez-faire doctrine in fiscal and monetary policy.
3 For a collection of contributions to this debate up to the mid 1990s, see Towse (1997, vol. II, Parts V–VIII, pp. 499–719); see also Frey (2003).
4 See further in Chapter 6.
5 See further in Chapter 13.

6 Indeed if the lessening of poverty provides perceived benefits to the community at large, for example by making everybody happier because a source of suffering in society has been removed, poverty alleviation itself becomes a public good, and government intervention to relieve it can be rationalised on grounds of promoting economic efficiency rather than as an aspect of equity policy; the classic paper on this topic is Thurow (1971).

7 See statistics collected in Department for Culture, Media and Sport (2006).

8 See Shim (2006: 28).

9 See UNCTAD (2008: 47).

10 See further in Chapter 7.

11 See further in Wiesand and Söndermann (2005: 9).

12 See, for example, Strom (1999). These issues are discussed further in Chapter 7.

13 For a discussion of the impact of cost inflation on performing arts firms, see Chapter 4.

14 For a more detailed analysis, see UNCTAD (2008: 110).

15 See further in McMaster (2008).

16 See further in Chapter 11.

17 See further in Chapter 13.

18 See further in Chapter 4. For a case-study of a specific example of conflict involving the public funding of controversial art, see Rothfield (2001); Brooks (2008).

19 See Chapter 14.

# 4 | Arts policy

JAKE: I live by literary hack-work, and a little original writing, as little as possible. One can live by writing these days, if one does it pretty well all the time, and is prepared to write anything which the market asks for.

(Iris Murdoch, *Under the Net*, 1954[1])

## 1 Introduction

The creative arts is a generic term covering a wide variety of activities, including the arts that produce things – the visual arts, the crafts, musical composition, and literature (nowadays often referred to as 'creative writing') – and the arts that involve interpretation, such as musical performance, drama, dance, opera and music theatre. Within each of these artistic categories there is a further division into specific forms of practice: painting, drawing, printmaking, etc., in the visual arts, for example, or rock, pop, folk, jazz, classical, etc., in music. But although a taxonomic exercise within the family 'creative arts' can construct a reasonably coherent basic classification of artistic genres, there are many blurred edges. Should narrative non-fiction such as biography be included in the literary arts? Does 'new media art' comprise a separate category on its own, or is it simply a variant of something else? Are all types of film-making classifiable within the creative arts, or only those producing films for 'art house' cinemas?

Such definitional issues raise longstanding arguments surrounding terms such as the 'high arts' or the 'serious arts'. These terms have been used in some artistic circles to differentiate genres or modes of practice that are considered worthy from those that are 'popular' or merely 'entertainment'. It is true that, in practice, arts policy has tended to focus on the so-called serious arts, allowing the inclusion of artforms such as grand opera and the exclusion of others such as soap opera. The concentration of traditional arts policy on the high arts has been interpreted within the cultural studies discipline

58

as reflecting the hegemonic role of an artistic elite or the cultural establishment in capturing and controlling the arts policy terrain. On the other hand, the orientation of arts policy towards those arts that are supposed to reflect upper-class tastes could indicate simply that the objectives of government assistance are interpreted as being most appropriately served at the non-commercial or not-for-profit end of the production spectrum, an area where the high arts are mostly to be found.[2]

Whatever the outcome of these debates – which will doubtless continue *ad infinitum* if not *ad nauseam* – the widening of cultural policy beyond the confines of a traditional arts policy, which we have described in earlier chapters, means that such disputes can be absorbed into a larger policy discussion where all forms of cultural production and consumption are under consideration, without the need for value judgements as to their respective artistic status. In these circumstances, arts policy simply becomes one element in a more general cultural policy framework, relating specifically to those individuals and organisations making original creative work in text, sound, image or performance. In the context of the concentric circles model of the cultural industries introduced in Chapter 2, these individuals and organisations make up the creative core.

We begin this chapter by asking how arts policy has changed in recent times and how its objectives are now being reinterpreted. Inevitably, considerations of value underlie the discussion of this question. We then go on to consider in detail the two major avenues through which arts policy is implemented: *direct support* for artists, arts organisations and consumers provided by a ministry of culture or an arts funding agency, and *indirect support* for the arts provided via the tax system. Finally, the chapter considers the role of the individual artist as an object of cultural policy.

## 2  What is arts policy today?

Most industrialised countries around the world, and some developing countries as well, have established policies of providing support for the creative arts in one form or another. In virtually all cases the traditional orientation of arts policy has been towards the importance of artistic production and participation for building a civilised and socially enriched society, and also towards the role of the arts in the education of children. In these terms it can be said that arts

policy has been based on a concern for the intrinsic or cultural values
of the arts. This is not quite an instance of the familiar slogan 'art
for art's sake', although there is an undeniable flavour in some policy pronouncements that the arts need no further justification than
their own self-referential importance. Rather, locating arts policy
within the domain of the arts' cultural significance can be taken as an
acknowledgement of the historical role of the creative arts, in all their
manifestations, as an essential ingredient in the evolution of human
civilisation. The link between this role and policy lies in the recognition that, although artists will always create art spontaneously
regardless of their circumstances, there has generally been a requirement, if sufficient art to serve society's needs is to be forthcoming,
for collective intervention of some kind. In the past, such supportive
action was taken by princes and potentates, by churches and royal
houses, by merchants and bankers, in short, by patrons of various
kinds with sufficient money and taste to pay for art that could serve
their own self-aggrandisement and that might also spread enlightenment and pleasure amongst those around them. Today these philanthropic duties are assumed by arts councils, ministries of culture,
private foundations and generous individuals.

In political terms, when a government enunciates an arts policy
built around the cultural importance of the arts in society, it may
be interpreted as acting on one or both of two motivations. Firstly,
the government may see such actions as according broadly with the
desires of its constituency. In other words it may judge that voters will
approve of some public expenditure being devoted to arts support,
whether such approval derives from an explicit willingness to pay for
perceived non-market benefits from the arts, or from some looser,
less formalised agreement amongst the electorate that it is somehow
'right' that governments should do such things. Secondly, the government may take it on itself to assert the appropriateness of spending on
the arts from the public purse regardless of whether or not the voters
agree; such a case would categorise the arts as what economists label
a 'merit good', i.e., a good or service provided by the public sector
irrespective of consumer demand, where the usual operation of consumer sovereignty is set aside in favour of the imposition of the government's own preferences.[3]

Whatever the underlying rationale, a traditional arts policy based
on the cultural value of the arts has generally interpreted its essential

mission in terms of the three objectives discussed in Chapter 3: promotion of artistic excellence, encouragement of work that might not
otherwise find a market, and spreading the benefits of artistic consumption and participation as widely as possible in the community.
In recent times, as we have noted, there has been a shift in the orientation of cultural policy away from the longstanding focus on the
arts per se towards a broader agenda. In this process arts policy as a
specific component of cultural policy has itself changed. Two sources
of this change can be identified.

The first is the general 'economisation' that has affected cultural
policy overall. In regard specifically to the arts, this process can be
traced back at least to the 1980s, when demonstrating the size of the
arts sector as a component of the national economy was seen as a
means of asserting the arts' importance as an object of government
concern. Studies that purported to show the economic contribution
of the arts industries to output and employment in the economy at
large, or the local economic impacts of an arts event such as a festival, were criticised in many instances as methodologically unsound,
and invalid as a justification for government support.[4] Nevertheless,
as Bruno Frey points out, such studies continue to find favour with
arts advocates determined to appear pragmatic and policy-relevant.[5]
The best that can be said of the current state of play in this area is
that measuring the economic contribution or impact of the arts, when
competently carried out, is now a somewhat more sophisticated science than it has been in the past.[6]

The second source of the shift in arts policy has been brought about
by wider trends in public sector management. In several countries
the concept of public value as promulgated by Mark Moore and his
colleagues at Harvard University took hold as a means of making
public-sector service delivery more efficient and more accountable. In
the UK, for example, cultural institutions such as the BBC undertook
major reviews of their performance calibrated against public-value
criteria, while in the US some state arts agencies assessed the application of public-value processes to their operations.[7]

The obvious question raised for arts policy by the introduction of
public value as a yardstick for measuring the effectiveness of government expenditure is: How can the contribution of artistic activity
to the creation of public value be assessed?[8] In the UK, the bureaucratic response was to tie arts funding criteria more closely to

those outcomes that could be measured: numbers of people visiting museums, for example, or more indirect indicators such as health or learning outcomes. This trend towards instrumentalism in arts policy brought a strong reaction. At a symposium on *Valuing Culture* held in 2003, and in a Demos pamphlet published in 2004,[9] a vigorous campaign was mounted to reassert the importance of the arts' fundamental purposes, a cry that was even echoed at ministerial level.[10] It was argued that although music ensembles, theatre companies, art galleries, and so on, may indeed contribute to promoting social cohesion, alleviating youth unemployment or improving community health, these are not the primary reasons for their existence. Funding that is made dependent on achievement of these sorts of instrumental objectives loses sight of the intrinsic cultural value of art to people and to society.[11]

At the same time, on the other side of the Atlantic, a report produced by the RAND Corporation on the benefits of the arts in the United States was also concerned about intrinsic benefits, which it labelled as the 'missing link' in a public debate that had become too preoccupied with instrumental objectives. The authors argued that although arts advocates were uncomfortable with having to make a utilitarian case for the arts, they were 'reluctant to emphasise the intrinsic aspects of the arts experience lest such arguments fail to resonate with funders'.[12]

Both the Demos and the RAND reports saw the trend towards instrumentalism as being prompted by the need for data. Policymakers, they argued, cannot translate vague and subjective assessments of artistic 'quality' into rigorous measures of public value, instead requiring quantitative results that can be set against benchmarked performance standards. But, as John Holden has declared,

the value of culture cannot be adequately expressed in terms of statistics. Audience numbers and gallery visitor profiles give an impoverished picture of how culture enriches us.[13]

Holden proposed a 'new language' of communication that would give fuller expression to the true value of culture, a theme taken up by Sir Brian McMaster in a report for the UK Department for Culture, Media and Sport. This report advocated evaluation methods that focus on objective assessments of excellence, innovation and risk-taking rather than on bean-counting, a proposition for a 'move from measurement to judgement' that, like the intrinsic-value arguments noted earlier, once again received the ministerial nod.[14]

Discussion of the purposes of arts policy and how it should be interpreted in a changing world will doubtless continue. On the one hand, political pragmatists seeking to bring the arts into a broader public-policy discourse will be accused of philistinism, while on the other side, those arguing for a return to the intrinsic or absolute values of culture will be labelled elitist and self-serving. In a rational world neither side should hold sway; rather in this area, as elsewhere, a sensible way forward would seem to rest on a recognition of the multiple dimensions of artistic experience. The transcendental purposes of art are undeniable, as is the fact that the arts contribute to community life, improve tolerance, enhance understanding, stimulate creative thinking, provide incomes and employment, and so on. We have portrayed these various attributes of the arts as expressible in value terms by reference to the dualism in cultural valuation processes. In this context the task of policy-makers can be construed as one of finding the optimal balance between the generation of economic value and cultural value from the arts, and calibrating funding decisions accordingly.

In the following two sections we turn to the major avenues by which arts policy is put into effect: through direct support measures administered by a ministry of culture or a public agency such as an arts council, and indirect support for the arts via the tax system. These avenues are not mutually exclusive, and the administrative arrangements in place in most developed countries contain some elements of both: for example, in countries such as the UK where national-level arts policy relies primarily on the arts council model, there are nevertheless tax incentives to encourage private-sector support, whilst in a country like the US where indirect support comprises the principal means for federal arts funding,[15] there are nevertheless state arts councils that administer active arts policies at the sub-national level.[16]

## 3  Direct support

Institutional structures providing direct support for the arts vary between countries in terms of the mix and importance of different administrative mechanisms. At one extreme is the straightforward arts or culture ministry that makes funding allocations direct to recipient organisations and individuals, as is the case in a number of European countries.[17] Ultimate decision-making powers in this model lie with the relevant government minister. At the other end of the spectrum is the system whereby decision-making responsibilities are transferred to an independent statutory body, usually called an arts council after the original such body established in Great Britain in the 1940s. The so-called arm's length principle in operation in this situation is intended to guarantee that funding decisions will be free of political influence. The arts council model is in use today in, amongst others, England, Scotland, Wales, Ireland, Canada, Australia and New Zealand. Nevertheless, in most of these countries the central arts ministry generally retains some functions, such as the funding of major public museums and galleries, or the international promotion of the nation's art.

In this section we consider three aspects of direct arts support in more detail: the objectives of arts funding authorities; the making of allocation decisions; and governance issues.

## Objectives

John Maynard Keynes, the inaugural Chairman of the Arts Council of Great Britain, proclaimed in a radio broadcast in 1945 announcing the forthcoming establishment of the Council that the organisation's purpose would be:

> to create an environment, to breed a spirit, to cultivate an opinion, to offer a stimulus to such purpose that the artist and the public can each sustain and live on the other in that union which has occasionally existed in the past at the great ages of a communal civilised life.[18]

Ever since then the mission statements of arts funding agencies the world over have been replete with references to the cultural importance of the arts, to creativity, to the striving for artistic excellence, to the need for expanding access to the arts, to the significance of the arts in identity formation, and, importantly, to the fundamental role of the individual artist. So, for example, the Canada Council for the Arts describes its 'ultimate goal' as 'a Canadian artistic life that is creative, diverse, resilient, and profoundly meaningful to

Canadians across the country and to the world'.[19] In New Zealand, the Parliamentary Act for the Arts Council (now called Creative New Zealand) enunciates guiding objectives for the Council that include participation, access, excellence and innovation, professionalism and advocacy.[20] These sorts of sentiments are summed up by the following statement promulgated by the Scottish Arts Council in 2007, which declared that the Council's mission was to

serve the people of Scotland by fostering arts of excellence through funding, development, research and advocacy. We believe the arts to be the foundation of a confident and cultured society. They challenge and inspire us. They bring beauty, excitement and happiness into our lives. They help us to express our identity as individuals, as communities and as a nation.[21]

The translation of these declarations of virtuous intent into realisable policy objectives can be interpreted in economic terms by reference back to the twin goals of efficiency and equity discussed in Chapter 3 – efficiency can be sought through increased quantity and quality of artistic output, whilst equity relates to how that output is distributed amongst different classes of beneficiaries. Expressed in these terms, the policy objectives can be seen to be congruent with those of the typical not-for-profit firm; a standard model of such a firm assumes utility to be a joint function of output quantity and quality (however measured), where utility is to be maximised subject to a break-even financial constraint. If the quality dimension of the objective function is summarised as the drive for the highest artistic standards, and the quantity aspect feeds into the achievement of increased consumption and participation, the policy objective can be reduced to one representing the joint pursuit of excellence and access. This point was made neatly by the first Chairman of the Australian Council for the Arts (later the Australia Council), Dr H. C. Coombs, who, like Keynes, was an eminent economist of his day with strong artistic sensibilities; in his statement for the First Annual Report of the Council, in 1973, he wrote:

The problem facing the Council and the Boards is essentially that of achieving a proper balance in the allocation of effort and resources to the various objectives – particularly between the promotion of excellence and the widening of participation in and experience of the arts.[22]

These twin objectives of excellence and access, quality and quantity, have remained more or less unchanged to the present day. Yet despite progress over the years in the fine-tuning of arts policies to changing modes of artistic production and to cultural trends in society generally, fundamental questions still remain as to whether such stated policy objectives are relevant or achievable, and whether their achievement or otherwise can be evaluated other than in the most general terms. In this respect the rhetorical question 'Does the Arts Council know what it is doing?', which was the title of Karen King and Mark Blaug's 1973 article on the then Arts Council of Great Britain, still remains relevant to arts funding authorities everywhere today, more than three decades later.[23] Perhaps the widening scope of cultural policy to which we have drawn attention provides at least a partial answer to the question, by opening the way towards a more clearly articulated policy for the creative arts, one which integrates art more fully into the broader concerns of public policy, and which celebrates quite naturally and unashamedly all aspects of the centrality of art in everyday life.

## Allocation decisions

Whether direct arts funding is provided by a government ministry or an arts council, decisions as to the allocation of a given budget amongst competing uses must be made, consistent with the stated objectives. An initial question to be answered is, 'At what point in the value chain should intervention occur?' If the artistic sequence of events begins with the creative artist at one end and finishes with the consumer at the other, with a series of value-adding processes along the way, the policy-maker has a choice as to where the injection of support funds will be most beneficial. At first glance it may seem obvious that if, say, the objective of improving artistic quality were paramount, assistance at the production end of the value chain would be appropriate, whereas if increasing access were the relevant goal, support should be directed towards consumers. However, the answer may not be so clear-cut, since funding provided at one point in the value chain may have beneficial effects upstream or downstream from the point of intervention. For example, a policy objective of widening access may be facilitated by support for a theatre company, if the funding enables ticket prices to be lower than they would otherwise be. Similarly, the theatre company's grant is likely to flow in the other direction as well, assisting individual artists through the payments to actors, playwrights, designers, and so on, which the grant makes possible.

Support directed to artists and arts companies serves both quantity and quality intentions of assistance. Increased quantity of output – more novels written, more plays produced, more art exhibitions mounted, more music performed – is consistent with the efficiency-related objective of correcting for market failure by raising artistic output to a more socially optimal level, whilst quality goals can be pursued through targeted support for work of a particular genre or aspiring to high-level artistic standards. In some circumstances the relationship between quantity and quality could be seen as competitive, in other respects complementary. For example, in classical music the more innovative, experimental or avant-garde is the work supported, the smaller are audiences likely to be; if the qualitative goal of funding is specified in this instance as the pursuit of innovation, a trade-off is likely to exist between increased quality and increased attendance goals in a funding authority's multiple-objective decision problem. On the other hand, in exhibiting visual art a public gallery might find that the higher the reputation of the artists shown (presumably implying higher quality standards in at least someone's estimation) the greater the number of visitors, suggesting in this case a positive connection between quality and quantity achievement.[24]

In economic terms the decision-maker's problem in this sort of situation can be cast as one of identifying the marginal contribution to the achievement of a given objective by an additional unit of funding – dollar, pound, euro, or whatever – amongst competing claimants for funds. Economic theory, if not ordinary intuitive common sense, suggests that the marginal effects of additional funding to a given recipient, measured in terms of an objective such as increased output, improved attendance figures, higher quality standards, etc., will decline as funding increases. If so, the decision-maker's task of allocating funds amongst applicants in pursuit of a particular objective can be portrayed as one of equalising the marginal benefits of the last unit of funding across all recipients; such an allocation would maximise the total benefit in regard to that objective.

Notwithstanding its apparent rationality, however, it is hardly surprising that applying such a principle in practice will be difficult, as measures of the 'productivity' of funding in terms of various objectives are unlikely to be available. In these circumstances decision-makers have to fall back on ad hoc judgements, juggling many variables in making a final determination. Nevertheless, even if solutions to real-world allocation problems cannot be reached by such formal calculations, at least an understanding of the concept of the marginal productivity of subsidy can help to inform decisions. To illustrate, consider the problem of providing assistance to not-for-profit performing companies with the aim of encouraging innovation. In areas such as drama, the production of new, risky and adventurous work tends to be concentrated amongst smaller and sometimes ephemeral companies, where a small amount of public funding means a great deal. The marginal productivity of the extra unit of subsidy to such companies is likely to be quite high, measured in terms of innovative yield. By contrast, the corresponding marginal productivity of the extra unit of finance to large enterprises that are more generously funded in absolute terms is likely to be relatively less, given not just their size but also their possible tendency to rely on safer and more conservative programming.

Mention of not-for-profit firms raises the question that is often asked in relation to public-funding allocations: 'Should *for-profit* firms in opera, theatre or dance have access to government grants?' Three points are relevant in answering this question. Firstly, commercial companies in the performing arts are financed by speculative capital that may or may not make a return on the investment involved. It is not the responsibility of governments to provide assistance to speculators who expect to take their chances in a risky marketplace. Secondly, commercial performing companies are already likely to have received significant benefits from public funding, for example if they are able to make use of artistic talent that has been trained or has gained experience at public expense. Thirdly, and perhaps most importantly, the not-for-profit status of subsidised firms in the performing arts means that they are forbidden under their act of incorporation to distribute any surplus they may make to the firm's owners. For-profit companies operate under no such constraint, opening up the possibility that if a subsidy were paid to such a firm, it could flow directly as profit into the pockets of the firm's owners or managers.

It is well known that public museums and galleries, theatre companies, symphony orchestras, etc., face perennial problems of financial hardship, with uncertain revenues and inexorably rising costs. To what extent should a funding body take cost pressures into account when making its decisions? For example, performing companies might invoke the well-known problems of the productivity lag in the live arts when putting forward their case for funding. This phenomenon was first identified by William Baumol and William Bowen in 1966 and subsequently labelled 'Baumol's disease' or 'the cost disease'.[25] Essentially, the hypothesis states that labour productivity in the live arts remains static over time – it still takes the same number of work-ers the same amount of time to perform a Beethoven string quartet today as it did in Beethoven's day. In a two-sector model in which one sector suffers from this technological disadvantage, wage rises in the productive sector are transmitted to the stagnant sector, causing a widening gap in the latter between revenues and costs, since firms in the stagnant sector cannot cover wage rises with improved labour productivity. Applying this to the live arts, Baumol and Bowen pre-dicted that performing firms would have to access increasing levels of non-box-office revenue, such as public subsidy, in order to stay in business.

Does the cost disease constitute a valid argument for subsidy to firms affected by it? Regrettably not. While the existence of high costs of production may earn some sympathy from a funding source, it does not of itself constitute a case for assistance; many businesses suffer from cost pressures of various sorts that are regarded as part of the normal conditions of production, and performing firms are no different. Nevertheless, the prospects for the live arts are not as bleak as a strict application of the cost-disease hypothesis might suggest. Empirical studies of this phenomenon have confirmed that costs of live performances have indeed risen as the model implies, but that the impact of these cost increases on firms has been somewhat muted. Most performing companies have been able to mitigate the effects of slow productivity growth through a variety of strategies, including tapping new sources of unearned revenue, exploiting the potential of new recording and distribution technologies, expanding ancillary activities such as merchandising, and so on.

Our discussion so far has focussed on the production end of the value chain, reflecting the predominant direction in which funding is delivered in the contemporary world. The goal of increased access has arisen only incidentally, met almost by chance on the assumption that increased output of the arts will be taken up by a growing number of consumers. In fact access objectives can be explicitly served via assistance to producers if it is targeted to specific projects or strategies designed to increase and/or widen audiences. For example, artists and companies can be encouraged through subsidy to take their art out into the community, to places where a broader cross section of people can experience their work; theatre companies can be subsidised to offer free performances; opera companies can set up screens in parks and squares, or broadcast their productions live into cinemas; and so on. And most public galleries run educational programmes to inculcate a taste for art in the young.

Even more pointedly, subsidy funds can be channelled direct to consumers via the provision of free or low-cost vouchers exchangeable for artistic goods and services, such as theatre tickets, books, etc. Economists with a belief in consumer sovereignty tend to favour such schemes, arguing that the resulting pattern of artistic production will follow consumer tastes rather than be determined by the self-interested wishes of producers or the ill-informed judgements of bureaucrats. Despite the appeal of voucher schemes to aficionados of the free market, however, designing workable schemes that are proof against mismanagement or subversion has proved difficult,[26] and few successful examples exist. Moreover, allowing consumers to choose what art receives the benefits of subsidy may undermine the quality objectives of assistance if consumers at large lack the necessary information to be able to recognise the value of, say, avant-garde or innovative art that happens to be the focus of a funding authority's quality objectives.

## Governance

The arts council model for direct provision of cultural support is based on two principles, which can be referred to as the 'arm's length' and the 'peer review' principle respectively. The arm's length principle requires that the council be set up as an independent body which has the capacity to make its own decisions without reference to any goverment minister and without influence being imposed on it from any part of the political machinery.[27] The advantage of such an arrangement from the viewpoint of the government is that if the council makes unpopular decisions, or funds projects or activities that some in the community may find obscene or distasteful, the minister can claim that he or she was not responsible and therefore cannot be blamed. Reference is then made to the second principle, peer review, which holds that funding allocations in the arts should be determined by experts – the 'peers' of those being funded – much as we rely on the judgements of experts in making financing decisions in other areas, such as medical research. Thus the provision of public funds to support controversial art is rationalised on the grounds that those in the know regard the work being supported as artistically worthwhile.

Although these two principles have managed to survive more or less unscathed in most arts councils, they came unstuck some years ago in the United States with the outbreak of the so-called 'culture wars' over funding decisions of the federally funded National Endowment for the Arts (NEA).[28] Grants to allegedly obscene or blasphemous projects were subject to sustained criticism from conservative political and social forces, to the point where, in 1990, the US Congress imposed a requirement on the NEA Chair that funding decisions must take into account 'general standards of decency and respect for the diverse beliefs and values of the American people'.[29] Funding for the Endowment was cut, and its activities have continued to be compromised ever since.

The peer review principle enshrined in the operation of arts councils outside the United States is also a controversial issue. Critics of this principle question whether artists and managers of arts companies who sit on panels to decide upon funding allocations are actually capable of making independent judgements, especially when the pool of applicants is relatively small and likely to be known personally to at least some of the judges. Despite the fact that procedures designed to resolve real or potential conflicts of interest are invariably contained in the operating rules of boards, panels and committees, the peer review process is still seen by some to be liable to the phenomenon of 'regulatory capture', the process whereby beneficiaries of government decisions gain control over the relevant decision-making machinery. In view of this, and in pursuit of a wider and more 'representative' frame of reference for allocation decisions, some arts-funding authorities have sought to dilute the influence of peers on their funding committees through the introduction of 'independent' individuals, for example bureaucrats from non-arts areas, community representatives, corporate executives from the private sector, and so on.

A final issue of concern under the governance heading relates to the question of public versus private ownership and control of government cultural institutions such as art galleries, museums, symphony orchestras, broadcasting organisations, and so on. In recent years there has been an increasing emphasis in most countries' economic policy on opening up the economy to market forces and reducing state involvement in economic activity. These trends have been evidenced in a variety of ways, including the breaking up of state-owned monopolies, the transfer of public assets to private ownership, the introduction of contracting-in and contracting-out into the operations of public business undertakings, an increased application of 'user-pays' principles by such organisations, and so on. All of these phenomena, and more, have been loosely gathered together under the heading of 'privatisation'. The question arises as to how these various processes of privatisation might affect, if at all, the traditional role of the state towards the arts and culture.

In the first place it can be said that the wholesale transfer of public assets to private ownership as has happened, for example, in the transport, telecommunications and energy sectors, has not occurred, and is unlikely to occur, in the case of state-owned cultural institutions, even when they operate effectively as monopolies. The reasons have to do with their cultural purpose. They are not commercial organisations striving for profitability in a competitive marketplace, even though their economic performance, measured in terms of their capacity to raise revenue, their cost-efficiency, their market effectiveness, and so on, is a matter of concern to the government. Rather, their raison d'être is their contribution to the cultural life of the community and of the nation.

Nevertheless, in managing their internal operations, such organisations may look to strategies in use in the private sector to improve the efficiency of their operations and management. For example, outsourcing of some functions may appear an attractive option to reduce costs. If outsourcing has to do with non-cultural aspects of an institution's function, such as catering services in an art gallery, the move can be judged against normal financial yardsticks. But if the outsourcing relates to cultural processes, quality concerns are likely to be raised. For example, a public broadcaster buying in news reports instead of using its own correspondents may lose control over vital aspects of the quality of its output.

There may be other lessons, both positive and negative, to be learned from existing privatisation experience in many countries that could be useful to cultural institutions, organisations, enterprises, etc., in helping them to cope with a variety of changes in their operating environment, including diminishing government budgets, pressures for greater efficiency, changing market demands, new regulatory environments, and so on. In particular, research showing the importance of corporate structures and incentives in affecting efficiency in business operations may suggest opportunities for redesigning management systems and procedures in a number of different types of arts organisations. Already there are cultural institutions in several countries that exemplify these trends. In the Netherlands, for example, the programme of re-establishing national museums and galleries as autonomous and independent business units is well underway. Under these arrangements, the state retains ownership of buildings and collections, and continues to provide financial support on agreed terms, but the governance and management of the institutions are freed up to be more flexible, responsive, dynamic and entrepreneurial in the operation of facilities and in the delivery of service to the public. The state symphony orchestras in Australia provide another example; their gradual corporatisation in recent years has retained their public-sector presence but given them a new sense of self-determination and independence to take on a more varied role in serving the cultural needs of their various communities.[30]

## 4 Indirect support

We turn now to the other main means by which governments implement an arts policy, i.e., by using the tax system to encourage private donors to support the arts, or to allow exemption from various taxes to eligible artists or arts organisations. The cost to the public purse of such indirect assistance is not observed in the government budget, but is realised in terms of the public revenue forgone as a result of reduced tax collections.

In considering private support for the arts, it is important at the outset that we distinguish between sponsorship and philanthropy.  The former is a means by which corporations can gain some exposure for their brand through supplying goods and services at zero or reduced cost to arts organisations, or by providing financial support in exchange for naming rights or for some other form of corporate recognition. Thus a sponsorship deal is a purely commercial transaction, in which the recipient arts organisation gains financial or other benefit and the sponsoring firm enjoys some advertising or marketing advantage. Philanthropy, on the other hand, refers to donations in cash or kind that are untied as to their use; the donor expresses support for the mission of the artist, arts company or organisation by giving money, but does not receive anything in return other than a 'warm inner glow' from having contributed to a worthy cause. However, the flow of benefit is not entirely one-way; apart from the desire to do good, a philanthropist is also likely to be motivated by the prospect of some tax relief flowing from his or her donation.

Another form of philanthropic action is seen in volunteering. Many people donate their time and their skills free of charge to an arts or cultural organisation because they are interested in the artform, because they admire the organisation, share its goals, and want to help in some way, or simply because they have time to spare and want to spend it in doing things they find enjoyable and rewarding. The cost to the individual can be measured in terms of the opportunity cost of the time donated, plus any associated expenses not reimbursed, and the benefit to the recipient organisation is enjoyed in the form of reduced expenditure on labour and sometimes in opportunities to access particular skills.[31]

In the following discussion of indirect means for providing arts support, we consider three aspects: the rationale for a tax-based policy, the mechanisms that can be used, and the economic aspects of manipulating tax incentives to encourage donations for artistic purposes.

## Rationale

There are two grounds on which support for the arts and culture via the tax system can be rationalised. The first is that such a system mobilises private support for the arts, bringing financial resources to the sector that it would not otherwise receive. In other words, a given cost in terms of public support leverages an additional pool of private funds, increasing the total amount of funding available. The second rationale is that decisions as to who and what is subsidised are effectively transferred from bureaucrats and politicians to a much larger number of individuals, who direct their donations to organisations and activities of their choice.

The first of these rationales would appear to be quite straightforward. Although worthy citizens and altruistic foundations might be inclined to support the arts even in the absence of tax incentives, the provision of such incentives clearly stimulates a larger volume of giving, and the tax revenue forgone could be seen as money well spent insofar as it has co-opted the general public into helping finance the achievement of government policy objectives at relatively little cost to the Treasury. Moreover, the recipient organisations would seem to be better off than they would have been had the equivalent amount in terms of cost to government been provided by a direct grant, without any private contribution.

However, the prospect of private sector involvement in support for the arts raises questions concerning the relationship between public and private financing. In particular, does the existence of some level of direct public support 'crowd-out' or 'crowd-in' private donations? *Crowding-out* occurs if donors, seeing an increase in public grants to a particular arts organisation or to the arts as a whole, reduce their giving accordingly. Such crowding could also occur in the opposite direction, if a government agency were to cut back its funding to a recipient organisation because it was doing so well in raising funds from other sources. *Crowding-in*, on the other hand, occurs when philanthropic donations are attracted specifically to arts organisations that receive funding from a public agency; such donations may be responding to the 'seal of approval' bestowed on the organisation by the receipt of a public grant, or they may be stimulated by a matching-grants provision contained in the public support.

Most research on relationships between private and public funding levels has been undertaken in the United States,[32] but the verdict on both crowding-out and crowding-in remains equivocal, with different results pointing in different directions according to the circumstances of the particular cases studied. In commenting on a number of studies, Arthur Brooks notes that:

the relationship between government subsidies and private philanthropy is highly dependent on the subsector, the level of government involved, and the specific dataset used in the analysis.[33]

So, for example, an early study by Burton Abrams and Mark Schmitz (1978) found some evidence for crowding-out of private charitable contributions by government transfers, whilst Patricia Hughes and William Luksetich (1999) found some crowding-in effect in donations to art museums, probably attributable to the use of matching grants in federal funding. However, Francesca Borgonovi and Michael O'Hare (2004) found no significant crowding-in or crowding-out over a long period in relation to NEA funding.[34] Apparently, no clear-cut set of conclusions can be drawn.

The second rationale for supporting the arts via the tax system relates to the decentralisation of responsibility for arts-funding decisions – the devolution from government to the people of decisions as to who gets what. There is an obvious ideological justification for favouring a decentralised decision process; those who generally advocate consumer sovereignty and a reliance on the market in preference to the allocation of resources by government will see virtue in the indirect system for arts support. Such a system, they will argue, diversifies not only the range of preferences that are expressed in arts funding allocations, but also opens up a wider range of financial sources for individuals and organisations than is available if there were only a single public-sector provider. On the other hand, the transfer of decision-making power in relation to arts policy from government to private individuals may make the achievement of some aspects of public policy more uncertain. This uncertainty may affect both quality and access dimensions of policy. In the first place, as noted earlier, there may be little public interest in providing philanthropic support for the sort of innovative work that is the research and development laboratory for future artistic growth, and whose encouragement is always an important arts-policy objective. Moreover, access goals may be compromised if arts donors are drawn predominantly from the wealthier income groups – their support will tend to be channelled in directions reflecting their own tastes and may not necessarily serve the needs of the less well-off members of society whose participation access goals seek to achieve.[35]

## Mechanisms

Governments have at their disposal a range of ways in which the tax system can be used to provide support for artists, arts organisations and consumers of the arts. The deployment of the various means, and their relationship to whatever direct arts support might be provided, varies enormously between countries, and, in some cases, even within a country. Here we simply list the most important mechanisms by which a policy of indirect support can be delivered, before proceeding in the next section to look at some of the economic aspects. The major tax-related measures in use are the following:

- *Tax treatment of not-for-profit organisations.* The regulatory environment under which not-for-profit organisations are established and operate their businesses allows them exemptions from income tax and often from other impositions, such as property and sales taxes. These conditions relate to the non-profit sector generally, which includes religious, educational, health-related, social welfare, and other types of businesses as well as cultural organisations. Thus the tax concessions involved are not unique to arts policy but benefit a broader spectrum of government interest. Nevertheless, measures may be implemented that are targeted specifically at arts and cultural organisations, such as sales tax exemptions for particular artistic inputs.
- *Tax treatment for individual artists.* It is possible to provide support for practising artists through the tax system by allowing them some concessions in income tax rates or exemptions from certain sales taxes, and/or by recognising their artistic expenses as legitimate deductions in calculating their taxable income. Whilst the latter provision would usually be expected for any business operation, artists sometimes have difficulty in convincing the tax authorities of the seriousness of their purpose because, as Alan Feld, Michael O'Hare and Mark Schuster put it, 'artists do for a living what many people do for fun'.[36] A further complication arises when artists seek to claim business losses from their arts work by offsetting their artistic costs against their non-arts income.
- *Tax treatment of charitable donations.* As in the case of non-profit regulations, discussed above, the allowance of a tax deduction for donations to good causes is a policy that extends far beyond the arts and culture. However, such a policy can be tailored towards the arts by specifying the types of donations affected, by identifying categories of eligible recipients, and by manipulating the tax rates involved. Individuals are likely to be particularly affected by marginal tax rates in determining the size of their donations, as we shall see further below. Corporate philanthropy is also responsive to tax incentives.[37] The means by which a policy of providing tax exemptions for arts donors may be delivered include the allowance of donations

as deductions from income before tax or the allowance of a rebate on tax payable; the associated decisions that the government must make include how to set the marginal tax rates, whether to place lower or upper limits on the amounts permitted, and so on.

- *Tax treatment on gifts and bequests.* Sometimes donations to arts organisations take the form of gifts in kind rather than cash, for example when a collector donates an artwork to a gallery. Governments can stimulate such generosity by providing exemptions from income taxes, death duties, inheritance taxes, etc., based on the value of the property donated. In some cases such gifts are prompted not so much by generosity as by a desire for a restructuring of a person's tax obligations when it is inconvenient or impossible to meet these obligations in cash. A particular type of gift that may be looked on kindly or otherwise by the tax authorities depending on the circumstances is gifts by artists of their own work; such donations, if accepted, raise difficult questions – should a work be valued at its cost of production or its market price, and if the latter, how is this to be determined?

- *Assistance through indirect taxes.* Tax-related assistance to the arts can be provided through special provisions relating to goods-and-services taxes, value-added taxes or wholesale/retail sales taxes – in other words, to indirect taxes that are applied in one form or another in virtually all jurisdictions. Specific reductions in, or exemptions from, such taxes can be allowed to cultural producers when purchasing inputs or to consumers when they buy artistic goods and services such as books, paintings, theatre tickets, etc. In fact wherever such concessions are applied, both producers and consumers may enjoy the benefits they yield, since the incidence of taxes is shared by both sides of the market depending on the relative price elasticity of supply and demand for the goods and services concerned. The policy measures that can be applied in this area relate to the rates of tax that are charged on the final good or service and also to the possibility of allowing eligible arts businesses full tax-exempt status, meaning that they can reclaim the tax paid on all of their inputs.

## Economic effects

All of the measures discussed above affect prices in one way or another – changing marginal tax rates affects the after-tax price of making a donation, changing value-added tax affects the price of a theatre ticket, etc. A question of critical importance to the implementation of an arts policy via the tax system has to do with how these price effects influence behaviour. For example, will the reduction in the price of books that would be expected to follow the removal of VAT lead to an increase in demand? If so, by how much? If marginal rates of tax on income were raised, what would be the effect on the volume of individual philanthropy? The important parameter that describes people's responsiveness in these circumstances is the price elasticity – the percentage change in the quantity demanded or the amount donated in response to a 1 per cent change in price. We can illustrate the importance of price elasticity by reference to a simple example.

Imagine a not-for-profit theatre company that hopes to receive charitable donations. From a donor's point of view the crucial question is the after-tax price of the donation. If, for example, the marginal tax rate is 40 cents in the dollar, the cost to the donor of a dollar donation is 60 cents, since every dollar she donates reduces her tax bill by 40 cents (and thus costs the government 40 cents in reduced tax revenue). To put it another way, of every dollar the theatre company receives by this means, 60 cents has been given by the individual donor, and 40 cents has been funded by the government. Now suppose that the marginal tax rate increases. This makes donating to the theatre a more attractive prospect because the after-tax price of a dollar donation has fallen, and the individual's tax saving on every dollar donated is correspondingly greater. The effect of a fall in the after-tax price of a donation can be described as follows. If an $x$-per cent fall in the after-tax price induces a greater-than-$x$-per cent increase in the amount donated (a 'price-elastic' response), the outcome is a win for both the theatre company and the government, whereas the reverse is true if the response is price-inelastic. The break-even point is where an $x$-per cent fall in the tax price leads to an equivalent $x$-per cent rise in the donation (a 'unit-elastic' response).

An empirical example of the responsiveness of donations to a change in the after-tax price is spelt out in detail in the Appendix to this chapter. Here it suffices to point out that for a government contemplating manipulating marginal tax rates or other variables governing the amount of charitable giving in pursuit of a policy aimed at increasing the flow of funds to the arts and culture sector, knowledge of the elasticity of donations with respect to the after-tax price is a vital piece of information – on it depends whether or not moving rates in one direction or another will succeed or will fail to achieve the desired objective. Regrettably, however, the empirical evidence is inconclusive. As Mark Schuster has noted, somewhat ruefully, 'even after some forty years of research on this question a clear consensus has yet to emerge'.[38] Policy-makers are thus obliged to rely on judgement and faith rather than on any ability to forecast the behaviour of an unpredictable public.

## 5 The role of the individual artist

We noted earlier that support for the individual artist has been a consistent feature, indeed a central plank, of arts policies in many countries over many years. Since governments do not generally support workers in specific occupations by payment of grants, etc., to enable them to pursue their calling, it is worth asking why artists receive this sort of policy attention. To answer this question it is necessary to describe the nature of individual artistic practice.

Artistic labour is characterised by three features that combine to set artists apart from other workers in their labour market behaviour.[39] The first is that financial rewards to professional artistic practice are generally lower than in other occupations with otherwise similar characteristics (education and training requirements, etc.); thus many artists' labour market profiles exhibit multiple job-holding. Typically artists allocate their working time between three types of jobs corresponding to three separate labour markets: the market for their creative work (including all preparation, practice, rehearsal, research, and similar time); the market for 'other arts-related work' such as arts administration or teaching in their artform (especially relevant to visual artists, instrumental musicians, singers and dancers); and the non-arts labour market (for actors this seems inevitably to involve work as a taxi driver or a waiter in a restaurant).

The second feature of artistic work is the level of variability of artistic earnings, which is generally higher than in comparable occupations, making an individual artist's attitudes to risk an important determinant of his or her labour market participation. Individuals who are risk averse will be deterred from entry into the artistic workforce but others may be attracted by the prospect of a winner-take-all lottery in which the prize is superstardom. Superstars are artists such as rock musicians and film actors whose incomes are greater than those of their competitors by a much larger differential than marginal productivity theory would suggest.[40]

The third aspect of artistic occupations that distinguishes them from others in the labour force is the role of non-pecuniary motives in determining artists' time allocations. Artists in general do not regard work as a chore where the only purpose is to earn an income. Rather, their commitment to making art means that they have a positive preference for working at their chosen profession, and empirical evidence indicates that they often forgo lucrative alternative employment in order to spend more time pursuing their creative work. This can be modelled as a time allocation problem, where a worker has to choose between preferred but less remunerative work in the arts on the one hand, and better-paid but less desired non-arts work on the other. The choice is subject to a minimum-income constraint necessary to prevent starvation, a condition often romantically associated with artists but rarely observed in practice. Such a 'work preference' model of labour supply yields predictions of behaviour at variance with the usual textbook construct – for example, a wage rise in the non-arts occupation may induce *less* work in that occupation because it enables more time to be devoted to the arts, a phenomenon akin to the backward-bending supply curve of labour in the conventional model.[41]

The derivation of psychic income from practice as an artist relates directly to the creative urge, i.e., the motivation that generates pursuit of an artistic vision as the artist's goal rather than response to financial incentives. Nevertheless, minimum-income constraints can be unavoidable, and this has led to efforts to model creativity as a constrained optimisation process, where the decision variables are proportions of time allocated to artistic work (preferred but poorly paid) and to non-artistic work (not preferred but lucrative), and the constraint is survival-income over a given time period.[42]

Artistic labour markets operate within the larger spheres of the demand for and supply of labour in the economy as a whole. As is well recognised, labour markets across the board in many countries are undergoing radical changes with greater casualisation and increased occupational mobility in the workforce. Markets for artistic labour have been caught up in these changes; as Pierre-Michel Menger points out, long-term employment in the arts has been replaced by a project-based system of production relying on short-term hiring, large parts of business risk are transferred downwards onto the workforce, and artists learn to manage risk and to stay alive through multiple job-holding, occupational versatility, diversification of job portfolios and occasional income transfers from social security or other sources.[43] Despite manifold deterrents to an artistic career, an excess supply of artists persists in many countries, attributable in part to the non-pecuniary attraction of work as an artist mentioned above.

In light of the above outline of the ways in which artists work, what is the policy interest? The answer lies in the critical, originating and central role that artists play in the creation of artistic work and its transmission to the public, and hence in providing the materials from which arts policy is fashioned. Artists are unique to the production of art; without them no original work would emerge and the central element of arts policy would be lost. If the justification for a policy of public assistance to the arts turns on the generation of public-good benefits from artistic activity, it follows that support for the work of artists as the primary source of that activity is warranted as one appropriate policy measure.

How might such support be provided? It is clear from the above discussion, and from empirical evidence from surveys of artists' working conditions, that the overwhelming constraints limiting pro-fessional art practice across all artforms are availability of time and financial return. Thus, measures to support artists have included the following:

- direct grants to 'buy time' or to allow full-time concentration on artistic work;
- commissions for the production of a specific work or works;
- special purpose financial assistance for research, mentorship, travel, etc.;
- support for companies to employ artists, such as a playwright-in-residence in a theatre company;
- support for work to be performed, published, and so on, i.e., to allow new or existing work by an artist to be disseminated to the public;
- income support provided via non-arts channels, e.g., via the social welfare system, whereby artists may be able to receive

unemployment benefits to enable them to remain in artistic practice; and
• support for education and training in the arts.

All of these measures and more are used in varying degrees in different countries. Together they help to sustain many professional artists in practice who would otherwise be unable to continue.

## 6 Conclusions

Over the past decade or so, arts policy everywhere has undergone some significant changes. The rigid distinction between high art and popular culture that permeated arts policy in earlier times and that inevitably identified it with the tastes of the upper echelons of society has been gradually relaxed. New communications technologies have opened up opportunities for cultural consumption to new cohorts of consumers and have generated new modes of artistic expression. Visitors to art galleries and audiences in theatre, opera, music and dance are drawn from ever-widening social groups as artists, performing companies and public cultural institutions engage with expanding ideas of what art is and how it can be experienced. In these circumstances policy-makers have looked to supporting a broader range of activities while remaining faithful to the fundamental arts-policy objectives of striving for excellence and access.

Whether arts policy is administered by an arts council, a culture ministry or some other authority, and whether it is implemented through direct assistance to artists, organisations or consumers, or indirectly through the tax system, the essential role of arts policy can be expressed as the creation of value for the society that it serves. Undoubtedly there are significant benefits from the arts that can be accounted for in monetary terms, through assessments of the market value and non-market value the arts create. But although these economic considerations are an essential element in the formulation of arts policy, they should not be allowed to drive the policy-making process, since the primary concern has to be with the cultural value that is the arts' ultimate rationale. As ever, the task is a balancing act between excellence and access, quality and quantity, efficiency and equity, and finally between the generation of economic value and cultural value.

## APPENDIX TO CHAPTER 4

### Illustration of the response of charitable donations to changes in the after-tax price

Consider a not-for-profit theatre company that is in receipt of charitable donations from a given donor. Assume the initial marginal rate of income tax is 40 cents in the dollar, making the after-tax price of a one-dollar donation 60 cents. Suppose the tax price falls by 10 per cent to 54 cents as a result of an increase in the marginal tax rate from 40 to 46 cents in the dollar. What effect will the fall in price have on the individual's initial donation of, say, $100? Consider three possibilities:

- Suppose she increases her donation by 20 per cent to $120. Her total cost has risen from $60 to about $65 (= $120 x 0.54), and the government's share of the donation has risen from $40 to about $55. Thus an increase of about $15 in government expenditure has produced a $20 increase in the amount going to the theatre.
- Suppose she increases her donation by 10 per cent to $110. Her total cost remains roughly the same ($110 x 0.54 = $59.40), while the government's share increases by around $10.
- Suppose that she increases her donation by only 5 per cent to $105. Her total cost is now $105 x 0.54, i.e., about $57. Thus the government's share has risen from $40 to about $48. In this case, the government's cost has increased by about $8 to produce an increase of only $5 going to the theatre.

These calculations are summarised in the table on the following page.

The first of these cases demonstrates a positive outcome – the fall in the tax price has stimulated a sufficiently large response from the donor to result in a win for both the government and the theatre company. In the second case, the donor's after-tax cost remains about the same, with the government providing all of the increase in the amount received by the theatre. In the final case, the donor's response has been weak, and the theatre would have been better off if the government had simply provided the $8.30 extra cost direct to the theatre instead of relying on the tax system. What is the difference between these cases? The relevant parameter is the elasticity of the amount donated with respect to the after-tax price. In the first case, a 10 per cent fall in

|  | Original situation | Following a 10% fall in after-tax price | | |
|---|---|---|---|---|
|  |  | Donation increases 20% | Donation increases 10% | Donation increases 5% |
| Donation amount ($) | 100.00 | 120.00 | 110.00 | 105.00 |
| Shared between: |  |  |  |  |
| Individual ($) | 60.00 | 64.80 | 59.40 | 56.70 |
| Government ($) | 40.00 | 55.20 | 50.60 | 48.30 |
| Absolute value of price elasticity |  | >1 | 1 | <1 |

the tax price induced a greater-than-10-per cent increase in the donation (a price-elastic response, i.e., the absolute value of the elasticity was greater than 1) whereas in the final case the donation increased by less than 10 per cent (a price-inelastic response). The critical or break-even value of the elasticity is an absolute value of unity, where a 10 per cent fall in price is just matched by a 10 per cent increase in the donation.

*Notes*

1 Quote is from Murdoch (1954: 23).
2 See further in O'Connor (2006).
3 For a reassessment of the theory of merit goods by its originator, see Musgrave (1990).
4 For a critique of arts impact studies, see Seaman (1987), Bille and Schulze (2006); the difference between 'contribution' and 'impact' is discussed in Throsby (2004).
5 See Frey (2008).
6 See, for example, Selwood (2001), Tohmo (2005).
7 See respectively Moore (1995); BBC (2004); Moore and Williams Moore (2005).
8 For a review of the literature in this field, see Keaney (2006).
9 See Ellis (2003), Holden (2004), and a series of commentaries on the latter published in *Cultural Trends* 14(1), 2005; see also Selwood (2006).
10 See the speech made in 2004 by Tessa Jowell, the UK's then Secretary of State for Culture (Jowell, 2004).

11 Note that Holden (2004) uses the term 'cultural value' to include the full range of values, including economic value, that culture generates; as such his usage is different from the more specific definition of cultural value used in this book.

12 See McCarthy, et al. (2004: 68); for a discussion of intrinsic value arguments in the context of US cultural policy, see DeVereaux (2006).

13 Holden (2004: 21).

14 In a foreword to the report, James Purnell, the then Secretary of State for Culture, Media and Sport, described this move as 'a vital one' (McMaster, 2008: 4).

15 See National Endowment for the Arts (2007).

16 For a discussion of the importance of sub-national cultural policy in the US, see Schuster (2002b).

17 For an account of the European situation, see Van der Ploeg (2006).

18 Broadcast by Lord Keynes published in *The Listener*, 12 July 1945, and reprinted as Appendix A, pp. 20–23 of the Arts Council of Great Britain (1945–46).

19 Canada Council for the Arts (2008: 17).

20 See Arts Council of New Zealand Toi Aotearoa Act 1994, Section 5.

21 Scottish Arts Council (2007: 5); see also Galloway (2008).

22 See Australian Council for the Arts (1973: 16).

23 King and Blaug (1973).

24 In fact it can be suggested that there is no necessary trade-off between excellence and access objectives, which John Holden identifies as a false dichotomy; see Holden (2008).

25 See Baumol and Bowen (1966); for a contemporary assessment, see Heilbrun (2003).

26 'Subversion' here meant that the scheme does not widen access but simply provides free tickets to people who would otherwise have paid the full price; for an early contribution in favour of arts vouchers, see West (1986).

27 Critics of the arms-length model argue that direct political manipulation of arts councils by governments has become inevitable with the greater accountability now required of them; see, for example, Brighton (2006).

28 For a collection of documentation, see Bolton (1992); see also Marquis (1995); Rushton (2000). A discussion of the culture wars in the UK can be found in Curran, et al. (2005).

29 Quoted by Netzer (2006: 1233).

30 For an overview of this field see papers collected in Boorsma, et al. (1998); for an assessment of the Netherlands case, see Engelsman (2006); the Australian orchestras are analysed in Boyle (2007).

31  See further in Bussell and Forbes (2006).

32  See the extensive documentation contained in Schuster (2006).

33  Brooks (2000: 213).

34  See respectively Abrams and Schmitz (1978); Hughes and Luksetich (1999); Borgonovi and O'Hare (2004). For further discussion of crowding effects, see Frey and Jegen (2001); Netzer (2006); Schuster (2006).

35  A vigorous advocate of the US system of decentralised support for the arts is Tyler Cowen; see, for example, Cowen (2006).

36  See Feld, et al. (1983: 17).

37  Such philanthropy, although altruistic and given without strings attached, is also likely to be influenced by the expectation of beneficial effects on the company's public image arising from a conspicuous donation to a prominent artistic or cultural organisation.

38  Schuster (2006: 1272).

39  For overviews of research on artistic labour markets, see Benhamou (2003), Alper and Wassall (2006).

40  The original article on this subject is Rosen (1981); for a recent assessment, see Adler (2006).

41  The original exposition of the formal 'work-preferences model' for artists is in Throsby (1994); see also Cowen and Tabarrok (2000); Robinson and Montgomery (2000).

42  See Throsby (2001, Ch. 6); Bryant and Throsby (2006).

43  See Menger (2006).

# 5 | *Cultural industries*

PHIL: We positioned the band. We located the band. You think music is
some great moment of inspiration. It's a product.

(Andrew Upton, *Riflemind*, 2008[1])

## 1 Introduction

In earlier chapters we have pointed to the growing importance of the cultural industries in reorienting cultural policy away from its traditional
focus on support for the arts towards a more economically motivated
set of priorities. In this process, creativity has emerged as a key concept in linking the production of cultural content in creative goods and
services with expanding market opportunities for all sorts of cultural
product. Rapid technological change, especially in the production and
uptake of audio-visual material, has fuelled the growth of industries
with low or zero marginal costs of reproduction and distribution, and
has catapulted the cultural sector into becoming an integral component of the global information economy. This focus on creativity has
led to the same terminological confusion that we noted when defining
cultural/creative goods and services in Chapter 2. Should these industries be called cultural or creative and does it matter?

There have been many contributions to the literature discussing this
question, some exploring theoretical origins, some getting entangled
in semantics, others more concerned with what's in and what's out of
any given classification.[2] In practical policy circles, the term 'cultural
industries' emerged in the UK and elsewhere in the late 1980s, and
was transposed to the 'creative industries' in Australia in 1994 in the
major government policy statement *Creative Nation*, which sought to
chart a cultural policy combining the arts with new communications
technologies.[3] The term subsequently gained much wider acceptance
following its adoption by the UK's Department for Culture, Media
and Sport, which set up its Creative Industries Task Force in 1997.

Richard Caves used *Creative Industries* as the title for his influential book, published in 2000, in which he defined these industries as those 'supplying goods and services that we broadly associate with cultural, artistic, or simply entertainment value',[4] in other words *cultural* goods and services.

Whilst the 'creative industries' nomenclature remains in use in the UK and some other European countries, in other places the term 'cultural industries' is more prominent. In UNESCO, for example, the cultural industries are regarded as those industries that 'combine the creation, production and commercialisation of contents which are intangible and cultural in nature. These contents are typically protected by copyright and they can take the form of goods or services'. An important aspect of the cultural industries, according to UNESCO, is that they are 'central in promoting and maintaining cultural diversity and in ensuring democratic access to culture'.[5] Similarly in France, the cultural industries have recently been defined as a set of economic activities that combine the functions of conception, creation and production of culture with more industrial functions in the large-scale manufacture and commercialisation of cultural products.[6]

For our purposes here the issue can be resolved in the same terms with which we disposed of the definition of cultural and creative goods in Chapter 2; i.e., we can define creative industries as those industries producing *creative* goods and services as defined there, and cultural industries as those producing *cultural* goods and services. Thus the cultural industries, according to this definition, are a subset of the wider group of creative industries. Since our concern in this volume is with cultural policy, we will pay attention primarily to cultural rather than creative industries.

What are the implications for government policy towards the cultural industries given the increasing importance of these industries to the economy? In this chapter we consider this question, looking first at ways in which the cultural industries' role in the contemporary mixed economy can be conceptualised, and discussing how their role in the economy can be assessed. Given that a significant feature of government interest in the creative economy is in the contribution of the cultural industries to economic growth, the chapter goes on to consider industry dynamics and the contribution of the cultural industries to growth, interpreted in both economic and cultural terms. Finally, policy measures to promote the cultural industries are discussed.

## 2 Conceptualising the cultural industries' role in the economy

An understanding of how the cultural production sector is structured is an essential prerequisite to effective policy formulation. We can identify two broad approaches to conceptualising the structural features of the cultural industries, deriving from the two words from which they take their name: 'culture' and 'industry'. Firstly, a *cultural* approach to these industries is pursued within the disciplines of cultural studies, cultural theory, sociology and political economy. Such an approach can be traced back at least as far as the writings of Theodore Adorno and Max Horkheimer, who coined the disparaging term 'culture industry' to describe the commodification of culture in the immediate post-war world that they inhabited.[7] In its present-day manifestation, a 'cultural' approach to the cultural industries is likely to ask how these industries reflect and shape the culture of contemporary capitalism, how power and class relationships affect the production and distribution of culture, and how the industrial system responds to the demands of consumers whose preferences are formed within a given social and political context.

Thus a structural model of the cultural industries as depicted within this intellectual framework would give a central role to those productive activities associated with the production, dissemination and consumption of popular culture through the broadcast and print media, film, the internet, and so on. In a construction such as this, the creative arts (in their 'high art' or 'fine art' interpretation) are likely to be relegated to peripheral status, since they are seen as a reflection of the tastes of a hegemonic cultural elite and hence are of lesser policy concern.[8]

The second approach, focussing on the *industry* aspect, is pursued within economics, political science and practical policy studies. It is best exemplified by the new wave of pragmatic efforts amongst policy-makers, especially those in Europe, to embrace the economic potential of the cultural industries. As noted above, a primary impetus in this direction grew out of the UK government's late 1990s vision for re-positioning the British economy as one driven by creativity and innovation in a globally competitive world. The UK Department for Culture, Media and Sport (DCMS) singled out for attention those industries that required creativity, skill and talent with potential for wealth and job creation through exploitation of their intellectual property. The DCMS labelled these industrial sectors as 'creative industries', even though virtually all of the thirteen industries included in the classification could also be interpreted as 'cultural'.[9]

The DCMS's concern with intellectual property as a principal source of economic empowerment for the creative sector is also evident in the definition of the cultural industries embraced by several European countries as well as by UNESCO, as observed above. An even more explicit emphasis on intellectual property is contained in the designation of creative industries as 'copyright industries' as proposed by the World Intellectual Property Organisation (WIPO), which defines these industries as those involved directly or indirectly in the creation, manufacture, production, broadcast and distribution of copyrighted works.[10] This classification thus extends considerably further than others, for example by including industries such as the manufacture of audio-visual hardware that provides the mechanical means for conveying copyright material to consumers.

An approach to conceptualising the structural features of the cultural industries that combines both the 'cultural' and the 'industry' concerns is the concentric circles model, introduced in intuitive terms in Chapter 2. The dual culture/industry characteristic of the model derives from the fact that it distinguishes between the cultural value and the economic value yielded by cultural goods and services. The model assumes that cultural content springs from the incorporation of creative ideas into the production and/or presentation of sound, text and image and that these ideas originate in the arenas of primary artistic creativity. This is an assumption that accords primacy to the processes of artistic (as distinct from scientific) creativity, and is the reason why the creative arts – music, drama, dance, visual art, literature – lie at the centre of the model, with successive layers of the concentric circles defined as the ideas and influences of these creative activities diffuse outwards. The economic content of the model is represented by the market and non-market value of the goods and services produced as either intermediate or final products in the various layers of the system.

Attributing a central role to the creative artist in cultural systems is, of course, nothing new. After all, it has been, and remains, a central element in arts policies as discussed in the previous chapter. But the distinctive feature of the concentric circles model is that it integrates this central role into the wider context of the cultural industries more broadly defined, by surrounding the arts with the industries that derive their cultural content from the creative core. The successive circles extend as far as activities that have a strong commercial focus, such as advertising and fashion, and could be extended even further to layers such as sports, tourism, gastronomy, theme parks, and so on.[11]

The concentric circles model in the form discussed here was enunciated in general terms in Throsby (2001: 112–113) and has subsequently been applied, adapted and developed in a number of studies.[12] In its basic form the model comprises four circles:

### Core creative arts
Literature
Music
Performing arts
Visual arts

### Other core cultural industries
Film
Museums, galleries, libraries
Photography

### Wider cultural industries
Heritage services
Publishing and print media
Sound recording
Television and radio
Video and computer games

### Related industries
Advertising
Architecture
Design
Fashion

Although the above designation of four industry groups, and the allocation of specific industries within them, is derived from the set of assumptions on which the concentric circles model is based, decisions as to which industry goes where are essentially ad hoc; they do not rely on any objective benchmarks for assessing the cultural or commercial content of the goods and services produced. For example, the allocation of Design to 'Related Industries' could be contested. Some features of design could be seen as a creative activity eligible for inclusion in the core of the model, whilst others such as industrial design are essentially utilitarian rather than engaged in conveying cultural content. In practice, the overall design industry, which embraces a wide range of fields, would seem best interpreted as being mainly involved with commercialisation, and hence is properly placed in the outer layers of the concentric circles of this model.

Notwithstanding the differences between the alternative conceptualisations of the cultural or creative industries described above, all of the approaches discussed lead in the end to much the same collection of industries to be included – the media, the creative arts, the audio-visual industries, heritage services, publishing, architecture, design, and so on.[13] Their definition accords with that of cultural goods and services as put forward in Chapter 2 above; all of these industries can be seen to require creativity as a significant input, all supply products with some degree of cultural content, and all involve to a greater or lesser extent the exploitation of intellectual property as the source of their economic power.

## 3  Assessing the economic contribution of the cultural industries

The economic functioning of an industry can be assessed in a number of different ways. The most basic approach is to measure the contribution that the industry makes to the usual macroeconomic aggregates: gross value of production, value added, fixed capital formation, employment, exports, and so on. Such statistics can be used to indicate the size of the industry, expressed, for example, as a certain percentage of whole-economy aggregates such as GDP. Studies of the economic contribution of the cultural industries carried out along these lines may be effective in demonstrating that the cultural sector is not some minor economic backwater, but a significant component of the economy. At a regional level, mapping exercises can plot the locational distribution of economic activity, enabling, for instance, the identification of areas where creative businesses tend to cluster. While all these data-gathering exercises have their uses, they can also be misused if the aim is simply to talk up the economic 'impact' of the cultural industries; in particular, they are most unlikely of themselves to provide any special case for policy intervention.[14]

The standard methods of industrial organisation theory are readily applicable to the cultural industries. The traditional approach is to evaluate the structure/conduct/performance characteristics of the industries: *structure* refers to the organisational characteristics of markets, with an emphasis on the degree of seller and buyer concentration, the nature of product differentiation and the conditions for entry and exit of firms; *conduct* refers to the ways in which firms in the industry behave in setting prices and output levels, marketing their products and competing with one another; and *performance* refers to how efficiently firms adjust to effective demands for their output in terms of costs, prices and product quality. These sorts of analyses are likely to be most relevant to those industries involved primarily in the commercial production of cultural goods and services; nevertheless, many of the methods of industrial organisation theory are also applicable to areas such as the not-for-profit arts, where economic concepts such as product differentiation, monopoly rents, price discrimination, non-price competition, and so on, all have considerable relevance.[15]

A higher level of analytical insight is provided by approaches that look at inter-industry relationships; whether the concern is 'contribution' or 'impact', it is important to understand the ways in which a particular industry interacts with others if a full picture of the industry's role in the economy is to be painted. Input-output analysis is one of the longest-standing techniques available for this type of study. Its capacity to depict the ways in which output is produced and distributed in the economy, and to capture the direct, indirect and induced effects on industries, consumers and government of a range of external stimuli is well known. Empirical application of input-output analysis to the cultural sector is constrained, firstly, by the relative scarcity of up-to-date input-output tables containing sufficient detail to enable useful identification of the cultural industries, and, secondly, by the heavy data demands that input-output analysis imposes. However, some successful studies have been carried out, such as that undertaken by Bryan, et al. (2000), who examined the economic impact of the arts and cultural industries on the economy of Wales for the year 1997. The study identified a range of industries across the performing arts, visual arts, craft, design, literature, publishing, media and heritage sectors, and collected data by survey for incorporation into the Welsh input-output table. The analysis estimated sectoral impacts on output, employment and incomes, and drew some policy implications concerning appropriate points of intervention.

What kinds of interactions do we observe between the cultural sector and other industries in the economy? And what of inter-industry relationships within the cultural sector itself? Several different interconnections can be identified:

## Inter-industry trade

The most direct ways in which firms in the cultural industries interact with other businesses and with the household sector is via the supply and demand for goods and services that are exchanged between them. Cultural products of all kinds are used in other parts of the economy, such as the purchase of live and recorded music by the hotel and restaurant industries, or the supply of museum and gallery services to members of the public. Likewise the production of creative goods uses inputs sourced from beyond the cultural industries; for example, visual artists buy materials from the paint industry, theatre companies hire accountants, and creators of computer games purchase their hardware from local retailers who may in turn get their supplies from the import sector. Similar interactions occur amongst the cultural industries themselves. Such interrelationships are of course characteristic of all industries in the contemporary economy; interest in the cultural industries might focus on how far-reaching and how significant such interdependencies are, in order to judge the extent of the impact on the rest of the economy of any change in economic activity within the creative sector. It is in this context that input-output analysis and related methods are useful, since they enable the short- and longer-run effects of exogenous change to be evaluated. The policy analyst can use these approaches to address questions such as: What would be the impact on the cultural industries of an increase in demand following an upsurge in tourist numbers? What would be the flow-on effect to other industries if artistic output were to fall because of cuts to public assistance?

## Movement of creative workers

A characteristic of the relationship between the cultural sector and the rest of the economy that has gained increasing attention relates to the supply of creative workers. Artists and other creators of original content in sound, text and image who are trained and who may gain experience in the core industries of the cultural sector may go on to work in other non-cultural industries. In the so-called 'creative trident' model of creative and non-creative employment in the creative and non-creative industries, these workers are called 'embedded', i.e., individuals employed in defined creative occupations but who are working outside the defined creative industries.[16] Estimates of the size of the embedded workforce for a given economy at a particular time will vary depending on the definitions used. For our purposes the broad-ranging creative industry definition adopted by Peter Higgs and colleagues (2008) can be narrowed to a specifically cultural focus by reference, for example, to the concentric circles model, while creative occupations can be identified by recognising the specific types of creative activity observable within the cultural sector:

- the production of primary creative output by individuals in occupations such as writer, composer, visual artist, film- and/or video maker, sculptor, craftsperson, etc.;
- creative interpretation as practised by performers in dance, drama, music, etc., in a variety of media; and
- the supply of creative services in support of arts and cultural production by workers such as book editors, lighting designers, music producers, and so on.

Whatever approach is used, empirical estimates point to significant numbers of creative people who work outside the creative or cultural industries, indicating important structural relationships in the labour market between the cultural and non-cultural sectors of the economy.

## Knowledge transfers

The emergence in recent times of concepts such as the information economy and the knowledge economy has drawn attention to the ways in which knowledge is generated, transmitted and accumulated during the process of economic growth. In particular, the production of new knowledge and the exploitation of new ideas through innovation have been recognised as important influences on business success.[17] In this context the creative industries, especially those built around new digital technologies, are a significant source of innovation-intensive information services. Thus knowledge transfers between economic agents in the cultural and other industries are a further consideration to be taken into account when analysing the interactions between the cultural sector and the wider economy. Such transfers of knowledge may occur in a variety of ways. They may arise from technical discussions, exchanges of information and joint ventures between businesses. In many cases, knowledge is 'embodied' in the goods and services exchanged. A further mechanism for knowledge transfer is seen in the movement of creative workers between firms, as discussed above. In all of these situations the information flows may be in either direction, through both forward and backward linkages in the supply chain for cultural goods and services. Thus, for example, the supply of artistic and creative inputs may be significant for innovation processes in other sectors of the economy, whilst reverse linkages may stimulate new forms of creativity in the cultural industries themselves. Using an input-output model for the UK economy, Hasan Bakhshi and colleagues (2008) derive empirical evidence demonstrating the role of supply-chain linkages in facilitating the transfer of ideas and knowledge between creative businesses and firms in other industries.

## Spillovers

If new ideas or processes developed by creative businesses are available to other firms without their having to pay for them, the knowledge transfer involved is technically a positive externality or spillover, defined in economic terms as an unintentional and uncompensated benefit flowing from one economic agent to another. A more important type of spillover that occurs in the cultural industries arises when firms locate near one another and enjoy reciprocal benefits from other firms involved in the production of similar cultural products. Such spillovers are referred to as 'network externalities' or 'agglomeration externalities', and help to explain the growth of centres of cultural production such as Hollywood or the fashion industry in Milan. We will return to the role of creative networks in the urban setting in more detail in Chapter 7.

## 4  Industry dynamics: economic and cultural growth

Much of our discussion of the cultural industries so far has referred implicitly or explicitly to the role of these industries in promoting economic growth. This is hardly surprising in a book about cultural policy, since the growth potential of these industries is what has captured the attention of governments around the world. Impressive statistics showing that output and employment in the creative sector have risen more rapidly in recent times than in most other sectors, together with the seductive rhetoric of the creative economy, have persuaded policy-makers that the cultural industries can be a source of economic dynamism when other more traditional economic activities such as agriculture or manufacturing are in decline.

How are the connections between the cultural industries and the processes of economic growth to be articulated? At its most basic, the growth performance of the cultural industries can be interpreted in terms of increasing demand for new cultural product and expanding supply dependent on rapid technological change, resulting in an inexorable rise in recorded output of a broad range of cultural goods and services. In addition, the effects of industry expansion on levels of employment tend to be more pronounced in the cultural sector because labour intensities in the cultural industries are generally greater than in other sectors of the economy.

But the relationships with economic dynamics extend further than these simple observations suggest. The transfers of knowledge and the stimulus to innovation in the wider economy, which were discussed earlier, indicate a more far-reaching role for the creative sector, one whereby the cultural industries introduce new ideas for the economy that diffuse outwards and stimulate innovation in other sectors. Just as in the endogenous growth theories of the 1980s and 1990s, which introduced human capital into growth models as the engine for generating technological change, so also can the role of creative activity be made endogenous, providing the ideas and skills to feed the growth process. One way of depicting these sorts of interrelationships is as networks, replacing the static, linear formulation of the value chain with a 'value-creating ecology', as we saw in Chapter 2. Such a system sees the creative industries as part of a web involving multiple interactions between suppliers and consumers. Similarly, the creative industries can be portrayed as complex social networks that foster and coordinate the production and consumption of novel ideas.[18] These approaches to interpreting the creative industries complement rather than replace the standard economic methods for industrial classification and analysis; their contribution is to provide an alternative lens through which to view the role of the creative sector in processes of structural change in the economy.

There is a distinct lopsidedness to most discussions of the growth performance of the cultural industries – growth is interpreted almost universally in economic terms, reflecting the dominating economic orientation of creative industry studies. But what about *cultural* growth? If cultural policy is concerned with culture as much as with the economy, its application to the cultural industries and their contribution to growth needs to widen its focus to consider artistic and cultural growth alongside the purely economic variables. Of course, there are difficulties; economic indicators of industrial performance are easily defined and measured, whereas the definition of what might be meant by cultural growth is not at all obvious. Three possibilities suggest themselves:

- Cultural growth could be interpreted simply as an increase in the per capita production and/or consumption of cultural goods and services. So, for example, data on rising trends in variables such as numbers of movies produced, or the sales volumes of artworks, or the consumption of music downloaded from the internet, or attendances at the theatre – any or all of these could be taken as indicators of growth in cultural output and cultural consumption in society.
- Capital accumulation in the economy is seen as a driver of growth and also as an indicator of economic growth itself. Accordingly, cultural growth could be defined as the accumulation of cultural assets, i.e., of cultural capital, to be discussed more fully in the next chapter.
- Parallel with the notion that *economic* growth in the cultural industries can be measured as the increased generation of *economic* value by these industries, it can be suggested that an expansion in the amount of *cultural* value yielded by these industries could be thought of as another indicator of *cultural* growth. In this context, innovation in the development of an artform could be seen as cultural growth; there is no denying, for example, that new directions in the arts brought about through the work of

innovators like Giotto, Mozart or James Joyce can be described in these terms. Of course artistic progress does not render what has gone before obsolete; it simply adds new qualitative dimensions to the accumulation of intangible cultural capital. Today, new technologies are pushing the boundaries of artistic and cultural production and consumption even further, expanding the concept of cultural value creation. If suitable indicators can be assembled, the significance of this aspect of cultural growth could be identified.

## 5  Policy strategies for the cultural industries

We turn finally to drawing together the threads of this chapter into a summary of the implications for cultural policy arising from the public sector's interest in the cultural industries. In keeping with the themes of this volume, we divide our treatment into economic aspects and cultural aspects.

### *Economic aspects*

A wide range of measures is available to governments at all levels to stimulate the cultural industries, to reinforce the linkages between these industries and the wider economy, and to promote the achievement of sustainable growth. These measures include small business development, regulation, innovation policy, market development, and education and training, as detailed in the following sections.

(i)  Small business development
As noted in earlier chapters, the predominant organisational form in the cultural industries is the traditional SME, the small-to-medium enterprise that is the target of economic policy across a variety of sectors of the economy. The policy strategies of particular relevance to the development of creative businesses include:

• provision of start-up assistance and business incubators, etc., to help small enterprises get underway;
• facilitating access to finance, including micro-finance, given that many SMEs find it difficult to secure start-up and/or operational capital;

- supply of information packages, workshops, etc., for the development of entrepreneurial skills in creative business strategy, financial planing, marketing, and so on, in order to overcome a possible lack of appropriate business skills; and
- assistance in areas such as convergence and digitisation of business operations, since many SMEs find accessing and using new information and communications technologies difficult.

(ii) Regulatory infrastructure

As noted in Chapter 3, the maintenance of the regulatory framework within which industries operate is an essential responsibility of government. For the cultural industries this responsibility extends to:

- contract law, especially relevant to enabling the efficient operation of cultural industries such as film-making, which involve multiple players and multi-stage production processes, and where the rights and responsibilities of the various parties must be identifiable and enforceable;
- copyright law, including the requirement for effective digital rights management, to be discussed in Chapter 13; and
- antitrust legislation and the regulation of competition, to control the market power of transnational corporations in cultural industries such as music production and distribution, where global conglomerates can colonise new markets and force SMEs out of business.

(iii) Innovation policy

Government policy targeted at innovation operates across a range of industries, including the creative sector. Strategies include:

- grants for research and development projects;
- public/private partnerships in new business investment, particularly targeted towards innovative businesses with a high growth potential;
- facilitating knowledge transfers, for example by encouraging business-to-business communication and establishing channels for the transfer of new knowledge from universities, colleges, research institutes, etc., to commercial exploitation; and
- use of investment incentives, relocation grants and other devices to encourage the growth of creative clusters that can stimulate innovation amongst firms in the cluster and increase the flow of creative ideas to other industries.

(iv) Market development

There are a number of ways in which governments in mixed economies can promote the development of markets for creative product, including:

- provision of information and market intelligence services;
- encouraging the establishment of industry advisory bodies; and
- development of specific market segments, including export markets, in areas such as cultural tourism and through support for expos, trade fairs and similar promotional devices aimed at increasing demand for creative products.

(v) Education and training

The long-term foundation of the cultural industries is built upon the talents and skills of artists and other creative workers, and, as we have seen above, these workers are important to other industries as well. We return to the question of education in the arts and culture in Chapter 11.

## Cultural aspects

A consideration of the cultural dimensions of policy towards the cultural industries brings us back to the concentric circles model. If indeed the creative arts represent the core of the cultural industries, then it is the instruments of arts policy (as outlined in the previous chapter) that will form an essential component of cultural industries policy. Furthermore, those cultural industries beyond the core – in the 'wider' and 'related' classifications in the model – also yield products and services with varying degrees of cultural content, so emphasising the cultural aspects of creative industries policy is by no means confined to the arts. Media policy, for example, although driven by economic concerns, also has significant cultural ramifications, as noted in Chapter 3.

Ultimately the challenge, as ever, is to strike the right policy balance between the generation of economic value and of cultural value through the operation of the cultural industries. But in drawing attention to the cultural dimension to the functioning of these industries, and in emphasising the role of the creative arts in the generation of cultural value, it is important to see the arts in a wider industrial context. Arts policy is an essential ingredient of cultural industries policy not only because of the arts' own cultural significance but also because a flourishing, dynamic, innovative creative core is essential to sustaining both the economic and the cultural health of the cultural industries across the board.

## 6 Conclusions

The phenomenon of globalisation that characterises the contemporary economic environment carries with it particular challenges for the cultural industries. New communications technologies, digital convergence and the growth of global markets for cultural products have transformed the cultural industries from minor players in an economic system with priorities that lay elsewhere, to a central element in the new economy driven by creativity, innovation and access to knowledge. But in the headlong rush to embrace the supposed wealth-creating potential of the creative economy, there is a danger that public policy loses sight of the cultural importance of the cultural industries. In this chapter we have pointed to the manifold ways in which the cultural industries do indeed contribute to the economy, but we have also argued that the cultural content of the goods and services produced has important policy relevance in its own right. Cultural policy, if properly conceived, has the task of balancing these often complementary roles for these industries in contributing to both economic and cultural development.

Despite the apparently inexorable influence of economic imperatives on policies towards the cultural industries in different parts of the world, the economic agenda does not always dominate to the exclusion of broader cultural concerns. For example, the cultural policy framework proposed by the Australian government in 1994 in its *Creative Nation* statement was an exemplary effort to balance artistic, cultural and economic objectives, even if the policy proposals put forward were never fully implemented. More recently, Susan Galloway has pointed out that in Scotland, cultural rather than economic considerations are driving discussion about public policy intervention within key parts of the creative industries; for instance, in debate about ownership and control of media companies in Scotland, the role of the press and the literary arts in maintaining a sense of Scottish nationhood and identity has been emphasised in contrast to purely commercial concerns.[19]

*Notes*

1  Quote is from Upton (2008: 80).
2  See, for example, O'Connor (1999); Garnham (2001); Flew (2002); the editor's introduction in Hartley (2005); Pratt (2005); Galloway and Dunlop (2007).
3  Commonwealth of Australia (1994).
4  Caves (2000: 1).
5  See www.unesco.org/culture.
6  Département des Études, de la Prospective et des Statistiques (2006: 7).
7  See Adorno and Horkheimer (1947).
8  See, especially, Hesmondhalgh (2007: 11–15) and papers collected in Hartley (2005).
9  It appears the UK government preferred the 'creative' nomenclature partly to avoid associations of 'culture' with the fine arts and partly to widen the scope of the industries covered to include activities such as computer software, where the economic potential was regarded as substantial. Nicholas Garnham argues that the enthusiastic embrace of the 'creative' label by the cultural sector is an attempt to buy into the 'unquestioned prestige that now attaches to the information society and to any policy that supposedly favours its development' (Garnham, 2005: 20).
10 See WIPO (2003) and various country reports issued by that organisation.
11 See, for example, the classification contained in Segers and Huijgh (2008: 13).
12 Including Gibson, et al. (2002), Sasaki (2004), KEA European Affairs (2006), and The Work Foundation (2007). A more detailed exposition of the model, including some empirical evidence, is contained in Throsby (2008b). A model of the supply chain for creative goods as a series of layers, beginning with the 'most creative' activities as the first layer, is presented in a report for the DCMS by Frontier Economics (see DCMS, 2007a), while Markusen, et al. (2008) identify 'core' and 'periphery' in defining cultural occupations.
13 The main exception is the WIPO model's classification, which, as noted above, extends much further than the others; for a more detailed account of the various models and the industries they contain, see Throsby (2008a).
14 For a recent US study of the economic impact of the arts, see Americans for the Arts (2008).
15 Bruce Seaman notes that the application of industrial organisation theory to the arts has been surprisingly sparse; see Seaman (2004).

16 See Cunningham (2006), Higgs, et al. (2008); note the particular definitions of 'creative' employment and industries used in these studies, which may not necessarily correspond with usage elsewhere.
17 For an account of the role of innovation in the contemporary economy, see Baumol (2002); a case study of creative skills transfers in the video game industry is contained in Izushi and Aoyama (2006).
18 See Potts, et al. (2008).
19 See Galloway (2008).

# 6 | *Cultural heritage*

> They took all the trees
> And put them in a tree museum
> And they charged the people
> A dollar and a half just to see 'em
> Don't it always seem to go
> That you don't know what you've got
> Till it's gone.

(Joni Mitchell, 'Big Yellow Taxi', 1970[1])

## 1 Introduction

As its dictionary definition indicates, heritage is something inherited from the past. Attaching the adjective 'cultural' defines its scope more precisely, relating it to inherited things that have some cultural significance, where the term 'cultural' is used both in its broad anthropological and in its more specific artistic interpretation. Three types of cultural heritage can be identified:

- built or immoveable heritage, such as buildings, monuments, sites or locations, including groups of buildings and sites found in historic city centres;
- moveable heritage, such as artworks, archives, artefacts, or other objects of cultural significance; and
- intangible heritage, existing as works of music or literature handed down to us from the past, or as inherited practices, language, rituals, skills or traditional knowledge that communities and groups recognise as culturally important.

Although the term heritage invokes images of the distant past, some heritage items may be of quite recent origin; for example, the Sydney Opera House, a building identified as being of World Heritage significance, was only completed in 1973.

Simple economic concepts such as scarcity and opportunity costs can be readily applied to the analysis of decisions concerning cultural heritage. What can be preserved and what cannot? How much renovation or restoration is warranted? Whose preferences should guide conservation decisions? Despite the obvious relevance of economic concepts to answering such questions, the initial efforts by economists a decade or so ago to enter the heritage arena were resented by heritage professionals, who feared a process whereby their 'cultural' decisions would inevitably be transformed into 'economic' decisions.[2] These experts preferred in any case not to have to be worried by financial concerns, and were quite content to go on making their decisions on purely cultural grounds. Two things happened to change this state of affairs. Firstly, shrinking budgets and tightened financial constraints on heritage managers around the world during the 1980s and 1990s meant they could no longer afford the luxury of assuming that money didn't matter. Secondly, after a while conservationists began to realise that not all economists were the insensitive philistines of legend, but that they could bring to the table analytical methods that could actually help to achieve better conservation outcomes.[3]

In this chapter we review the basic concepts of cultural capital and cultural value as a means towards understanding the economic dimensions of cultural heritage in whatever form it occurs. We then go on to discuss policy issues in heritage management, both from an overall point of view and in relation specifically to each of the three types of heritage identified above.

## 2 Heritage as asset

Items of cultural heritage can be brought into the economic calculus by regarding them as assets with the usual characteristics attributable to economic capital: they require investment of resources in their manufacture or creation; they function both as stores of value and as long-lasting sources of capital services over time; and they will depreciate unless maintained. It can be suggested that heritage items are members of a class of capital which is distinct from other forms of capital; this class has been called *cultural capital*.[4] The distinction lies in the type of value that is embodied in these assets and is yielded by the goods and services they produce. A historic building certainly has the characteristics of an ordinary building as an item of physical capital, but in addition it has historical and other attributes which an ordinary building does not. Using the terminology introduced in earlier chapters, we can describe these attributes as the building's cultural value, and the same type of cultural value can be attributed to the flow of services it provides.

Treating heritage as cultural capital has some attractions to the economist and policy analyst. Defining heritage as capital enables concepts such as investment, depreciation, rates of return, and so on, to be applied to its evaluation and management. In particular, the way is opened to applying investment appraisal techniques such as cost-benefit analysis to the assessment of public and private expenditure on heritage conservation, as we shall see further below. Furthermore, regarding heritage as cultural capital builds a link with the well-established theory of natural capital which forms a core component of the discipline of ecological economics.[5] The elements of natural capital comprise renewable and non-renewable resources, the ecosystems that support and maintain the quality of land, air and water, and the vast genetic library referred to as biodiversity. The economic dimensions of all of these natural phenomena have now been extensively analysed and their policy implications discussed; these discussions indicate the potential contribution that the parallel concept of cultural capital can make to the formulation of cultural policy.[6]

## 3  Value

Cultural capital, like any capital item, exists both as a stock of assets and as a flow of capital services over time. The value of the capital may be assessed in terms of its asset value at a given point in time or as the value of the flow of services to which it gives rise. Either way, the particular characteristic of cultural capital is that it embodies or gives rise to the two types of value, economic and cultural, that are a guiding theme throughout this volume. Let us consider the nature of these two types of value when applied to the specific case of cultural heritage.

### The economic value of heritage

In a neoclassical world peopled by rational fully informed utility-maximising consumers, value arises through processes of exchange in perfectly functioning markets. Even when markets fail, as in the case, for example, of public goods, it is the willingness-to-pay of individual consumers that expresses the value of the goods in question. So when we think about the economic value of heritage within this model, we are thinking of the sorts of values that individuals recognise and are prepared to pay for in one way or another. The categories into which the value of heritage can be classified in these terms are well known and are clearly spelt out in the heritage economics literature referred to above. The categories correspond to the ways in which individuals experience heritage: by direct consumption or 'use'; by indirect means through 'non-use'; or as a beneficial externality.

(i) Use value

Use value is the value that accrues to individuals, households or firms through the direct consumption of heritage services. It may be experienced in different ways, for example through the ownership of heritage assets, or through the enjoyment of the services of such an asset by living in a heritage house or working in a heritage building; such values are reflected in market processes, and can be observed, for instance, in the actual or imputed rental value of heritage buildings used as dwellings or commercial premises. Direct-use value of heritage also accrues to tourists visiting heritage sites; in this case the relevant value can be measured by entrance fees, or, if appropriate data are available, by consumer surpluses estimated using methods such as travel-cost analysis.

In assessing the direct-use value specifically attributable to the heritage qualities of, say, a historic building used for commercial purposes, it should be remembered that the heritage value per se is actually a marginal value: the building would presumably have some rental value as commercial space in the absence of any heritage quality, and the question to be asked is whether the rent is higher or lower as a result of its heritage characteristics. The rental value of such buildings might be higher if people prefer to live in heritage houses or to work in a listed building, or it might be lower if, for example, the building were inconvenient because of its antiquated design or facilities. On the whole, the market seems to suggest that these sorts of direct-use values are positive, insofar as studies of the effect of heritage listing on the price of houses or other buildings mostly indicate a positive premium;[7] this is not surprising since in general heritage properties are demanded by people who do value heritage services and so are prepared to bid up the purchase or rental prices of such properties.

(ii)  Non-use values

The second aspect of individual valuation is the non-use or passive-use values which are experienced by individuals but are not reflected in market processes since they are derived from those attributes of cultural heritage that are classifiable as non-rival and non-excludable public goods. Over the last twenty years or so, research in environmental and ecological economics into demand for the non-market benefits of the natural environment has identified three categories of passive-use value that are equally relevant to heritage. We noted these in Chapter 2 as relating to the public-good component of cultural goods and services in general. Now we can state them more specifically as applying to cultural heritage. The values are:

- *existence value*: individuals may value cultural heritage simply because it exists, even if they themselves have not directly experienced particular heritage items;
- *option value*: individuals may wish to preserve heritage items in order to leave open the option that they or somebody else may visit them or consume their services in some way in the future; and
- *bequest value*: individuals may wish to pass on heritage assets to future generations.

All of these sources of value give rise to non-market demand for the conservation of heritage, expressible as individual willingness to pay.

Methods used to assess non-market demands for heritage can be classified as *revealed preference* and *stated preference* approaches. Amongst the former, hedonic-price and travel-cost methods have been used; however, their applicability to estimating the public-good demand for heritage is limited on conceptual and methodological grounds.[8] Thus it has been stated preference methods such as contingent valuation methodology (CVM) or discrete choice modelling that have been most widely employed. These methods are usually administered via sample surveys of individuals in the relevant population under given assumptions as to the respondent's liability to pay, the means for payment, and so on. Despite lingering scepticism in some quarters about the validity of CVM, its acceptance as a useful means for assessing the value of non-market benefits of public goods has grown as the number of successful applications has increased, especially following the (somewhat cautious) endorsement given to CVM by a panel of disinterested experts in the early 1990s.[9]

The application of stated preference methods to cultural heritage has drawn heavily on theoretical insights and refinements of empirical technique that have arisen as a result of extensive applications of CVM and choice modelling to environmental projects and amenities.[10] Nevertheless, the use of these methods in informing actual decision-making in heritage policy matters remains limited by the fact that undertaking CVM or other stated preference studies requires time, resources and expertise that may not be readily available to policy-makers.[11] One means of overcoming this constraint is the application of benefit-transfer methods that have been used in the environmental field, whereby the non-market effects of a particular project can be inferred by reference to estimates made for a similar project elsewhere.[12]

(iii)  Beneficial externalities

A third type of value of cultural heritage experienced by individuals stands somewhat apart from the above two categories, although it incorporates both use and non-use characteristics. It derives from the fact that heritage may generate positive spillovers. A heritage building or site, for example, may give rise to a beneficial externality if passers-by gain pleasure from observing its aesthetic or historic qualities; for example, people walking about in a city such as Rome or Paris may enjoy the sight of the historic buildings, monuments and squares that they encounter. In principle the economic value of such a benefit could be estimated, but it seldom is – its transitory nature and the difficulty of constructing even hypothetically a basis for payment render application of CVM in this case problematical. Nevertheless, the fact remains that positive spillovers are an identifiable and possibly significant value of heritage that accrues to individuals.

## The cultural value of heritage

We have identified cultural value as the characteristic of cultural capital that distinguishes it from other forms of capital. In Chapter 2 we pointed out that, in contrast to economic value, cultural value has no single unit of account that can capture its multidimensional nature.

A sensible approach to evaluating it would seem to involve trying to disaggregate it into its component elements.

Consider an item of tangible or intangible cultural heritage such as a building, a group of buildings, an artefact, an artwork, a tradition, or a ritual. The elements that go together to make up the cultural value of any of these examples of heritage can be detailed, following Throsby (2001: 84–85), as follows:

- *Aesthetic value* exists because the item displays qualities of beauty, harmony, etc., recognised by individuals and groups, whatever criteria might be used to define aesthetic significance. Examples could be drawn from almost any area, as most heritage items are likely to have some aesthetic qualities contributing to their value.
- *Spiritual value* arises because an item may provide people with a sense of connection with the infinite or with a particular faith or belief, or it may convey religious meaning or messages. Examples include shrines, churches, cathedrals, mosques, etc., as well as artworks that depict religious themes or, in a secular sense, that help to define the nature of human existence.
- *Social value* derives from the definition of culture as shared values and beliefs that bind groups together. Heritage items convey social value if they inform people about the nature of society or if they contribute towards social stability or cohesion in the community. Examples are the traditional meeting houses used by New Zealand Maoris and by other groups throughout the Pacific Islands.
- *Historical value* is intrinsic to any heritage item and is one of the most readily identifiable of the components of cultural value. Its principal benefit is seen in the way historical value assists in defining identity by providing a connectedness with the past and by revealing the origins of the present. Examples abound across all heritage areas, though the importance of historical value as a component of overall cultural significance for different items of similar age will vary markedly.[13]
- *Symbolic value* relates to the general characteristic of cultural goods and services as vehicles for conveying cultural meaning. When attached to a heritage item, symbolic value refers to the way the item helps individuals or communities to receive and interpret cultural messages of various sorts, particularly those relating to cultural identity. An example is the monument in Arlington, Virginia,

depicting the flag-raising at Iwo Jima that conveys a symbolic message about American military heroism.

- *Authenticity value* is attributable to the fact that a particular item is real, not fake, and is unique. A concomitant characteristic is integrity, meaning that the item has not been altered, tampered with or defaced. An example is an actual painting by, say, van Gogh that is in original condition and certifiable as the work of the artist; because of its authenticity, the cultural value that people assign to the painting is likely to be significantly greater than that of an exact reproduction or copy.[14]
- *Locational value* arises when cultural significance attaches to the physical or geographical location of a heritage item. Included in this component of value is the agglomeration of value that springs from the interrelatedness of items existing in proximity to one another, as in historic urban districts. Locational value can also be ascribed to cultural landscapes of various sorts, and to sites that are the scenes of past events of cultural importance. Many examples can be cited, ranging from the value that individual buildings in Venice acquire from being located in that unique urban setting, to the significance of an otherwise anonymous field in England where some historic battle was fought.

The methods for assessing cultural value that were discussed in Chapter 2 might be a workable means of systematising an approach to decision making in regard to the cultural value of heritage. These methods may be especially useful in comparing or ranking items, assuming that the judgements on the various aspects of the cultural value of all the items were made in a consistent manner. Thus, for example, Nathaniel Lichfield discusses a checklist with scores for evaluating the cultural quality of heritage buildings, whilst Peter Nijkamp provides a hypothetical illustration of ascribing cultural value to a number of historic urban districts according to 'profiles' reflecting socio-economic, geographical-environmental and cultural-architectural criteria.[15]

## 4  Policy issues in heritage management

The task facing public policy towards any type of cultural heritage can be stated in general terms as follows. Heritage assets may be held in public or private ownership but their common characteristic is that they engender significant public-good benefits. This being so, the policy task is to manage the publicly owned cultural capital, and to oversee the management of privately owned heritage, in such a way that the public interest is best served. Conceptualising heritage as cultural capital, with the long-lasting asset properties that such a proposition implies, leads naturally to thinking of sustainability and sustainable development as appropriate policy frameworks within which heritage management can be analysed. Again the link with natural capital can be exploited, since it was in regard to natural resources that the idea of sustainable development originated.

A standard definition of sustainable development arising from the Brundtland Report[16] refers to the management of natural resources in a way that provides for the needs of the present generation without compromising the capacity of future generations to meet their own needs. A key element of this definition is the concept of equity in the treatment of different generations over time, i.e., the principle of intergenerational equity. When applied to *cultural* sustainability, this concept can be considered as relating principally to the management of cultural capital, because the stock of cultural capital, both tangible and intangible, embodies the culture we have inherited from our forebears and which we hand on to future generations.

In addition to intergenerational features, the notion of ecological sustainability also implies several other principles, including attention to equity within the present generation, the maintenance of biodiversity, and observance of the precautionary principle (taking an extreme risk-averse stance when confronted with decisions that may cause irreversible change). Principles of sustainable development in relation to cultural capital can be proposed along similar lines. Thus, for example, intragenerational equity concerning heritage would imply fairness in access to cultural heritage services across social classes, income groups, locational categories, etc. Likewise the principles of maintaining cultural diversity through heritage conservation would derive from the proposition that the diversity of ideas, beliefs, traditions and other artistic and cultural manifestations yields a flow of cultural services that is quite distinct from the services provided by the individual components. The precautionary principle, too, has a parallel in the heritage sphere. In the natural world this principle is invoked when species loss is threatened; the same situation arises when, for example, historic buildings are in danger of demolition or indigenous languages are faced with extinction.

At a practical level, the question facing policy-makers is a more immediate one: How is it possible to choose amongst alternative heritage projects when finance for preservation, restoration, adaptive re-use, etc., is limited? The choice can be portrayed as one where the benefits and costs of alternative projects have to be evaluated and compared, i.e., as an application of the methods of cost-benefit analysis (CBA). Heritage items have an existing asset value, require real resources for their maintenance, and yield flows of benefits and costs into the future; hence any of the CBA methods for evaluating capital investment decisions could be applied. For example, a project involving the rehabilitation of a historic site or the restoration of a painting could be evaluated in economic terms by identifying all the market and non-market benefits and costs involved, and then using CBA to compare investment in this project with other alternative opportunities.

As in other areas of investment appraisal, a distinction must be made between private CBA and social CBA. In the case of a heritage project such as the conservation or adaptive re-use of a privately owned property, a CBA undertaken from a *private* viewpoint would use the actual financial flows and opportunity costs as experienced by the individual owner; it is also likely to use the opportunity cost of capital as the appropriate discount rate. A *social* CBA of the same project would adjust the private analysis to:

- account for taxes and transfers;
- use shadow prices, not market prices;
- use a lower discount rate reflecting (perhaps) a social time preference rate; and
- include all non-market effects (public goods and externalities).

Once these adjustments are made, the private and social rates of return can be compared as a basis for decision-making. It should be remembered, of course, that the CBA, at whichever level it is undertaken, does not make the decision, it simply acts as an important piece of information to be put on the table as part of a more wide-ranging decision-making process. For public policy purposes it has to be, by definition, the social assessment of value that must guide the processes of policy formation and implementation, since there is a clear obligation on government instrumentalities at all levels to be the guardians of the public interest. At the same time, however, the legitimate property rights of private individuals and firms must be respected and this is frequently a source of conflict between the heritage listing authorities and private owners, as we shall see further below.

So far we have considered the application of CBA to the assessment of the *economic* effects of a heritage project. But there is a further dimension: cultural capital yields both economic value and cultural value, so an assessment of the latter is also required. In principle there is no reason why a form of CBA could not be applied to assessing the time-stream of *cultural* value arising from a given heritage project; indeed it is the prospect of this flow, more than of the economic return, that is likely to have generated the project in the first place. Furthermore, cultural benefits can accrue both to individuals (as rival excludable benefits) and to society at large (as non-rival non-excludable benefits), suggesting that a division into private and public components is just as relevant to the assessment of cultural value as it is for economic effects. In addition, it is reasonable to suggest that a unit of cultural benefit at some time in the future will be worth less to the project's stakeholders than a unit now, making some form of discounting of future benefit streams appropriate. The difficulty, of course, lies in measurement. However, the disaggregated approach to evaluating cultural value outlined above does at least offer promise of progress in this endeavour.

A significant dilemma confronting heritage policy is the matter of identifying beneficiaries, since those who benefit from heritage should in principle be the ones who pay for it. This issue has both sectoral and locational elements. In the first instance, a distinction is possible between those benefits experienced as private goods by an individual consumer – for example, as an owner of a heritage property or as a tourist visiting a heritage site – and those benefits accruing as public goods to the community at large. The latter, as we have noted, provide a prima facie case for public support; the larger this component is relative to the private benefits from a given heritage item, the stronger that case is likely to be, and the greater the financial share that is appropriately borne by the public sector.

Regarding the locational element, the issue is one of how widely those enjoying non-market benefits from the heritage item are dispersed – are they confined to the local community, to the national population, or do they extend to the citizens of other countries or indeed of the whole world? In some instances the distribution of beneficiaries happens to coincide with a convenient tax base from which to fund heritage expenditure in the public interest – paying for locally significant heritage projects from local government rates, for example, or using national tax revenue to finance the conservation of heritage of national importance. But if the beneficiaries extend to other countries, as they do for iconic 'superstar' heritage, the problem of finding an equitable financing arrangement becomes virtually insurmountable, since no workable means exists for revenue to be collected. Voluntary financing, and actions by international cultural organisations, may be of some assistance in such cases but a significant burden no doubt remains, to be shouldered by the domestic taxpayer.[17]

## 5  Public policy and built heritage

We turn now to some policy issues relating specifically to the three types of cultural heritage described in the introduction to this chapter, beginning with the first – heritage building, sites, locations, etc. The actions that public authorities or private individuals or companies that own heritage property might contemplate as investment projects in regard to the cultural capital under their control include:

- *Preservation*: ensuring the continued existence of the asset;
- *Conservation*: caring for the asset and maintaining it in proper condition according to accepted professional standards;
- *Renovation or restoration*: returning an asset that has deteriorated to its original condition; and
- *Adaptive re-use*: any or all of the above when applied to an asset when its function or use is altered.

The last-mentioned case arises because in some situations preservation of heritage in its original condition and use may be either impractical or inappropriate. Think of industrial buildings such as city warehouses that can no longer be used for their original purpose, but which are significant items for conservation because of their architectural or historical importance. In this instance, renovation or restoration is likely to involve a redevelopment or a change of purpose, so that the building can remain useful while at the same time its heritage significance can be maintained. A typical redevelopment might involve using the building for office space, for housing, or for use as a museum or theatre. Adaptive re-use of heritage properties is generally subject to strict limitations. For example, in historic sites being redeveloped for tourism, controls may be necessary to forestall what could be called 'Disneyfication', i.e., turning the heritage location or site into a consumer-oriented entertainment package – a Disneyland – in pursuit of greater economic profit; this sort of strategy entails a disregard for, or insensitivity to, the cultural content of the heritage, and focusses primarily or exclusively on financial returns.

The policy instrument of most relevance in regard to the built heritage is regulation, i.e., setting criteria to determine which heritage items are sufficiently significant to warrant some public control over their use, and laying down standards for the ways in which heritage buildings and sites can be renovated, restored, altered or re-used. A distinction can be drawn between 'hard' and 'soft' regulation when applied to the built heritage.[18] Hard regulation comprises enforceable directives requiring certain behaviour, implemented through legislation, and involving penalties for non-compliance. Such regulation includes preservation orders; constraints on the appearance, function or use of buildings; land-use zoning; imposition of process requirements for development applications; and so on. Soft regulation on the other hand is not compulsory, but refers to unenforceable directives calling for or encouraging certain behaviour, implemented by agreement, and not involving penalties. It includes treaties, conventions, charters, guidelines, codes of practice, and other instruments that operate through voluntary compliance rather than coercion (other than moral persuasion).

Economists generally frown upon regulation as a policy instrument in most circumstances, and urban heritage conservation is no exception. They argue that it creates inefficiency; can be expensive in terms of both administrative and compliance costs; offers no incentive to do better; and can be captured both by private owners (e.g., through manipulation of planning controls) and by special interest groups such as the 'heritage lobby'. However, regulation has a number of advantages in this area, including its applicability when there are all-or-nothing choices (e.g. preservation versus demolition); when there is a high risk to the public interest; when certainty of outcome is required; and when short-run flexibility is advantageous. All of these policy requirements are delivered more effectively by regulation than by market-based alternatives.

The main mechanism that public authorities around the world use to regulate the built heritage is *listing*, i.e., the establishment of lists of properties within a given jurisdiction – international, national, regional, local – that are considered to be of cultural significance. Criteria are generally laid down to specify the characteristics that define cultural significance such that any property meeting these criteria will be eligible for inclusion on a particular list. In many cases, multiple lists exist specifying different grades of significance, often identifying the level according to the beneficiaries, ranging from local to national or international. In most jurisdictions the inclusion of privately owned buildings or groups of buildings on an official publicly sanctioned heritage list is compulsory, and the owners have no alternative but to comply with whatever requirements the list carries with it. In some cases, however, accession of properties to an official heritage list is voluntary; in these instances the representativeness and comprehensiveness of the list is dependent on the willingness of private owners to subject themselves to whatever obligations the listing process brings with it. In addition to lists maintained and enforced by public sector agencies, there are often 'unofficial' lists maintained by interest groups, non-government organisations, and so on, such as National Trusts, local history societies, etc.

The obligations imposed by a public regulatory authority on those owning or managing heritage properties vary among and within countries, and may include:

• restrictions on the extent to which the property can be altered;
• requirements for maintenance of the property in good condition;
• a prohibition on demolition;
• specification of standards of materials, etc., used in renovation or restoration;
• conditions attaching to sale; and so on.

These sorts of regulations are usually legally binding, such that non-compliance will incur penalties. In cases where some public funding may be made available to assist private owners of heritage properties with their maintenance or restoration, the regulatory authority will spell out the conditions on which finance is provided and the amounts involved.

Despite the acceptance in many countries of compulsory listing as the appropriate instrument for implementing public heritage policy towards the built environment, calls are sometimes heard for a more market-oriented approach to dealing with privately owned heritage properties.[19] For example, the question is asked: 'Why not implement a process of voluntary negotiation between the owners and the public authority in place of compulsory listing?' Such a process, it is argued, can provide a basis for determining the optimal amounts of financial assistance that owners could receive to help in their conservation efforts. The feasibility of using a negotiation process between the affected parties in these circumstances would rely on the well known Coase Theorem,[20] which requires three necessary conditions:

- that interested parties can be identified and property rights can be assigned;
- that transactions costs are negligible or zero; and
- that contracts can be enforced.

A moment's thought can establish that none of these conditions is likely to be met in a voluntary heritage-listing scheme. A series of individual negotiations would be necessary in which identifying the monetary value of the public interest would be extremely difficult. In addition, the process would be unduly costly to all parties, and the monitoring and enforcement of contracts under such a scheme would be likely to be ineffective.

Nevertheless, complaints that the listing of heritage properties may in some circumstances impose significant costs on private owners must be taken seriously. For some owners the costs imposed by regulatory controls, or simply by the physical task of restoration and repair, are excessively burdensome in relation to the individual benefits the heritage bestows on them. In such cases – where in effect the benefits of conservation are substantially public rather than private – it is appropriate that public assistance should be provided if the size of the public benefit warrants it. The difficulty then is assessment of the extent of public benefit involved, since even with a more generous financial contribution from the public sector, not all old buildings can be preserved. In many countries, present processes for assessing the public value attributable to privately owned heritage lack common standards across jurisdictions, and resources are generally insufficient to allow a full accounting for non-market benefits to be undertaken.

Furthermore a stronger recognition of the precautionary principle is required, whereby decisions concerning irreversible actions such as demolition should be considered only from an extreme risk-averse viewpoint. Thus, the policy recommendation should be pointing to sharpened techniques of economic value and cultural value assessment at all levels of government in the application of regulatory controls.

To sum up, in considering means of dealing with cases where private owners claim to be disadvantaged by listing or its consequences, it is incumbent on the government not to lose sight of the primary purpose of heritage regulation, i.e., to protect the public benefit arising from the built heritage at whatever level it occurs. In particular, it is important that the short-term financial exigency of some property owners should not be allowed to override the longer-term public interest. The key to achieving the appropriate balance between private interest and public interest in heritage conservation lies particularly in two policy directions: the application of objective, consistent and thorough procedures for heritage assessment, and the provision of adequate resources for compensation when a demonstrated need for it can be shown to exist.

## 6 Public policy and moveable heritage

Moveable cultural heritage differs from the other two types because it is generally small in physical scale, transportable, and readily saleable. Moreover the private benefits of such heritage are more easily appropriated by individuals, to the point where access to any public-good properties that an item may potentially possess can easily be excluded. Indeed, much moveable heritage is privately owned and unavailable for public enjoyment and enlightenment. Although the private owners of significant heritage items such as old master paintings are often identifiable, the works they possess only come under public scrutiny if they are put up for sale or are lent to a gallery for exhibition purposes. Moveable heritage items such as paintings and other collectibles are traded on private markets; such markets function as a service to individual and corporate dealers and collectors, and are of public concern only through normal market regulations, such as those designed to protect consumers or to guard against anti-competitive practices.[21] Nevertheless there are some situations where public involvement in the art market is required, for example when specific market provisions apply (resale royalty schemes are a case in point), or when important items are for sale that might be bought by agencies such as public art galleries or museums.[22]

A category of moveable heritage of particular interest is archaeological material or 'portable antiquities' that may be unearthed in scientific digs or that may be found by treasure hunters using sophisticated equipment such as metal detectors when searching for coins, jewellery or other metallic objects on the sites of former settlements. Such artefacts may be valuable both in monetary terms and in their historical or cultural significance. To the extent that such moveable heritage has public value, it is likely to engage the interest of museums, and dealing with this material becomes an important issue for cultural policy at both national and international levels.[23] Similar remarks relate to underwater heritage to be found in shipwrecks in all parts of the world.[24]

Public policy towards moveable heritage is exercised mainly through the ownership and management of collections of such heritage held in museums, galleries and archives, or in public buildings such as parliament houses and municipal offices. Sometimes museums with heritage collections are privately owned and operated, especially in the United States, and as such are not directly subject to public regulatory control. Nevertheless, regardless of ownership, heritage museums all over the world are almost always constituted as non-profit organisations with explicit cultural, scientific and educational objectives that could be regarded as congruent with public-sector cultural policy. Indeed, whether art galleries and museums are publicly or privately owned and operated, their boards, trustees and management face a common set of issues and tasks. These can be listed under four interrelated headings:

- *Collection management*: The care and conservation of artworks and artefacts is a primary responsibility. Collections are not static, but are constantly being added to through purchases, gifts, etc. There is a widespread reluctance amongst museums to dispose of items from their collections (deaccessioning), though occasionally objects or works are sold off to make way for new additions.[25] The costs of storing, maintaining and restoring items in collections forms a major component of most museums' expenditure. At the same time, the financial value of the collection is likely to comprise the most significant item on the asset side of the organisation's balance sheet.

- *Exhibition*: Museums function as major cultural centres where members of the public can come for learning and enjoyment. In many museums only a relatively small proportion of the collection can be displayed at any one time, and what is on show is constantly changing. Museums do not only exhibit their own collections but also put on shows of items lent by collectors or other museums. These are often themed shows that are shared sequentially amongst institutions in several locations; as 'blockbusters', these shows may prove to be a significant source of revenue through entrance charges and merchandising. For management, the economic attractiveness of putting on a popular exhibition may have to be weighed against the value of a show considered deeper and more challenging in artistic or cultural terms.
- *Education*: Most museums rank their educational mission amongst their highest priorities, whether it is pursued through the general exhibitions open to everyone, or through specific programmes targeted at young people. Education specialists on the staff of large museums arrange many activities for children and cooperate extensively with educational institutions in organising visits of student groups.
- *Research*: Many museums carry out pure and applied research in their area of expertise, host visiting scholars to work with their collections, and organise seminars and conferences to disseminate their research findings.

In all of these areas, museums are interested in monitoring and measuring the impact of their activities. Over the last few years considerable effort has gone into specifying and refining outcomes-based measures of impact as a means of improving their own operations and strengthening their case for financial support from public and private sources.[26]

From a public policy viewpoint, governance issues affecting museums and galleries are of particular concern. The costs of running public museums have risen steadily over time and the provision of public funding has come under increasing scrutiny. Cultural institutions have been obliged to search further afield for sources of revenue, raising questions about whether entry fees should be charged and requiring the commitment of more time and effort into securing donations and sponsorship deals.[27] Government policy-makers in turn need to assess the level of public value being created by museums and to calibrate funding decisions accordingly. A notable area of policy interest has been in new models for structuring the ownership and operation of public cultural institutions, following the success of initiatives such as the so-called 'privatisation' of major art museums in the Netherlands over the last decade. In fact, as we noted in Chapter 4, the Dutch model has not involved privatisation in the conventional sense, but rather a judicious withdrawal of hands-on government engagement, allowing a freeing up of the management of the museums and a renegotiation of the processes by which funding is provided. Ownership of buildings and collections in this system remains firmly in public hands.

Despite the enthusiasm engendered by the possibilities for *désétatisation* of cultural institutions, public policy must be on guard against excessive commercialisation of museum activities in the face of economic hardship. One of the most significant threats is 'mission displacement': when cultural institutions come to rely too heavily on earned income, they may be enticed away from their artistic or educational goals towards a greater reliance on entertainment-oriented offerings with greater earning potential. Moreover, if they become too commercial, they may jeopardise both their non-profit status and their access to various tax exemptions.[28]

An issue of increasing importance to all cultural institutions associated with moveable heritage, which includes not only museums and galleries but also libraries and archives, is the matter of dealing with new technology. The impact of new information and communications technologies on these institutions has been profound. Collection management has been revolutionised through digitisation and through the advent of software applications in registration, cataloguing and information retrieval. Exhibitions are increasingly adopting new media technologies for presentation and interpretation. Online access to museum services has greatly extended audience reach. From a policy perspective it can be suggested that such developments consolidate the position of these cultural institutions as core components of the creative sector, and as such come under the policy prescriptions for the cultural industries discussed in the previous chapter.[29]

## 7 Public policy and intangible heritage

We noted earlier that the concept of intangible cultural heritage can be somewhat difficult to pin down. The recently formulated UN *Convention for Safeguarding of the Intangible Cultural Heritage* (2003) defines it as

the practices, representations, expressions, knowledge, skills – as well as the instruments, objects, artefacts and cultural spaces associated there-with – that communities, groups and, in some cases, individuals recognise as part of their cultural heritage. This intangible cultural heritage, trans-mitted from generation to generation, is constantly recreated by communities and groups in response to their environment, their interaction with nature and their history ... (UNESCO, 2003: 2).

As such, intangible heritage can be interpreted as cultural capital, existing as a stock of assets and giving rise to a flow of services. Furthermore, the management of intangible capital from a policy viewpoint has much the same dimensions as managing its tangible counterpart, although the use of regulation is likely to be less appropriate as an instrument; rather, less formal and more wide-ranging policy approaches will tend to be more useful. So, for example, ensuring the preservation and transmission of traditional knowledge might require assistance delivered through policy measures such as: grants to individuals and businesses employing inherited skills to produce various goods and services; support for education, training and skills-development programmes; assistance to research projects; and so on.

The other component of intangible cultural heritage as defined earlier is the stock of inherited music and literature. Items in this category of cultural heritage exist as non-rival public goods that are also non-excludable once they are in the public domain. It is indisputable that such heritage can have significant cultural value. Furthermore, inherited music and literature display both market and non-market economic value, the former in the various ways it can be packaged and sold (books, recordings, performances) and the latter in the community's willingness to pay for existence, option, and bequest benefits. Much of the preservation, conservation and transmission of inherited music and literature happens without any need for public intervention; the significance of these forms of cultural heritage is widely appreciated and the normal processes of demand and supply will ensure that music from the distant or recent past continues to be performed, plays continue to be produced, novels read, and so on. However, assertion of the public interest regarding this type of intangible cultural heritage requires a recognition of the extent of non-market benefits (and hence of market failure) and an assumption of responsibility towards those aspects of cultural value that might escape a monetary evaluation. This might involve, for example, public support for performing groups, publishers and others specialising in the conservation and presentation of inherited cultural forms.[30]

## 8 International dimensions to heritage policy

Public policy towards both tangible and intangible cultural heritage is addressed by international conventions that recognise heritage items in particular countries that are of 'universal significance' and seek to ensure their conservation and proper management. The two most important instruments are the World Heritage Convention, which relates to tangible immoveable heritage, and the Intangible Heritage Convention, both administered by UNESCO.[31]

The World Heritage Convention was adopted by the UNESCO General Conference in 1972, and entered into force in 1977 when the required minimum number of countries had ratified it. Its primary vehicle is the World Heritage List, the international equivalent of the domestic listing process described earlier. The List covers both natural and cultural heritage. Countries nominate particular buildings, collections of buildings, locations, etc., for inscription onto the List, and their acceptance or otherwise is determined by a representative committee. Originally the sole criterion for inclusion on the List was a requirement that the item be judged of 'outstanding universal value'. A more detailed specification has subsequently evolved, which identifies the aspects of the item that must be able to be described in terms such as 'outstanding', 'exceptional' or 'superlative'.[32]

Inclusion of a cultural heritage item on the World Heritage List carries with it some implications for domestic cultural policy. Listing confers international recognition, with concomitant benefits flowing from increased tourist numbers, and possibly opening up potential for partnerships and projects to participate in the conservation and development of the site.[33] It also raises the profile of the site domestic-ally, and this may make it easier for governments to allocate funds to support the capital or operating expenditures involved in managing the facility. At the same time, listing carries with it responsibilities for ensuring the preservation of the site and for the regulation of its management such that the natural or cultural values that were the justification for its listing are properly maintained. Listing can on occasion be a double-edged sword, as, for example, when it attracts such an increase in tourist numbers that threshold visitation levels are exceeded and damage to the site ensues.

The Intangible Heritage Convention, as noted earlier, covers oral traditions and expressions (including language); traditional perform-ing arts; social practices, rituals and events; traditional knowledge; and traditional craftsmanship. The Convention dates from 2003 and entered into force in 2006. It is an effort to do for intangible heritage what the World Heritage Convention does for cultural heritage in its tangible immoveable form. It comprises a list of the specific items that have been nominated by signatory countries and accepted by the evaluation process, and a smaller list of items that are considered 'representative' of the creativity of humanity either in general terms or in relation to a specific community. The obligations assumed by the government of countries acceding to the Convention include the compilation of inventories of intangible heritage items and a commit-ment to safeguarding the items by whatever means are appropriate. As in the case of its sister treaty, the machinery for implementation of the Intangible Heritage Convention seeks to draw special attention to heritage items in danger, with an implied or explicit message to the government concerned and to the wider international community that urgent safeguarding measures will be needed.[34]

## 9  Conclusions

This chapter has reviewed the concept of cultural capital as it relates to the interpretation of heritage, noting its similarity to natural cap-ital – a comparison that opens up both theoretical and empirical possibilities for adapting concepts and methods from ecological and environmental economics to the study of culture. The parallels can be extended further, to the area of sustainability, allowing the specifica-tion of principles for culturally sustainable heritage management.

These discussions have also highlighted the fundamental role of concepts of value in the heritage arena, and emphasise the importance of the distinctions between different types and levels of value – individual/collective, economic/cultural, and private/public. Economic analysis using well-established methods for benefit assessment such as CVM, and applying them using equally well-established techniques such as CBA, allows these distinctions to be clarified in ways that can make a substantial contribution to heritage policy and practice. Yet much remains to be done in areas such as the development of market-based instruments, the evaluation of non-market effects, the possibilities for benefit transfer, and the assessment of those aspects of cultural value not captured via standard economic analysis. Given the multidimensional nature of the value of heritage, a great deal will depend on cooperation between economists and heritage professionals in identifying problem areas and in seeking solutions.

*Notes*

1  Quote is from the song 'Big Yellow Taxi' appearing on the album *Ladies of the Canyon* (1970) © Siquomb Publishing Corp.
2  See, for example, Cannon-Brookes (1996).
3  For some contributions to the economic analysis of cultural heritage, see Hutter and Rizzo (1997); Schuster, et al. (1997); Peacock (1998); Rizzo and Towse (2002); Benhamou (2003); Rizzo and Throsby (2006). An annotated guide to the literature is contained in Mason (2005). For a comprehensive overview of legal aspects, see Hoffman (2006).
4  See Throsby (1999); Ulibarri (2000); Shockley (2004); Cheng (2006).
5  See Costanza (1992); Jansson, et al. (1994); Edwards-Jones, et al. (2000); Tisdell (2003).
6  There are also links in conservation practice between natural heritage and cultural heritage; see Harmon (2007).
7  See, for example, Shipley (2000); Leichenko, et al. (2001); Deodhar (2007).
8  Application of hedonic-price techniques requires market data that are rarely available for cultural heritage; the most successful applications of hedonic pricing have been to the valuation of heritage qualities in urban housing, where real-estate sales prices can be readily obtained. Travel-cost techniques, which enable estimation of consumers' surplus, may have difficulty attributing costs to a specific heritage item or site, and in any case are an indicator more of use- rather than non-use values.

9 See the report of a panel appointed by the US National Oceanic and Atmospheric Administration, chaired by Kenneth Arrow and Robert Solow (Arrow, et al., 1993).

10 For overviews of the application of these methods to cultural heritage, see Frey and Oberholzer-Gee (1998); Klamer and Zuidhof (1999); Navrud and Ready (2002); Noonan (2003).

11 An example of a choice-modelling study that provided policy-relevant data on the non-market demand for heritage is that undertaken in Australia by Jeremy Thorpe and colleagues (see Allen Consulting Group, 2005).

12 See, for example, Provins, et al. (2008).

13 It might also be noted that antiquity alone may be sufficient to endow an otherwise unremarkable item with heritage status; for instance, pieces of pottery unearthed in an archaeological dig take on a historical value as examples of material culture from an earlier age.

14 Authenticity also contributes to the economic value of such artworks; for a discussion, see McCain (2006: 154).

15 See Lichfield (1988, Ch. 10); Nijkamp (1995).

16 The report of the United Nations World Commission on Environment and Development, chaired by Gro Harlem Brundtland (WCED, 1987); see especially p. 43.

17 Of course this is a particular problem for countries with substantial endowments of iconic heritage. For example, Italy has the largest number of cultural heritage items on the World Heritage List (more than 40 in 2009), the non-market benefits of which are enjoyed by people the world over. Yet the cost of maintaining these assets largely rests with the Italian taxpayer. See further in Zan, et al. (2007).

18 For a fuller discussion of this distinction and of the use of regulation in heritage policy, see Throsby (1997a; 1997b).

19 See, for example, the Draft Report of the Australian Productivity Commission's inquiry into the built heritage; for the final report of the inquiry, see Productivity Commission (Australia) (2006).

20 Coase (1960).

21 An illustration of the latter is the celebrated action against the major art auction houses Christie's and Sotheby's for anti-competitive behaviour during the 1990s; see Ashenfelter and Graddy (2005); Ginsburgh et al. (2005).

22 Public policy in this area may also include the control of the import and export of cultural objects; see further in Chapter 9.

23 See further in Bland (2005).

24  See Strati (1995); Grenier et al. (2006). This form of heritage is protected by the UNESCO *Convention on the Protection of the Underwater Heritage* (2001), which entered into force in January 2009.
25  See Frey and Meier (2006).
26  See, for example, Weil (2000); Anderson (2004); Scott (2006).
27  On the question of free admission, see Cowell (2007).
28  See further in Toepler (2006).
29  For a discussion of the impact of new technologies on museums, see for example, Rayward and Twidale (1999); Rocchi, et al. (2004); Geber (2006).
30  Bill Ivey argues that the musical heritage of the United States is endangered by the market-driven activities of big music corporations. Corporate interests acquire rights to cultural material that, Ivey argues, properly belongs to the general public; see Ivey (2008).
31  Their full titles are, respectively, the *Convention Concerning the Protection of the World's Cultural and Natural Heritage*, and the *Convention for the Safeguarding of the Intangible Cultural Heritage.*
32  For a full list of criteria currently in use, visit the World Heritage website at http://whc.unesco.org/
33  See the case study in Tisdell and Wilson (2002), and papers collected in Leask and Fyall (2006).
34  For further discussion of the Intangible Heritage Convention and its effects, see Kirshenblatt-Gimblett (2006) and papers collected in Smith and Akagawa (2009).

# 7 | *Culture in urban and regional development*

> Such was Venice, the wheedling, shady beauty, a city half fairy tale, half tourist trap, in whose foul air the arts had once flourished luxuriantly ...
>
> (Thomas Mann, *Death in Venice*, 1912[1])

## 1 Introduction

A consideration of the arts and culture in the economic life of towns, cities and regions opens up the spatial dimensions of creative activity. Where do creative businesses locate? What impact do art galleries or performing companies have on their surrounding communities? How do cultural factors affect the quality of life for the urban population? A consideration of these questions will draw extensively on the previous two chapters' discussions of the cultural industries and of heritage, and will also look forward to the following chapter on tourism. Indeed, since local economies are in a sense microcosms of larger national systems, virtually every topic treated in this volume has its own particular interpretation when applied at an urban or regional level.

It has been recognised for some time that the arts and culture contribute to urban life and to the economic development of towns and cities in a number of ways, including the following:

- Artistic and cultural activities at the local level can provide social engagement and employment-creation opportunities that may be useful, for example, as a means of re-engaging displaced social groups such as marginalised youth.[2]
- Strong cultural infrastructure and an active artistic life can be important in creating 'sustainable cities' and in attracting inward investment to an urban region by providing agreeable living and working conditions for staff of in-migrating enterprises.
- A single cultural facility or institution can on its own provide a stimulus to urban economic growth; the Guggenheim Museum in

Bilbao, Spain, is often cited as a paradigm case of a cultural investment that has led to revitalisation of a depressed urban area. Other
iconic cultural buildings and structures, such as the Leaning Tower
in Pisa, or the Taj Mahal in Agra, or the Great Wall of China,
are magnets for tourism and, over time, become important cultural
symbols for local residents and overseas visitors alike.

- The cultural identity of a city may also be enhanced through the
staging of artistic events and festivals. For example, long-standing
festivals such as those in Bayreuth, Edinburgh or Salzburg, are
inextricably bound up with the image of those cities.[3]

- Cultural industries can benefit from network and agglomeration
externalities available in urban settings. The growth of 'creative
clusters' in the cultural industries in a number of cities – fashion in
Milan, theatre in London, film-making in Hollywood – reflects the
economic advantages of co-location.

In this chapter we discuss the above effects, beginning with some
basic concepts such as cultural capital, sustainable urban development and livability. Creativity remains a central theme, and we discuss the implications of ideas such as the creative class, the creative
city and creative clusters. Architecture has a particular role to play in
an urban context, not just as one of the cultural industries but as a
major determinant of the quality of urban environments; we consider
the special prominence in this regard taken on by buildings housing
cultural facilities – museums, galleries and performing arts centres. A
final section to the chapter outlines the various ways in which urban
and regional cultural policy is delivered.

## 2  Concepts

The fundamental unit of account when dealing with the economics
of sub-national systems is the urban or regional economy. A bound-
ary is drawn around the area of interest, usually corresponding to
an administrative entity such as a metropolitan area, a municipal-
ity, a county, a state, etc. With the enclosed area defined, its internal
economic transactions can be identified, the levels of key economic
indicators such as incomes, output, employment and growth can be
monitored, and its trading relationships with the larger economy in
which it is located can be measured. Defining the regional economy is

especially important in analysing the economic contribution of businesses and industries at a local level. For example, an assessment of the economic impact of an arts festival needs to identify how much expenditure generated by the event originates from within and from outside of the region, in order to distinguish between real additions to local incomes on the one hand and intra-regional transfers on the other, in arriving at the net financial effect.

In considering questions of urban cultural policy, we can divide the areas of concern into two interrelated groups: the provision of cultural infrastructure, and the encouragement of creative industries and cultural activity. In the remainder of this section we consider the first of these issues by outlining some basic concepts that are relevant to an assessment of the role of infrastructure in the cultural life of cities. A useful approach to addressing this question in the context of urban growth and renewal is to think of cities as collections of capital assets:

- physical capital (buildings, economic infrastructure, etc.);
- natural capital (the natural resources and ecosystems on which cities depend to maintain their environmental integrity);
- human capital (the skills and capacities of the city's inhabitants); and
- cultural capital (tangible and intangible cultural assets).

In these circumstances, interventions in the form of urban development projects of various sorts can be construed as investments that have one or more of the following intentions:

- to create new assets in one or more of the above categories;
- to improve efficiency in the management of existing assets; and or
- to renovate, restore, recycle or re-use old assets, as is the case with cultural heritage.

These projects may be undertaken by government (national, regional, local), private corporations, international aid donors and lending agencies, and/or other stakeholders; in many cases partnership arrangements between these different parties will be involved. The expected payoff from the project will be measured in terms of desired outcomes, and a decision as to whether or not investments are warranted can be determined via an assessment of the benefits and costs to all those with an interest in or affected by the project.

Clearly it is cultural capital in the above list that is of most relevance to our present discussion. The aggregate of urban cultural capital in any given city comprises tangible assets – buildings, open spaces, public places, art collections, monuments, and so on – and also a range of intangible assets, such as traditions, the sense of place, customary behaviours, networks of artists and consumers, and other immaterial things, all of which can be described as elements of the cultural infrastructure of the city. These various capital stocks produce that variegated flow of services which, when combined with other inputs, yields the continuing array of artistic and cultural benefits consumed by inhabitants and visitors alike. Of course, individual cities will vary in the extent and complexity of the cultural capital they contain. In some, the accumulation of cultural capital is localised, built around a single item of cultural heritage, or congregated in a 'cultural district', where theatres, galleries and other arts activities are located; in others, the cultural capital is more diffuse in both its tangible and intangible manifestations.

In some cities the concentration of cultural capital is so intense that they qualify for description as 'cities of art', a popular term in Europe used to describe cities whose entire character is defined by their art and architecture – examples include Florence, Venice, Granada, Paris, Prague and St Petersburg.[4] The cultural capital in these cities is so dense and interconnected as to render it all but pointless to try to separate out the component contributed by any one element of it. It is the accumulation of the items of cultural capital that such cities contain that gives them their unique status. Moreover, the flow of services from this stock of tangible and intangible cultural capital, which in these cities has been generated continuously over centuries, is of a particular self-reinforcing kind where, in short, art creates art.

Cities of art provide an especially important opportunity to observe the cultural capital paradigm in action, because of the unequivocally rich cultural value that they possess. Recognition of this by local authorities in these cities means that, typically, evaluations of urban development projects that affect the urban fabric are strongly or even overwhelmingly constrained by cultural value considerations. These examples provide a useful illustration of priorities (if not the urban planning methods), which might be applied more frequently in other cities where the role of art and architecture might not be so pervasive or of such a quality, but is no less important for that. Indeed in such cases it could be argued that an even heavier responsibility rests on planners and decision-makers to recognise the cultural value of the city's art and architecture, especially given that economic forces are invariably seen as the sole or primary determinant of the direction of urban development.[5]

Carrying forward our discussion of heritage from the previous chapter, we can suggest that the paradigm of sustainable development can guide our consideration of the management of specifically urban cultural capital. In particular, applying the established principles of sustainability to the arts and culture involves emphasising society's ethical responsibility to pass on the inherited stock of cultural capital to future generations. It also implies taking a holistic view of the workings of cultural systems, and provides an overarching framework wherein both economic value and cultural value can be taken into account. In the urban environment, these concerns translate into the concept of 'sustainable cities'. Whilst most attention to date has focussed on an environmental interpretation of sustainability when applied to cities, there are strong grounds for extending that concern to the sustainability of art and culture, as essential components of the urban experience.[6] The concept of cultural capital provides an effective theoretical structure within which this can be done.

All of these considerations can be brought together under the objective of improving the *livability* of cities. Livability is a concept used by urban scholars, including geographers, sociologists and planners, to describe the characteristics of urban environments that make them attractive as places to live. These characteristics include tangible features, such as the existence of public infrastructure (public spaces, urban transit, availability of health and education services, effective means for providing clean air and water, efficient sanitation and waste disposal, etc.), and intangible features, such as a sense of place, a distinctive local identity, well-established social networks, etc. Empirical evidence of livable environments can be documented in particular cities if inventories are drawn up of these tangible and intangible assets; indicators can also be sought through observation of the characteristics of citizens themselves, where behaviours such as active civic participation (governance) and active cultural and recreational involvements (creativity, artistic production and consumption, sporting activities, etc.) can be taken as signs of responsiveness to a livable environment.

### 3 Creativity in an urban context

Just as creativity is seen as a driving force in processes of innovation and technological change in the macroeconomy, as discussed in Chapter 5 above, so also is it important at a local and regional level. In the most immediate economic sense, creativity is the key to the expansion of cultural industries that are sought out and encouraged by local authorities in their efforts to boost regional economic growth and employment and to revive depressed areas in towns and cities – initiatives that contribute to a broader social agenda as well. Creativity is also involved in three concepts relating to the artistic and cultural life of specifically urban environments: the creative class, creative clusters, and the creative city.

### *The creative class*

A writer who has had a significant impact on awareness of creativity in the life of cities is the controversial American regional economist Richard Florida, who argues that creativity has replaced raw materials, physical labour and flows of capital as the primary driver of urban economic success (Florida, 2002). He sees the emergence of a new social class – the 'creative class' – as an innovative source of urban dynamism. It can be argued that these ideas are not particularly original – urban theorists such as Lewis Mumford, Jane Jacobs and Peter Hall have all pointed in one way or another to the phenomenon of creativity as an engine of innovation and urban growth.[7] But whereas these writers have suggested that creativity arises spontaneously, such that its appearance cannot be orchestrated, Florida maintains that cities can actively encourage the growth of the creative class, and in so doing can improve their economic performance. He points to technology, talent and tolerance ('the three Ts') as the economic sparks that will ignite creativity.

In his empirical work, Florida sets out a series of indices that purport to measure, for a given city, its labour market diversity, its lifestyle characteristics, its social interaction, and so on. Taken together these indices say something about a city's identity and provide numerical means for ranking of cities according to the strength of their creative class. In his more recent writing, Florida lays great stress on sense of place, arguing that *where* people live matters more to them than the work they do or the people they live with.[8]

The idea of the creative class has been subject to a great deal of criticism.[9] In particular, the concept of creativity to which Florida refers is a fuzzy one, extending as it does to encompass a very wide range of occupational categories in defining the creative class. His solutions to problems of inequality generated in cities with a strong creative-class presence have also been criticised.[10] The construction of the various indices by which the existence of the creative class is assessed has been seriously questioned, as has the proposition of causality implied by Florida's argument. In the latter respect, although he has asserted that he did not mean to suggest one-way causation, whereby a city's success is determined by the size of its creative class, many city mayors and urban policy-makers have interpreted Florida's message in precisely these terms and have proposed strategies to attract and retain creative people as a means, they hope, of boosting the city's economic prospects.

Whether or not the concept of the creative class has any analytical substance over and above its purely rhetorical power as a rallying cry for city politicians, the essential empirical fact to which it relates – namely the clustering of creative people in urban locations – remains an observable phenomenon. Many such concentrations of creative people can be observed in major cities around the world.

## Creative clusters

The phenomenon of the clustering of economic activity has been recognised for some time. Alfred Marshall drew attention to the internal and external economies of localised industry in his *Principles of Economics* of 1890.[11] More recently the development of 'cluster theory' by Michael Porter has stimulated a widespread interest in locational issues in business management strategy.[12] Porter argues that, through the effects of proximity to other firms, participation in a cluster contributes to competitive advantage in terms of productivity and the capacity for innovation. It is not only economic connections that are influential in these processes; social networks can also be important in promoting cooperation, flexibility, joint ventures and information-sharing.

Several sorts of creative clusters can be identified that exemplify the ways in which these ideas can be translated into a specifically cultural context. Firstly, the existence of urban cultural precincts is an illustration of the clustering of firms in proximity to input and output markets. Theatres, concert halls and museums are often located near one another in a city, taking advantage of the concentrations of visitors who are attracted to a cultural precinct. Likewise various input suppliers tend to cluster around major users of their goods and services, as happens in Hollywood where a variety of highly specialised input-providers such as actors' agents, special-effects firms, post-production service companies, and so on, are located around the major film production houses.[13]

Secondly, businesses in the creative industries may follow standard clustering patterns in their search for economies of scale and scope, looking for the sorts of networking and agglomeration benefits that underlie clustering processes in any industrial sector. The roles of creativity, knowledge-production and information-exchange, particularly in high-tech creative industries, may act as important drivers towards the clustering of content-creating businesses in urban or regional centres.

Finally, we can point to a special type of cluster, the cultural district that is based on securing a trademark for its product, which can be used in market promotion and as a means of protecting local producers.[14] Such districts exploit the notions of networking, agglomeration and inter-firm cooperation that are fundamental to the clustering phenomenon, but carry them a step further by using intellectual property law and regulation to formalise and protect their particular brand identity.

From a policy viewpoint, the question arises as to whether creative or cultural clustering occurs spontaneously, and/or whether it can be initiated or at least encouraged by policy intervention. Certainly the incentives to private firms to seek the advantage of co-location can arise without any external assistance; many examples of cultural clusters exist that have arisen of their own accord. But policy measures may also be used, although seeking to stimulate cluster formation as an article of regional cultural policy is by no means a straightforward issue. The conditions under which a local network of cultural producers can become viable and sustainable vary greatly in different countries and for different types of goods and services, such that no universal rules can be laid down. Nevertheless, the various instruments of creative industries policy (discussed in Chapter 5) do have important relevance to urban and regional development. We return to these questions below.

## Creative cities

The concept of a 'creative city' describes an urban complex where cultural activities of various sorts are an integral component of the city's economic and social functioning. Such cities tend to be built upon a strong social and cultural infrastructure; to have relatively high concentrations of creative employment; and to be attractive to inward investment because of their well-established arts and cultural facilities. Charles Landry contends that cities have one crucial resource – their people; creativity, he says, is replacing location, natural resources and market access as a principal key to urban dynamism. He points out that

Today many of the world's cities face periods of transition largely brought about by the vigour of renewed globalisation. These transitions vary from region to region: in areas like Asia, cities are growing, while in others, such as Europe, old industries are disappearing and the value added in cities is created less through what is manufactured and more through intellectual capital applied to products, processes and services.[15]

UNESCO has built up a 'creative cities network', the members of which include Bologna and Seville, where the focus is on music, and Buenos Aires, Montreal and Berlin, where the creative theme is design. The UNESCO network extends to include food as a cultural dimension; the city of Popayán in Colombia, where families and communities celebrate their distinctive recipes, rituals and ingredients in promoting their cultural identity, has been named as the network's first City of Gastronomy. A somewhat similar triumphalism is evident in the designation of successive European cities as the 'cultural capital' of Europe, a title held for one year before being passed to the next lucky recipient. Whilst such a focus of interest on the cultural life of the chosen city doubtless does much to stimulate production and consumption of the arts and culture in the urban environment, at least for 12 months, the longer-term impacts are less certain.[16]

As a general proposition, however, the concept of the creative city is a persuasive one, so much so that many urban authorities use the idea in their promotional material and their vision statements for the future. Sometimes such efforts are no more than a facile attempt to exploit the creative class hypothesis in the mistaken belief that encouraging creative businesses and the in-migration of creative workers will somehow work an economic miracle. At its best, however, a creative city strategy will pay attention to cultural infrastructure, local cultural participation and involvement, the development of a flourishing and dynamic creative arts sector, community-oriented heritage conservation, and support for wider creative industries that are fully integrated into the local economy.

## 4 The role of architecture

Any discussion of the role of the arts and culture in cities cannot ignore the significance of architecture, particularly what can be called cultural architecture, in the urban environment. Many cultural institutions are housed in heritage buildings and as such their contribution to the built environment is easily recognisable. But a contemporary phenomenon of apparently ever-increasing importance is the design of new cultural facilities as pieces of iconic architecture, to be visited as much for their reputation as buildings as for what goes on inside them. Let us consider three examples.

The first illustration is the Opera House in Sydney, one of the most remarkable buildings of the twentieth century. Set on a promontory in Sydney Harbour, its billowing white sails create the impression of a majestic ship launched upon the water against a backdrop of towering city buildings. It was designed by the Danish architect Joern Utzon and opened in 1973. It is more a performing arts complex than simply an opera house, since it contains a large concert hall, three drama spaces and several exhibition areas, as well as an opera theatre. Its distinctive silhouette has become a symbol of Sydney that is recognised around the world.[17]

The second example is the Guggenheim Museum in Bilbao, a building that has all the appearance of a spaceship that has landed by mistake in an industrial wasteland. Frank Gehry's titanium-clad structure could scarcely seem more out of context with its surroundings, yet somehow it has become, in the short time since its completion in 1997, an accepted part of Bilbao's urban landscape. International visitors who might not otherwise have ever heard of the city now flock there to see the building and the art it contains. To the Basques, it is an important symbol and a spearhead of the revitalisation of an economically depressed region.[18]

The third city in this trio is Los Angeles. In the late 1980s the J. Paul Getty Trust was looking for somewhere to centralise its museum, its research facilities, its conservation institute, and other activities, and chose a hilltop on the edge of Los Angeles as the appropriate site. The American architect Richard Meier designed a spacious collection of buildings and piazzas, called the Getty Center or simply the Getty, and no expense was spared in the realisation of his vision. The resulting complex, overlooking the wide freeways and the endless urban sprawl of the city, with views beyond to the Pacific Ocean, resembles a university campus, and conveys an air of both calm and cultural expectancy to the arriving visitor.[19]

These three examples, drawn from cities in three separate continents, have several things in common. All are outstanding pieces of late twentieth century architecture, each in its own way having a profound impact on ideas about building design and construction in a postmodern world. All three are cultural institutions, serving both as repositories and as purveyors of art to a broad clientele ranging in each case from domestic to international visitors and from cultivated connoisseurs of art to members of the general public. Furthermore, a reading of any of these buildings is dependent on the urban context in which the building is situated. At the level of physical design, this dependence is obvious – the buildings are viewed in relation to their urban surroundings and they would not have the same effect or the same interpretation if they were sited in, say, the middle of a desert. So, for example, the Sydney Opera House relates to the harbour that embraces it on three sides, and the Guggenheim in Bilbao seems to absorb and be absorbed by the tangle of bridges, roadways, railway yards and other urban paraphernalia surrounding it. Even the Getty Center, which stands somewhat aloof from the city of Los Angeles, rises like a majestic acropolis that has somehow grown out of the urban landscape. However, the urban interdependence as exemplified by the three examples just described goes deeper than just their physical presence. The role of these buildings as cultural centres also becomes an integral part of the *intangible* urban fabric of their respective cities, contributing to the cities' sense of themselves as recognisable places for civilised communal existence. These two characteristics – the buildings' real physical presence and their more diffuse role in representing a focus of cultural identity – help to define the relationship between cultural architecture and the community's experience of the art and culture of their city.

It is important to note that the visitor's cultural experience, whether it involves listening to music, watching a play or looking at paintings, is inseparable from the experiencing of the building itself. To attend a performance at the Sydney Opera House, for example, is like approaching and entering a piece of sculpture, even before one takes one's seat in the auditorium. Similarly, the siting of the works of artists like Richard Serra or Jenny Holzer in the Bilbao gallery profoundly affects the viewer's reaction to them, and works in the Getty collection seem to take on a new life when seen in Meier's stately paradise on the hill. In other words the enjoyment of art in an urban context cannot be isolated from the means by which that art is conveyed, and the more refined those means are, the more intense the consumer's experience of cultural consumption is likely to be.

Can we draw any policy implications from the above discussion? Certainly it would be unwise simply to recommend yet another international competition to design yet another iconic building to house yet another cultural facility to add to the proliferation of such architectural showpieces around the world. Yet it cannot be denied that good architecture that makes the most of the specific urban environment and that responds to demonstrable cultural needs can make a significant contribution not only to a city's cultural life but to its economy as well. The phenomenal success, in terms of visitor numbers, of the Tate Modern in London, for example, is due in no small measure to the attraction of the building itself as an exemplary instance of adaptive re-use and as an engaging and stimulating place in which to enjoy modern art. Fortunately for public authorities, the private sector is often willing to help finance the design and construction of highly visible cultural facilities, at least during prosperous economic times.

## 5 Policy conclusions

In this chapter we have drawn attention to some of the policy issues that arise when considering the role of the arts and culture in the life of cities. We have also pointed out that the policy instruments discussed in earlier chapters – especially in regard to the arts, the cultural industries and heritage – have a specific application in the context of urban and regional development. As always, it is unlikely that a single policy measure will be capable of optimising the contribution that the cultural sector can make to the urban economy. Rather a cultural development strategy for a town, a city or a region is likely to contain a package of different instruments, in particular one or more of the following:

- *Provision of infrastructure*: We have seen how both tangible and intangible cultural capital underpin the entire range of cultural activity in the urban environment, from the enjoyment of heritage to the functioning of the cultural industries. In addition, public infrastructure such as transport and communications facilities, financial services, market information, and so on, are as important for creative businesses as for any other type of enterprise.
- *Finance and investment*: Access to start-up and working capital for businesses in the cultural sector can be an especially important prerequisite to successful establishment and growth in an urban context. Government provision of incentives for small enterprises through business incubators, and for larger corporations through targeted public/private partnership arrangements, may be useful in stimulating the growth of local creative clusters.
- *Capacity-building at local level*: One of the principal characteristics of a creative city is the quality of community life, where a sense of social cohesion and cultural identity is generated by people's active participation in grassroots-level arts and cultural activities. Experience shows that generally management of such activities is best devolved to the local level, but higher levels of government can assist through strategies aimed at building the capacities of communities to handle their own affairs.
- *Inter-jurisdictional cooperation*: Because of the multifaceted nature of the creative economy, the responsibilities for policy towards the cultural sector at an urban or regional level will not be confined to a single office or agency or government department, but are likely to be spread across a number of different areas. It is therefore essential that policy strategies are developed on a cooperative basis, with input likely from several different areas, though coordinated, for example, through an urban or regional planning agency.
- *Support for the core creative arts*: A sustainable cultural sector requires a healthy and dynamic creative arts at its centre, as implied by the concentric circles model of the cultural industries discussed earlier. Thus, although a strong programme of support for artists and arts organisations can be justified for purely cultural reasons,

it can also be rationalised in economic terms as underpinning broader cultural production in the creative industries in the urban or regional economy.

Finally, it is important to acknowledge the need for reliable data and sound analytical methods as the foundations upon which good urban policy must be built. Cultural planners confront difficult questions of measurement and assessment on a daily basis. In particular they are required to make judgements about relative values. What is the value of a street festival to the local community? What is the economic contribution that individual artists make to the urban economy? What is the net value of tourist flows to the city during the summer season? Is the investment in building a new cultural centre likely to be worth it? All these are questions requiring assessment of both economic value and cultural value. Comprehensive statistical services and a capacity for competent economic and cultural analysis are essential requirements for a planning authority at local level if good decisions in the long-term interests of the community are to be made.

*Notes*

1  Quote is from Mann ([1912] 2005) p. 104.
2  See Bailey, et al. (2004); Miles and Paddison (2005); Bille and Schulze (2006); Vickery (2007).
3  See further in Quinn (2005).
4  See, for example, the case of Florence discussed in Lazzeretti (2004).
5  For a discussion of the incorporation of culture into urban planning, see Young (2008).
6  For a discussion of urban cultural sustainability in the context of globalisation, see Jelin (1998).
7  See respectively Mumford (1958); Jacobs (1970); Hall (1998).
8  See Florida (2008).
9  See particularly the Review Roundtable discussions of Florida's work at the annual meeting of the Association of Collegiate Schools of Planning, held in Portland, Oregon, in October 2004, and published in the *Journal of the American Planning Association* 71(2): 206–219, which also includes Florida's response to his critics; see also critical overviews in Peck (2005) and Rausch and Negrey (2006).
10  See especially Markusen (2006); Donegan and Lowe (2008).
11  See Marshall (1890: Book IV, Chapter X).
12  See especially Porter (1998, 2000); see also Palazuelos (2005).
13  See, for example, Scott (2005).

14 This form of cultural district has been prominent in areas producing wine, cheese, ceramics, textiles, and so on; see, for example, Santagata (2002; 2006).

15 Landry (2000: xiii).

16 For case-studies of Porto and Rotterdam, which held the title jointly in 2001, see respectively Balsas (2004) and Richards and Wilson (2004).

17 For a recent assessment, see Drew and Browell (2002).

18 See van Bruggen (1997); for a discussion of the economic and cultural impacts of the museum, see Plaza (2000); Baniotopoulou (2001).

19 The architect's own account is contained in Meier (1997).

# 8 | Tourism

'Are you pleased with the Pantheon [*a building in London*]?'
'Very much; I have seen no building at all equal to it.'
'You have not been abroad. Travelling is the ruin of all happiness! There's no looking at a building here after seeing Italy.'
(Fanny Burney, *Cecilia*, 1782[1])

## 1 Introduction

Analyses of the tourist industry usually make a distinction between *mass tourism*, characterised in business terms as being a high-volume low-yield operation, and *niche tourism*, referring to tourism products that cater to small numbers of discriminating tourists with high revenue yield per person. The arts and culture are deeply involved in, and affected by, both types of tourist market. The term *cultural tourism* is used to relate to both aspects of tourist activity. Cultural attractions of various sorts appear as components of packages put together for the mass tourist, including visits to museums and heritage sites, outings to performing arts events, and participation in entertainments staged in tourist resorts, hotels, etc. Such activities are also undertaken by individual tourists not involved in any organised tour. Either way, 'cultural tourism' in its broad mass-tourism sense means large numbers of people, a matter of particular concern to superstar attractions such as the world's major museums, art galleries and heritage locations, which have to deal with the pressure of visitor numbers on a daily basis.

Cultural tourism in its more specific sense, on the other hand, involves smaller numbers of people seeking a more specialised experience. Used in this context, the term 'cultural tourism' refers to the niche market of the well-informed and culturally-sensitive tourist, whose trip, whether part of an organised package or undertaken independently, is primarily or solely for cultural purposes. The range of experiences sought by cultural tourists includes the following: attending particular performing arts events or specific types of museums and galleries; attending an arts festival; engaging in a pilgrimage to a religious or cultural place; touring places with literary or other cultural connections; visiting archaeological or other cultural sites, perhaps with an expert guide; living amongst particular communities in order to experience their culture; and so on.

Both types of interaction between tourism and the arts and culture are of interest to cultural policy. In this chapter we review the *economic* ramifications of both types of tourism with particular reference to the cultural sector. We then proceed to examine *cultural* issues raised, firstly, by mass tourism and, secondly, by the specialised cultural tourism market. Finally, some policy conclusions are drawn.

## 2 Economic aspects of tourism

### *Tourism as an industry*

The first task in discussing the tourism industry is to define who is a tourist. Various definitions exist based on distance travelled and/or length of stay away from home. A widely used approach is to define tourism as all travel of more than 40 km from the usual place of residence, except for commuting. Such a definition includes both domestic and international travel, and both business and leisure trips. Further distinctions can be made between overnight-stayers and day-trippers, and other criteria can be introduced to eliminate groups such as migrants, refugees, students, etc., from the definition of a tourist. Still more classifications can be introduced when considering arts-related tourism, for example, visitors to a theatre performance can be identified as 'arts-core' or 'arts-peripheral' depending on their motivation for being there.[2]

Drawing boundaries around the tourism industry and defining its components is not as simple as might first appear. At the core of the industry are those individuals and companies whose entire business is dependent on tourism: package tour operators, tourist guides, heritage sites, resorts, and so on. Depending on the definition of who a tourist is, other industries, such as hotels and long-distance passenger transportation, can also be counted as integral components of the tourism sector. The borders of the industry can also be drawn to include industries with some partial dependence on tourism, such as restaurants, theatres, museums and galleries, and so on; in these industries the level of tourism involvement of individual firms will vary from zero to 100 per cent depending on location and other factors.

The contribution of the tourism sector to the economy can be measured by the direct effect that tourist expenditures on goods and services have on output, incomes, employment and exports, and the indirect and induced effects as initial expenditures diffuse through the economy. These effects can be analysed using the inter-industry methodologies discussed in previous chapters, including input-output analysis and computable general equilibrium models.[3] The extent and quality of data collected for such studies will be greatly improved if tourism satellite accounts are available;[4] in some cases there may be sufficient sectoral disaggregation in the accounts to enable analysis of the specific case of cultural tourism. These sorts of analyses focus on the generation of economic value, but in principle it is also possible to imagine that models depicting financial and resource flows between industries could be extended to map exchanges of cultural value. In practice, such an exercise is still a long way off; as we have noted, the data demands of input-output models are substantial and already limit their application, and it is not hard to see how much more problematical such applications would be in the cultural arena, given that we do not yet have reliable means for empirical representation of the cultural value which would be needed to quantify the model. Nevertheless, a great deal can be learned from the application of these methods to those effects that *can* be measured – broadly characterised as flows of economic value – when culture and tourism are both implicated, and doubtless we can look forward to a range of such applications becoming available in the future.

As in other cultural industries, tourism is affected by new communications technologies. The internet has brought about profound changes in the ways in which tourist producers market their product and potential tourists acquire information about destinations, transport, accommodation, and so on. Moreover, new technologies are beginning to affect the tourist experience itself. For example, global positioning devices can be used to enable tourists to follow personalised itineraries in a town, with commentary custom-made to their own requirements. Cultural institutions that tourists visit provide a range of media to enhance the visitor's experience. These sorts of developments are causing a re-thinking of the tourism value chain, with consequent implications for the business models of arts and cultural institutions that have involvement with the tourism industry.[5]

## Impact studies

The economic effects of tourism on the arts and culture relate to the generation of revenue and employment for cultural enterprises, which in some cases is essential for their viability. For example, live theatre in London's West End draws significant audience numbers from tourists, to the point where its economic survival has been described as being dependent on the tourist market.[6] In these cases tourism comprises simply a specific revenue source for the cultural facilities concerned, though one subject to particular variability resulting from the sometimes unpredictable ups and downs of the tourism market. For many heritage sites and attractions, tourism is virtually their only source of revenue; thus investment in restoration, conservation, etc., is heavily dependent on future income streams from this source. For example, the approval of a loan by the World Bank to a developing country for the restoration of an item of its cultural heritage may be predicated on a required level of income from tourism expenditure as the primary source of loan repayment.[7]

Not only is tourism a significant generator of income and employment for some arts companies, cultural institutions and heritage sites, it can also be important to entire local or regional economies. Arts festivals and other cultural events, for example, draw tourists to a town or city and the economic impact on the local economy of their expenditure can be significant. We discussed the economic impacts of arts and cultural activities in the previous chapter; now, in the context of tourism, we can simply add that when tourists are attracted from outside the local region, their spending and associated multiplier effects may be regarded as a net gain to the regional economy, whereas the spending of local visitors should be regarded simply as a transfer from alternative lines of expenditure. In terms of the national economy, an impact study of a festival or other event requires a distinction between international tourists and domestic tourists in order to differentiate between net revenue inflows and displacement expenditure. Moreover, discovering the motivation of visiting tourists is also relevant here, to find out whether it was the event that specifically attracted them; on this depends the proportion of their expenditure and its impact that can be counted as a net gain.[8]

## Sustainable tourism

The phenomenon of 'sustainable tourism' is now a well-established paradigm for tourism management strategies that seek to avoid short-term exploitative practices in favour of long-term solutions that maintain and enhance the economic, environmental, social and cultural capacities of a site, a city, a region or a country to continue delivering valued tourism services. In the case of tourist destinations where environmental assets are a particular attraction (coral reefs, wilderness areas, etc.), the principles of sustainable tourism have been seen as a means of reconciling the possibly conflicting objectives of tourism developers (who seek economic gain) and conservationists (who seek environmental preservation); the policy mix in this case can be described as a search for 'win-win' outcomes where what is good for the tourism operators is also good for the environment and for society. Likewise, mutually beneficial policy strategies can be sought in regard to cultural aspects of tourism.

The concept of sustainable tourism in its application to culture can be defined more precisely by specifying the following three requirements for a sustainable project such as restoration of a heritage site that is to rely on tourism as its primary income source:[9]

(i) *Economic sustainability*: The project should produce a stable and predictable flow of net economic benefits into the future, where both market and non-market effects are included in the assessment. Market effects include revenues from tourist admission charges and, if appropriate, the net incremental value ('impact') of tourist expenditures. If externality or public-good benefits or costs are significant relative to direct market revenues, the project may need to incorporate some means for revenue capture in order to ensure continued financial viability of the project; for example, such capture may be effected via taxes levied on those enjoying the external benefits or imposing the external costs. For tourists, revenue capture is typically achieved through arrival/departure levies at airports, or through hotel occupancy taxes. Application of the sustainability principle of intragenerational equity would also ensure, for example, that local residents in an area affected by the tourist project would have equitable access to the project's economic benefits and that they would not be culturally disadvantaged by the project.

(ii) *Ecological sustainability*: Ecological sustainability is relevant in the case of cultural heritage when the tourist experience involves both natural and cultural capital assets together.[10] Given that the key requirements for ecological sustainability are the maintenance of natural capital stocks, of biodiversity and of ecosystem balance, the project should ensure that tourist impacts are kept to levels that ensure these principles are satisfied. In some cases this involves simply controlling numbers via pricing or regulatory measures, in other cases it is the qualitative nature of impacts rather than their volume that requires attention.

(iii) *Cultural sustainability*: The formal parallels between the concepts of cultural capital and natural capital noted earlier suggest that the key requirements for cultural sustainability will focus particularly on the same principles as are important for ecological sustainability, namely maintenance of cultural capital stocks, of cultural diversity and of the balance of cultural ecosystems. Again, the control of tourist impacts to a level that ensures compliance with these principles is indicated. For example, an archaeological site subject to pressures from daily tourist visitation will not be sustainable in cultural terms if threshold carrying capacities are constantly exceeded. Similarly, a historic town centre will not meet criteria for cultural sustainability if the cultural networks that support the variety of its cultural activities are threatened by excessive tourist numbers. These matters are discussed further below.

## 3  Cultural issues in mass tourism

The effects of mass tourism may be felt by all types of cultural enterprise at all levels of activity, from the individual museum or performing arts venue to whole towns and cities. The sheer size of the mass tourism phenomenon brings with it enormous economic potential to contribute to revenues at all of these levels. However, it also brings costs, especially when numbers become excessive; congestion costs arise with overcrowding, and physical damage may be caused to sites, artworks and facilities. Moreover, mass tourism may bring adverse

cultural consequences, for example, when the cultural integrity of a
site or community is threatened by a flood of visitors.

The concept of *threshold carrying capacity* has been developed
to describe the maximum number of visitors per hour or per day
to an institution or a site that can be absorbed without causing an
unacceptable level of congestion or risk of damage.[11] The concept has
been used in connection with natural heritage sites such as national
parks, coral reefs, wilderness areas, and so on. It is equally applicable
in the cultural sphere. Its usefulness is in guiding operational policy
in the management of attractions and sites by setting control param-
eters on visitor numbers per unit of time. Many organisations rely on
the threshold carrying capacity concept either explicitly or implicitly,
mostly implementing it through the imposition of quantitative controls on admissions.

The issues discussed above that arise in the relationships between
mass tourism and culture have some specific implications for public cultural policy. Local and national governments that are keen to
exploit the economic potential of the mass tourism market will frequently engage the cultural sector as one of the drawcards for attracting visitors, but in doing so they need to be aware of both the positive
and negative impacts that exposure to mass tourism can bring for
individual businesses in the arts and cultural industries. If negative
effects are encountered or are foreseen, for example because numbers
become excessive, policy-makers need to be prepared to take appropriate action. Possible instruments include pricing measures, regulatory controls, and information/marketing/education campaigns.

## 4  Cultural tourism as a niche market

We turn now to issues involving cultural tourism as defined in the
specialised sense of the term. The phrase 'cultural tourism' in this
context can be interpreted in terms of the product presented (for
example, a tour in Europe taking in opera performances at major
houses on a defined circuit) or from the viewpoint of the tourist's
motives (to seek new cultural experiences, to expand cultural knowledge, and so on). However it is approached, this form of tourism has
all the hallmarks of a niche product, insofar as it is demanded by a
relatively small number of highly discriminating, well-informed and
well-off consumers. It bears many similarities to eco-tourism – the

market for specialised ecological and environmental tourism experiences – and indeed the two sometimes go hand in hand, for example, when both environmental and cultural attributes are attractive features of a particular tourist destination.

Given the cultural sensitivities of the tourists involved, it would not be expected that cultural tourism of the niche variety would have a negative impact on the institutions, sites or communities visited. An illustration is provided by indigenous tourism, where the tourist may stay with indigenous communities for a period of time in order to experience and learn at first hand about the people's culture and way of life. Such tourism is likely to have the explicit intention of respecting local cultural values and of not disrupting the community's cultural life. Nevertheless, no matter how unobtrusive the tourist tries to be, some adverse impact may be inevitable, pointing to a need for careful planning and management of tourism projects in indigenous areas.[12]

Another area where the specific form of cultural tourism is important is in island tourism. Small island states or regions that exist in the Caribbean, the Mediterranean, the Pacific Ocean, the Indian Ocean and elsewhere have stocks of natural and cultural capital that are typically a significant drawcard for tourists, and the tourism sector is frequently an important contributor to the island economy. Issues of economic, ecological and cultural sustainability are brought into sharp relief in these circumstances. Looking particularly at cultural sustainability, we can note that in some cases the maintenance of island traditions may depend on the commodification of the traditional experience for selling to visitors, as David Fisher points out in the case of a tourism project in Fiji.[13] But the sorts of impacts brought about by tourism demand may threaten cultural sustainability; for example, Veronica Long and Geoffrey Wall studied the provision of small 'homestay' facilities operated by locals in Bali to show off their culture to visitors, and demonstrated that the culture is in fact changed by the visitors' presence.[14]

The *economic* sustainability of tourism in small island states can also be called into question. Such states have sometimes looked to tourism as a magical means of overcoming their economic difficulties, even to the point of regarding tourism as a sort of cargo cult in its capacity to deliver economic wealth. However, inter-island competition, broader competitive pressures and sudden international shocks, not

to mention internal political and social instability, can cause significant cyclical and secular downturns in tourist numbers, making the
tourism sector a risky prospect for export development in a number of
island economies. Furthermore, the tourism industry may also have
adverse effects on internal economic indicators such as income distribution, if the economic benefits from tourist expenditures accrue only
to a small segment of the population.[15]

## 5  Policy conclusions

This chapter has discussed the various ways in which the tourism
industry affects, and is affected by, the arts and culture, whether at
local, regional, national or international level. Our discussion has
built upon a number of issues raised in earlier chapters, particularly
those relating to heritage (Chapter 6) and urban and regional development (Chapter 7). Much of the policy analysis contained in those
chapters is relevant to the particular context of tourism – the management of heritage sites, for example, or land-use planning at the
regional level. More generally, public policy towards the tourist sector
tends to be expressed in the form of a 'tourism strategy' containing a
package of measures in which the arts and culture may be given particular attention. The components of such a package at the national
level might typically include:

- a marketing campaign to promote the industry both at home and
  abroad;
- revenue-raising measures, such as occupancy taxes, arrival and
  departure taxes, etc.;
- expenditure measures such as assistance to tourist-related small
  businesses, some of which may be arts groups, organisations, etc.;
- regulatory measures, such as land-use planning and zoning;
- provision of information for tourists, such as city guides listing cultural attractions; and
- education campaigns to make individuals and communities more
  aware of the positive and negative aspects of tourism development.

Similar ingredients may be found in tourism development strategies
formulated at a local level. A particular area in which local cultural
policy directed at tourism is important is in the management of heritage sites, which, as we have noted, are likely to look to tourism as

a principal source of revenue. In a number of countries there exist specific cultural heritage sites that, for all their national or even international cultural significance, are essential to the character and cultural identity of the local population. The management of such sites – including their restoration, conservation, and operation as tourist venues – will frequently require the professional expertise of skilled people from outside the local area, such as conservationists, historians, archaeologists, business managers, etc. However, planning methods applicable to such sites are unlikely to be successful if they do not engage the local population in the 'ownership' of the project. An illustration of this is provided by UNESCO's 'LEAP' project ('Integrated Community Development and Cultural Heritage Site Preservation in Asia and the Pacific through Local Effort'), emanating from the Culture Unit of the Asia-Pacific Regional Office of UNESCO located in Bangkok.[16] This project fostered the creation of key networks within heritage and tourism sectors in a number of case study sites scattered throughout the region, bringing together heritage site managers and heritage experts from private and public sectors, and involving local people and resources in the sites' operations. An outcome of this project was a series of models laying down procedures for various aspects of the planning process aimed at achieving sustainability of the cultural heritage resource base and its supporting infrastructure (the 'Lijiang models'). Although oriented towards heritage management in developing countries, the principles on which these models are based are widely applicable to the management of tourist sites of cultural importance across the globe.

## Notes

1 Quote is from Vol i, Book 4, Ch. II of the two-volume edition published by George Bell, in London, in 1882; see Burney (1782 [1986]: 267).
2 See further in Hughes (2000: 54–60) and references cited therein.
3 See, for example, Dwyer, et al. (2000; 2004).
4 See Blake, et al. (2001); Jones, et al. (2003); Smeral (2006); Liberos, et al. (2006).
5 See further in Minghetti, et al. (2001); Sigala (2005).
6 But this may have effects on the type of theatre presented which some may regard as unfavourable; see Hughes (1998).
7 See further in Cernea (2001), and some case study examples in World Bank (2001; 2007).

8  A case study of a well-known festival, the Edinburgh Festival, is contained in Gratton and Taylor (1995); for discussion of methodological issues in analysing the economic impact of tourist events, see Tyrrell and Johnston (2001); Hodur and Leistritz (2007).

9  See Lindberg (1999); McKercher and du Cros (2002); Gilmore, et al. (2007).

10 For example, a number of items on the World Heritage List are classified as having both natural and cultural heritage significance.

11 See, for example, Brown, et al. (1995); Winter (2008).

12 For a discussion of some of these items, see Wall (1999); Ryan and Aicken (2005); Johnston (2006); Macleod (2006).

13 See Fisher (2003).

14 Long and Wall (1995).

15 Further discussion of island tourism is contained in Briguglio, et al. (1996); Tisdell and McKee (2001); Kokkranikal, et al. (2003); Harrison (2003).

16 See links to the project at www.unescobkk.org

# 9 | *Culture in the international economy*

Death to Hollywood.

(John Maynard Keynes, 1945[1])

## 1 Introduction

There are few areas where cultural policy and economic policy intersect more directly than in the international arena. At a fundamental
level the internationalisation of the world economy provides the context
within which much cultural production, distribution and consumption
takes place; indeed, as we saw in Chapter 1, globalisation has been one
of the key factors influencing the transformation of cultural policy in
recent years. In more immediate policy terms we can point to the following areas where culture engages with the international economy:

- international trade in tangible cultural products such as artworks,
  books, CDs, etc.;
- international trade in intellectual property rights relating to intangible cultural commodities such as television programmes, movies,
  digitised music, etc.;
- international labour movements affecting the cultural industries,
  such as the mobility of artists;
- international cultural exchanges such as touring by performing companies, the circulation of artworks and artefacts on loan
  between museums and galleries, etc.;
- international cultural diplomacy and the exercise of 'soft power';
  and
- international cultural tourism.

In this chapter we consider the above aspects (apart from tourism,
already discussed in Chapter 8) by distinguishing between the trade-
related and non-trade-related dimensions of international cultural
policy.

## 2 Cultural trade

International trading of cultural products has been going on for as long as trade itself. Indeed much of present-day cultural trade still reflects long-standing traditions in the international circulation of cultural products such as artworks, artefacts, and so on. However, the nature of cultural trade was transformed during the second half of the twentieth century as a result of the effects of three major developments: the expansion in trade in services; the changing architecture of world trading arrangements; and most recently, the emergence of the internet. In this section we discuss trade in both tangible and intangible cultural products as it has developed over the past decade or so and as it is likely to develop further in the future.[2]

### *The cultural exception*

Cultural goods and services have always proved an irritant in international trade negotiations, providing a paradigm case of the conflict between economic values and cultural values in decision-making. Consider the case of the international market for audio-visual product such as film and television programmes. On the one hand, producers of these goods in countries such as the United States, who have access to scale and other economies in production and who see lucrative markets in many parts of the world, are likely to oppose any intervention in international trading arrangements that will limit their market access. On the other hand, many importing countries see their culture swamped by foreign product against which their local cultural industries are unable to compete without some form of protection. Thus a fundamental question arises: Should cultural goods be treated simply as commercial merchandise, with the economic gains from trade being the only concern in trading negotiations, or should the fact that these goods convey cultural messages be taken into account, having regard for the profound quantitative and qualitative effects they have on the circulation of cultural value?

Concern over this issue goes back to the immediate post-war years when the General Agreement on Tariffs and Trade (GATT) was being negotiated. The basic principles of the GATT that were laid down in 1947 and that still apply today are:

- reducing import tariffs;
- treating different countries' imports equally, i.e., on 'Most Favoured Nation' (MFN) terms; and
- treating imported and domestic products on the same terms ('national treatment').

The GATT was intended to apply to all commodities, although at the insistence of the French during the original negotiations an allowance was made (Article IV) for countries to impose screen quotas in the cinema in order to protect national film industries. Apart from this, there has been no special treatment for cultural goods in the GATT. Nevertheless, the term 'cultural exception' has been widely used to describe any effort to provide for differential treatment of culture in trade negotiations. So, for example, in the formulation of the 1988 Free Trade Agreement between the United States and Canada, a sort of cultural exception was agreed to, though it proved to be of limited effectiveness.[3]

In the lead-up to the formation of the World Trade Organisation (WTO) in 1993, France and Canada argued for a cultural exception that would bring about the exemption of audio-visual media from WTO processes. This proposal failed, but a way out was found through the General Agreement on Trade in Services (GATS), established in 1995, which allows for flexibility in regard to the audio-visual sector. Specifically, members can decide whether or not to accept commitments with respect to market access, MFN and national treatment provisions in relation to particular services traded; most countries have not made such commitments in respect of audio-visual products, in order to uphold their existing cultural policies. Nevertheless, these arrangements were only intended to be temporary and further liberalisation was foreshadowed. However, progress in the ensuing years was slow and suffered a further setback with the collapse of the Doha Round at the end of 2008.

The arguments for treating cultural goods and services differently and therefore for accepting the case in favour of a cultural exception can be summarised as follows:

- cultural products are vehicles for symbolic messages that transcend the products' purely commercial value, such that normal market processes will not be capable of fully capturing their value to society;

- cultural products are essential to the expression of national identity and hence their protection is warranted in the public interest;
- a wide range of domestically produced cultural products is important for cultural diversity;
- cultural products may be subject to unfair competition from the dumping of cheap imports, and are therefore worthy of protection under competition law; and
- industries producing cultural products may be eligible for infant-industry protection if their growth prospects indicate eventual self-sufficiency.

The case against the cultural exception is based on the following propositions:

- protection involves market distortion and creates economic inefficiency by inhibiting the achievement of gains from trade that arise as a result of specialisation and comparative advantage;
- protection is a reflection of regulatory capture by a self-interested cultural lobby, enabling rent-seeking behaviour by privileged groups;
- protection is a denial of consumer sovereignty and a deprivation of individual freedom of choice;
- openness to cultural imports promotes cultural diversity; and
- cultural protection is simply a cover for broader ideological agendas, such as anti-Americanism, anti-globalisation, etc.

The above arguments on both sides of the fence contain a mixture of economic, cultural, ideological and ethical propositions. It can be suggested that if a decision for or against the cultural exception were to be based on economic criteria alone, the arguments against would be likely to prevail, at least in principle, whereas the opposite is probably true if a choice were motivated in purely cultural terms. On ethical grounds the outcome may be less clear, depending on the extent to which a trade-off is possible between the liberty of the individual and the occasional necessity of collective choice. Whatever the upshot of these speculations, the fact remains that trade negotiations are traditionally all about economics, whether on a multilateral basis through the WTO or in the many bilateral free-trade agreements that have been appearing on the international scene in recent years. Any suggestion that cultural value should be taken into account in determining the rules of the game is likely to be dismissed by economists as counter-productive, tender-minded and impractical. Yet the fact that cultural identity, self-recognition and self-esteem are important to people, and that cultural trade has an impact on these values, should give pause for thought. Economic policy-making in this area may need to temper its assertion of the supremacy of economic goals and accept that ultimately the needs of different societies extend beyond immediate material concerns.[4]

## Towards a new world order for cultural trade

It is noteworthy that in the above list of arguments for and against the cultural exception, the concept of cultural diversity is invoked on both sides. Opponents of the exception point to the increased range of cultural product that is potentially available to domestic consumers if there are no barriers to imports, whereas supporters of protection argue that openness results in market domination by a few major suppliers, driving out many small local producers. In these circumstances, there is a certain irony to the fact that an important impetus towards finding a new pathway for dealing with cultural trade has come through increased international interest in cultural diversity as an essential element in local, national and international cultural development. We consider the question of cultural diversity in detail in the following chapter. Here our attention is limited to the relationship between cultural diversity and trade.

Continuing dissatisfaction in a number of countries, especially in the developing world, with the incapacity of existing mechanisms governing world trade to reconcile the economic and cultural dimensions of trade in cultural goods and services was one of the concerns that led to the formulation of UNESCO's *Convention on the Protection and Promotion of the Diversity of Cultural Expressions* (known for short as the Cultural Diversity Convention), which was adopted in 2005 and which entered into force in 2007. The Convention was seen as a new standard-setting instrument for cultural trade which had the potential to resolve the tensions and ambiguities surrounding trade in audio-visual services and other cultural commodities that existed under the WTO and the GATS.

The Convention uses the word 'protection' in its title. It is important, in interpreting this usage, to distinguish between 'protection' and 'protectionism'. The latter is generally understood to mean an automatic resort to trade restrictions to shield otherwise uncompetitive domestic industries from foreign competition. It is generally agreed that knee-jerk protectionism imposes more costs than benefits, no matter how high-minded the rhetoric about protecting workers' jobs, etc., which is used in its justification. Moreover, cultural protectionism might be equated with the equally undesirable notion of cultural isolationism. The Convention does not advocate any of these forms of protectionism. On the contrary, the concept of protection enshrined in the agreement implies taking care of something regarded as valuable, as understood in the phrase 'child protection'.

From the outset of the process that led to the final drafting of the Cultural Diversity Convention, safeguarding *vulnerable* cultural expressions was a key element motivating the Convention's purpose. The threat to culture was identified rather vaguely as arising from 'globalisation', but in reality it was market dominance by the transglobal corporate giants in the audio-visual media industries that was seen as the main cause for concern. In its final form, the Convention deals with these issues by allowing signatories to take measures to protect and preserve cultural expressions when they are 'at *risk of extinction*, under *serious threat*, or otherwise in need of *urgent safeguarding*' (Article 8, para. 1, emphasis added). How are these terms to be interpreted by governments as they endeavour to implement the Convention's various provisions? It is appropriate to discuss their interpretation in the following stages:

(i) *What is being protected?* In the case of cultural expressions that are generated by tangible items of cultural capital such as heritage buildings, sites, artefacts and artworks, and by intangible cultural capital such as languages, traditions, rituals, etc., the protection required is directed at the asset itself. On the other hand, in the case of cultural expressions experienced by means of the production and consumption of cultural goods, services and activities such as the performing and visual arts, music, literature, films, television programmes, video games, etc., the protection required will be of the production and consumption processes of the goods, services and activities involved.

(ii) *Threat*: The literal meaning of the verb 'to threaten' is 'to be likely to injure', or 'to be a source of danger to' someone or something. In the case of cultural expressions, threats may be classified as external or internal to a country, and as arising from economic,

Table 9.1: *Possible threats to the diversity of cultural expressions*

|          | Economic | Cultural | Physical |
|----------|----------|----------|----------|
| External | competition from global markets; 'dumping' of cultural product | imposition of cultural symbols or messages from imported product | weather damage to heritage buildings and sites |
| Internal | insufficient demand; market failure; high cost of production | consumer indifference towards local cultural expressions | neglect, failure to maintain fabric of tangible cultural capital |

cultural and/or physical sources. The types of threat that may affect the diversity of cultural expressions according to this scheme are shown in Table 9.1.

The most obvious illustrations of threats to local cultural expressions arising from *economic* sources can be found in the competitive pressures affecting the production and consumption of film, television programmes, music, and other audio-visual product. An example of a *cultural* threat is the possible crowding-out of minority languages by a dominant national or international language.

It is apparent that economic and cultural threats and consequences are closely interconnected. Economic threats might have purely economic consequences, seen in loss of domestic incomes, loss of export earnings and loss of jobs. Economic threats may also have cultural effects through loss of cultural identity or diminution in the diversity of cultural expressions. Similarly, cultural threats might have economic consequences if, for example, the dominance of foreign cultural symbols directs consumer tastes away from domestically produced product, whilst cultural threats could have cultural effects, for instance, if living cultures are transformed into Disneyland-type experiences aimed particularly at tourists.

(iii) *In need of urgent safeguarding*: This phrase implies vulnerability, which may be defined as being susceptible to injury. Safeguarding, in turn, may be defined as keeping secure or protecting from the danger of injury. Vulnerability might arise from the same three sources that were identified in Table 9.1. Firstly, *economic* susceptibility might occur:

- if the scale of domestic cultural production is too small and/or costs of production are too high in comparison with international competitors;
- if domestic markets are too thin and/or demand for local cultural product is insufficient; or
- if the infrastructure to support domestic cultural industry is inadequate – this infrastructure might relate to the supply of managerial or entrepreneurial skills, the provision of financial services, the existence of efficient marketing and distribution channels, etc.

Secondly, *cultural* vulnerability could arise, for example, if there is insufficient community interest in maintaining a particular cultural expression, or if the holders of traditional knowledge are dying out and are not being replaced. Thirdly, *physical* susceptibility of tangible cultural items might arise simply through processes of decay and the ravages of time.

How should the word 'urgent' be interpreted? Some degree of exposure to threat and even some curtailment of the extent or diversity of output of cultural expressions may be both expected and tolerated as part of the normal economic and cultural dynamics of national and international affairs. However, such effects would be regarded as serious, and remedial actions seen to be urgently required, if the injury being caused was likely to be long-lasting or permanent, and/or if the harm was going to be difficult to repair. For example, the absorption of a traditional music genre into the world-music sphere might seriously undermine a country's long-term capacity to maintain the skills and talents of artists in this genre in production.

(iv) *Risk of extinction*: The extreme case of the circumstances described above is where a cultural expression may die out altogether. The word 'extinction' implies that, as with species in the biological sphere, the disappearance would be permanent and irrevocable. In this situation the precautionary principle should be invoked, requiring decisions that may have irreversible consequences to be taken with extreme caution. The possibility of extinction is most obviously illustrated when applied to tangible and intangible cultural capital, as in the destruction of a heritage building or the dying out of a traditional language, but it is also relevant to cultural goods, services and activities of other sorts, the disappearance of which would reduce cultural diversity.

It still remains to be seen whether the Cultural Diversity Convention will provide any lasting solution to the problems that continue to beset cultural trade. Although the Convention does not impose enforceable obligations on its signatories regarding the protection of vulnerable cultural expressions, it can be seen as a first step towards resolving potential conflicts between trade and culture arising in the world trading system. Nevertheless, a considerable challenge remains for countries that have ratified the Convention, most of which are members of the WTO, to find a workable way of integrating the Convention with existing WTO rules.[5]

## International movements of culturally significant objects

An aspect of trade in cultural goods and services that attracts public attention from time to time is the international movement, actual or potential, of artworks or artefacts that are regarded as being of cultural significance. Much of this trade is carried on between dealers, museums, collectors, etc., and is of no particular public concern, except insofar as the prices involved may stir the public's imagination.[6] But there are two circumstances in which the public interest is brought into play: when so-called 'national treasures' are likely to be exported, and when some culturally significant property is a candidate for repatriation to its country of origin.

In the first case, some governments require owners wishing to sell a significant cultural object to an overseas buyer to submit to an assessment procedure before an export licence is granted. In the UK, for instance, a set of standards known as the Waverley Criteria is used to assess whether a particular item is of such significance to the national cultural heritage that its export should be deferred to allow time for alternative ways for retaining it for the nation to be investigated, e.g., by purchasing it for a public collection. The criteria are applied by asking the following questions:

- Is the item so clearly connected to the history or national life of the country that its departure would be a misfortune?
- Is the item of outstanding aesthetic importance?
- Is the item of outstanding significance for some branch of art, learning or history?

A determination is made by an independent expert committee, which aims to strike a balance between the rights of owners and the need to protect the nation's heritage. Over the years this system has led to the retention in the UK of a number of important works of art that would otherwise have been exported.[7]

The second aspect of the international movement of culturally significant objects is the repatriation of cultural property. Although the long-running saga of the Elgin Marbles, held by the British Museum in London since 1816, is probably the most widely known example that springs to mind, there has in fact been a considerable number of less-publicised cases in recent years where objects and artefacts held in museum collections have been returned to indigenous communities in different parts of the world. Many major museums that have acquired cultural property in the past, as a result of colonial conquest or from archaeological or anthropological expeditions, have come to appreciate the importance of these items in their collections to the descendants of the people from whom the objects were taken, and have reached agreement in many instances as to their return.[8]

### 3  Non-trade issues in international cultural relations

*Cultural exchange*

International cultural movements and exchanges that are not trade-related occur in many forms, including the following:

- Artists have a long history of moving between countries in search of creative and income-earning opportunities, such as the migration of painters to Paris in the late nineteenth century or the inflow of actors and other film workers into Hollywood in the twentieth.
- Many performing companies, music ensembles and individual artists tour their wares on an international circuit.
- Museums and galleries put together exhibitions that travel around the world, and arrange exchanges of curatorial staff, etc., to improve their skill base.
- Film production companies and distributors in different countries enter into co-financing arrangements with each other to make movies, television programmes, etc., which will be seen in many countries.

Much of this activity is, and always has been, a response to purely artistic or commercial incentives. But there may also be a policy interest in encouraging international cultural exchange. In particular, governments may see it as worthwhile for the cultural experiences available to the domestic population to be expanded through exposure to art and artists from abroad, in accordance with motives of cultivating educational and cultural development. Thus, for example, an arts-funding authority may underwrite the showing of an imported exhibition at a public gallery, or provide financial help to a local folk-music festival featuring international artists.

More importantly, governments are likely to be interested in movements in the other direction, and indeed the exposure of a country's art and culture to an overseas audience is generally seen as an important aspect of international relations. The motives behind providing government support for an international tour by a local theatre company or symphony orchestra may be purely altruistic, aimed at promoting intercultural dialogue and understanding; such outcomes are regarded as important as a means of improving a country's image abroad and fostering harmonious diplomatic relations.[9] But there may also be a hidden (or not so hidden) economic motive; namely to promote the country's trade prospects. The old adage 'where culture leads, trade follows' may be an expression of faith rather than fact, but it is at least plausible to propose that the improved understanding and better communication that accompanies cultural exchange is likely to facilitate rather than hinder the development of trading relationships.

Furthermore, there may be a wider political or diplomatic purpose behind international cultural relations. Culture is a key component of what has been called *soft power*,[10] i.e., the use of cooperation, cultural contact, educational programmes, etc., as instruments of foreign policy rather than aggression, coercion and displays of military might (*hard power*). Many examples of the use of non-military means to influence other countries can be found, such as the role of the Voice of America in spearheading the spread of information from the West into the Soviet Union during the Cold War. Cultural exchange is also argued to have been influential in bringing down the Iron Curtain.[11] More recent illustrations of the role of arts and culture in the exercise of soft power can be seen in other parts of the world; indeed the ongoing cultural activities of organisations like the British Council, the

Goethe Institute, the Japan Foundation and the Alliance Française can be interpreted as being consistent with the soft power hypothesis.[12]

## Intercultural dialogue

The origins of an interest in intercultural dialogue as an element of cultural policy go back as far as the founding Constitution of UNESCO of 1946, which speaks of the need for nations to work together for peace and progress based on mutual understanding. Twenty years later, in 1966, the *Declaration of the Principles of International Cooperation* identified international cultural relationships covering all aspects of intellectual and creative activities as an important means of spreading knowledge, developing friendship and peace between the peoples of the world, and raising the level of spiritual and material life. Although essentially focussed on relationships between rather than within member states, the intention of this Declaration was clearly based on the proposition that dialogue is essential to the process of achieving mutual understanding.

A workable definition of intercultural dialogue has been proposed by ERICarts in a report for the European Commission. This report defines intercultural dialogue as:

a process that comprises an open and respectful exchange or interaction between individuals, groups and organisations with different cultural backgrounds.[13]

The ERICarts report goes on to outline the ramifications of intercultural dialogue – it is not simply an exchange of words but is aimed at developing a deeper understanding of diverse perspectives, increasing participation, promoting equality and enhancing creative processes.

It is important to recognise that dialogue is not an abstract process but a real interaction amongst people. At the outset, a comprehension is required of the subtleties of the similarities and differences between cultural groups in the process of intercultural communication and exchange. A necessary condition for dialogue is the recognition of common human characteristics that make people similar to one another; at the same time, the differences inherent in the concept of cultural diversity are intrinsic to notions of personal identity and the uniqueness of particular cultures.

Intercultural dialogue, for all its good intentions, is not necessarily easy or straightforward. It requires an abandonment of stereotyping and of reducing a cultural group to a single characteristic, such as religion or language. It encompasses a range of actors including government, NGOs, other civil society participants, and diverse individuals. It occurs at many levels; internationally, nationally, regionally, locally. Significantly, dialogue involves risks. As Arjun Appadurai points out, there are dangers of misunderstanding and, paradoxically, of understanding too well when 'too much' is revealed. Dialogue, he argues, is a process of negotiation, and there is a risk that negotiation may purport to represent or speak for a particular group when internal differences make finding a single representative voice impossible.[14]

Despite the problems, however, there can be no doubt that, just as dialogue between individuals is an essential component of interpersonal relations, so also is intercultural dialogue, when properly pursued, a primary means of fostering understanding and respect between cultures. It is likely to become a more important component of international cultural policy in the future.

## 4  Conclusions

This chapter has looked at the many ways in which the arts and culture enter the international economy, ranging from the long-running tensions raised by trade in cultural goods and services to the use of the arts as an instrument of foreign policy. In all of the areas discussed, questions were raised as to the appropriate means to value what is going on, so that sound policy decisions can be made. As always when cultural and economic aspects of value are implicated, we have suggested that a clear articulation of the distinction between economic value and cultural value can assist in the decision-making process. Sometimes these values appear to be at odds, as in the case of the cultural exception that may be invoked in trade negotiations; at other times they are in harmony, as when an artistically rewarding cultural exchange between countries brings economic benefits as well. Either way, a rational means of accounting for both types of value is a necessary prerequisite for good policy-making.

We have noted that pursuit of cultural policy at an international level has been given a significant new focus by the entry into force of UNESCO's Cultural Diversity Convention. This treaty addresses many of the issues discussed in the present chapter. It also signals a broader concern with the concept of cultural diversity as a critical element in domestic cultural policy in the modern world. We turn to the role of cultural diversity in national affairs and its relationship with economic policy in the next chapter.

*Notes*

1 Quote is from a radio broadcast made on the BBC in July 1945; see Arts Council of Great Britain (1945–46: 23).
2 For an overview of the field, see Acheson and Maule (2006).
3 For a discussion of cultural trade from a Canadian perspective, see Grant and Wood (2004) Chap. 16.
4 For sceptical views in favour of and against the idea of the cultural exception, see respectively Delacroix and Bornon (2005) and Galt (2004); see also Farchy (1999); Benhamou (2006).
5 For further discussions of these issues, see Papandrea (2005); Graber (2006); Hahn (2006).
6 For an account of the international art market, see Robertson (2005).
7 The Secretary of State for Culture, Media and Sport makes an annual report to the UK Parliament on the export of 'objects of cultural interest'; see, for example, DCMS (2007b). See also Maurice and Turnor (1992).
8 See Glass (2004); Greenfield (2007).
9 For a discussion of cultural exchanges as a means of enhancing a country's 'image', see Bellamy and Weinberg (2008); for a case study from an earlier era (the 1950s), see Prevots and Foner (2001).
10 See Nye (1990; 2004).
11 See, for example, Richmond (2003; 2005).
12 For an Asian example, see Lam (2007), who argues that Japan uses its popular cultural forms of cartoons and comics to project a 'soft' image in its relationship with China.
13 ERICarts (2008, p. xiii).
14 See Appadurai (2006).

# 10 | *Cultural diversity*

World is crazier and more of it than we think,
Incorrigibly plural. I peel and portion
A tangerine and spit the pips and feel
The drunkenness of things being various.

(Louis MacNeice, 'Snow', 1935[1])

## 1 Introduction

Whether it is called multiculturalism, pluralism, interculturality or some other descriptor, the idea of cultural diversity has different connotations for different people. For some it is a source of tension and hostility between social groups, even leading to vilification and violence. For others it represents a joyful recognition of the richness and multiplicity of human life, an avenue to greater dialogue, mutual understanding and creativity. Whichever way it is viewed, the phenomenon of cultural diversity has grown over recent years to become a significant feature of cultural policy both within and between nations.

In this chapter we consider the origins of the debate about cultural diversity and its development over the second half of the twentieth century, leading eventually to the UNESCO Convention on Cultural Diversity, which we began discussing in the previous chapter. The Convention as it is now in operation provides an appropriate framework within which to think about the role of diversity in informing the making of cultural policy in the contemporary world. First, however, it is necessary to consider the perennial question of value and valuation.

## 2 The value of cultural diversity

Motivating the international interest in cultural diversity has been an appreciation that for a variety of reasons cultural diversity is valuable. How does this value arise? In economic terms, cultural diversity can be regarded as an element of cultural capital; it is an intangible asset that gives rise to a flow of valued services. Thus, as with other aspects of cultural capital, we can draw parallels with natural capital. Indeed over recent years cultural diversity has increasingly been compared to the vast differentiation observable in nature, e.g., biodiversity. As scientists have been able to articulate the value of biodiversity more and more clearly, it has proved possible to carry the parallel forward and to point to similar ways in which the value of cultural diversity can be expressed. Four sources of the value of cultural diversity emerge from this exercise.[2]

To begin with, we know that biodiversity is valued for its own sake. People appreciate the infinite variety of plant and animal life on the planet for its aesthetic qualities and for the knowledge simply that such an amazing profusion of species exists. By the same token it can be argued that the variety of cultures and cultural expressions are seen as important per se, and as having qualities that are valued as a part of the 'human mosaic'. These sources of value, in economic terms, are public goods deriving from the existence value of the diversity in question – people gain benefit from the knowledge that both biodiversity and cultural diversity in all their richness are simply there.

The second source of value lies in the interconnectedness of the cultural world, which resembles that found in nature. No species exists in isolation, neither do cultures. If species are isolated from each other, they stagnate and die; so do cultures. Thus the webs of relationships in both biological and cultural spheres are valued. If these are damaged, diversity is diminished.

Furthermore, these natural and cultural 'ecosystems' are necessary to support economic activity. Over the past decade or so there has been a growing awareness of the interdependence between the economy and the air, land and water systems that make up the natural environment. Recently, we have begun to understand more clearly that cultural ecosystems – the invisible networks and relationships that bind cultures together and give meaning to people's lives – are just as important in underpinning the economic processes of production, consumption and exchange. This then is the third source of value; people are not automatons working in a vacuum, and they cannot be economically productive if their cultural infrastructure breaks down.

Finally, biodiversity is valued because some species *may* have economic value as yet unrecognised. Society should therefore be concerned by any loss of species diversity because this could incur economic costs or forgone opportunities in the future. A similar proposition can be made in the cultural sphere: certain cultural manifestations *may* have both economic value and cultural value that is not yet evident. Hence cultural diversity is valuable because it keeps options open for the future. Moreover, and as we noted in Chapter 6, preservation of those options requires adoption of the precautionary principle, demanding extra vigilance if the permanent loss of some item of cultural capital is threatened.

In light of these benefits it is apparent that the same duality of value that we have referred to in considering other aspects of cultural capital can be applied to cultural diversity. In other words, diversity yields both economic value and cultural value, and any assessment of policy in this area should give appropriate weight to both, as we shall see further below.

Let us turn now to considering how the idea of diversity has evolved in cultural policy over recent times.

## 3 The origins of diversity as an issue in cultural policy

Ever since its inauguration in the immediate post-World War II years, UNESCO has provided a focus for discussion of cultural diversity. The evolution of UNESCO's understanding of what diversity means and how it should be dealt with can be divided into four phases:[3]

- an initial phase during the 1950s and 1960s when cultural policy was mostly concerned with the arts, and pluralism was only an issue at the inter-country level, if at all;
- a phase during the Cold War period characterised by interpreting culture as identity, whereby independent countries could appeal to their differentiated cultural make-up as a means of opposing the ideological imperialism of powerful states;
- a phase that grew through the 1970s to the 1990s linking culture and development; and
- a more recent broadening of the idea of cultural diversity to embrace basic concepts of democracy and human rights.

The current period is one in which a multiplicity of meanings is attached to the notion of cultural diversity, with many political, cultural, economic and social ramifications. Nevertheless, two broad approaches can be distinguished. The first is to look at cultural diversity *within* countries. Nina Obuljen describes this approach as follows:

[It] regards individuals as potential denominators of multiple identities
and heterogeneous cultural characteristics that together eventually build
a national or other form of identity. It focuses on basic human rights, promotion of cultural democracy, equal participation of all minorities (ethnic,
gender, linguistic, racial, sexual orientation, etc.).[4]

The second approach considers cultural diversity *between* countries,
with emphasis on intercultural dialogue, cultural exchange, fairness
in participation in the international economy, and coping with the
threat of cultural homogenisation posed by globalisation.

At a practical level, policy interest in cultural diversity has increased
steadily over the last ten years or so, stimulated particularly by the
work of the UN World Commission on Culture and Development,
chaired by Javier Pérez de Cuéllar, which completed its deliberations
in 1994. In the Commission's report, *Our Creative Diversity*, and in
the two subsequent editions of the *World Culture Report*, published
in 1998 and 2000, the groundwork was laid for a broad-ranging treatment of cultural diversity in both its domestic and its international
interpretation.[5] The issue was also stressed as a guiding policy direction in the final communiqué arising from the Stockholm Conference
on Cultural Policies for Development.[6]

These various strands were brought together within the UNESCO
agenda with the formulation of the *Universal Declaration on Cultural
Diversity*, a document adopted by the UNESCO General Conference
towards the end of 2001. The *Declaration* is based on the premise
that intercultural dialogue is the best guarantee of peace, rejecting
the proposition that the 'clash of civilisations' is an inevitable condition of the contemporary world.[7] So what sort of cultural diversity
did the UNESCO member states endorse? The twelve articles of the
*Declaration* encompass identity, human rights, creativity and international solidarity. Together they comprise a comprehensive account
of how far the notion of cultural diversity can be taken to extend in
contemporary international discourse. According to this document,
cultural diversity may be defined in the following terms:

• Diversity is seen as being embodied in the 'uniqueness and plural-
  ity' of the identities of various societies and groups, a common heritage of humankind. Since culture itself is intrinsic to the realisation
  of human aspirations, it is argued that cultural diversity will be an
  important factor in promoting economic, social and cultural development in both industrialised and developing countries.

- Promotion of cultural diversity can take place only in accordance with respect for fundamental human rights. No one should invoke cultural diversity in order to defend, for example, 'traditional' cultural practices that deny basic rights and freedoms, such as those of women or of minorities.
- The distinctive nature of cultural goods and services such as movies, artworks, television programmes, music recordings, and so forth, must be recognised. Apart from being commercial commodities, these goods and services have an important role as purveyors of cultural messages. Since cultural goods and services arise from human creativity, it follows that cultural diversity will be enhanced in conditions conducive to creative activity and to the production and distribution of a wide range of cultural product.
- Finally, the UNESCO member states declared that to enable the benefits arising from cultural diversity to have effect worldwide, international cooperation and dialogue will be required involving public institutions, the private sector and civil society.

The *Universal Declaration* painted a glowing picture of an idealised world, one where people of all races, social classes and stages of economic development lived together in mutual harmony, expressing their own cultural identity while engaging in dialogue and fruitful exchanges with people from other cultural backgrounds. But the real world in the first year or two of the third millennium seemed a long way from such a vision. The Cold War might have ended, but new sources of instability had emerged. Terrorism was increasing, and the media were reminding us daily of the violence and intolerance that were affecting people's everyday lives in so many parts of the world. In these circumstances the *Universal Declaration*, for all its good intentions, could easily have been dismissed as empty rhetoric. Alert to this reality, the UNESCO member states realised that something more than just a declaration would be needed. Accordingly, a process was set in train that was to lead to the formulation of a new international treaty that would be established and implemented through the United Nations systems and that would carry with it all the authority that the world body could muster.

## 4  The UNESCO Convention process

The call for a new international legal instrument on cultural diversity was formally incorporated into the very first paragraph of the

Action Plan agreed to as an appendix to the Universal Declaration.[8] However, the impetus towards such a treaty had been building for some time, principally as a result of three interrelated pressures:

- a growing consensus that existing mechanisms for dealing with cultural goods and services in international trade were not working and that a separate instrument covering cultural trade was called for, as discussed in the previous chapter;
- a widespread concern that globalisation, taken in its broadest sense, was undermining people's sense of their cultural identity, and that a convention could provide a platform for a stronger assertion of the role of culture in national and international policy circles; and
- a profound sense that countries of the Third World were losing out in the process of economic and cultural development, and that the interests of such countries in achieving sustainable development paths could be served through specific development-related provisions in an international agreement on cultural diversity.

Given the tortuous and time-consuming processes that are usually required to reach agreement in international negotiations, the passage of the Cultural Diversity Convention from initial draft to final entry into force happened with lightning speed. The first step, undertaken in 2003–2004, comprised the work of an expert committee, which began with wide-ranging discussions on the scope of the proposed convention, and concluded with an agreed draft to submit to the next stage. Between 2004 and 2005 an intergovernmental committee considered this draft, agreeing on some aspects of it, disagreeing on others, until a final consensus on the text of the document was reached in mid-2005, for submission to the General Conference of UNESCO in October of that year. At that meeting, 148 member states voted in favour of adopting the Convention, with only the United States and Israel voting against, and with four countries abstaining (Australia, Honduras, Liberia and Nicaragua).[9] Less than two years later a sufficient number of signatories had ratified the Convention, and it entered into force in March 2007.

The adoption of the treaty provided at last an agreed definition of cultural diversity, one in fact that had remained more or less intact from the drafting work of the original experts. Article 4, paragraph 1 of the Convention defines this basic concept as follows:

'Cultural diversity' refers to the manifold ways in which the cultures of groups and societies find expression ... Cultural diversity is made manifest not only through the varied ways in which the cultural heritage of humanity is expressed, augmented and transmitted through the variety of cultural expressions, but also through diverse modes of artistic creation, production, dissemination, distribution and enjoyment, whatever the means and technologies used.

Moreover, the preamble, objectives and principles as spelt out in the treaty clearly recognise the distinction between economic value and cultural value in relation to cultural goods and services. For instance, one of the statements in the preamble to the Convention refers to UNESCO member states' conviction that 'cultural activities, goods and services have both an economic and cultural nature, because they convey identities, values and meanings, and must therefore not be treated as solely having commercial value'. Similarly, Article 2, Principle 5 notes that the cultural aspects of development are just as important as its economic aspects.

## 5 Policy implications

Notwithstanding its origins in the discourse on cultural diversity, which we have noted above, the UNESCO *Convention on the Protection and Promotion of the Diversity of Cultural Expressions* might just as well have been called a *Convention on Cultural Policy*, so pervasive are its provisions across the broad field that explicit cultural policy covers. It provides a framework within which a comprehensive suite of national-level cultural policy measures can be developed, and its international scope is directed at raising the profile of culture in a world where policy-making is thought by many to be dominated by a narrowly focussed economic agenda.

At the *national* level the Convention sets out the rights of parties to adopt policy measures in relation to culture (Article 6), including the following:

- fiscal and regulatory measures aimed at supporting and protecting artistic and cultural activity;
- measures to promote the free exchange and circulation of ideas and to stimulate creativity;

- measures to support artists, non-government organisations and public cultural institutions; and
- measures to enhance media diversity.

In subsequent articles some of these measures are spelt out in more detail, including means to safeguard and protect vulnerable cultural expressions (Article 8), as discussed in the previous chapter; strategies to promote education and public awareness (Article 10); and the integration of culture into sustainable development (Article 13), to be discussed further in Chapter 12. Many of the domestic policies relating to cultural diversity fall within the ambit of social policy, having implications for the enhancement of community relations, the cultivation of social cohesion, and so on. The creative arts have an important role to play in this context, as a means of breaking down barriers between people and promoting mutual understanding.[10]

*International* dimensions to cultural policy that are identified in the Cultural Diversity Convention include:

- information-sharing between member states relating to their experiences in cultural policy implementation;
- promotion of cultural exchanges and partnerships;
- international cooperation to strengthen the cultural industries in developing countries through improved market access, collaboration, capacity-building and technology transfer; and
- provision of financial support for cultural development in Third World countries, in particular through the establishment of an International Fund for Cultural Diversity to be administered by UNESCO.

As the above listings indicate, the Convention provides both a specific direction towards enhancing cultural diversity and a more general stimulus towards legitimising cultural policy at national and international levels. What is not immediately obvious from a quick reading of these provisions, however, is the Convention's implications for cultural trade, which were outlined in Chapter 9. Yet for some participants in the negotiating process, notably the United States, trade was the major issue at stake, and certainly the media reportage of the Convention's overwhelming adoption in October 2005 portrayed the outcome as a defeat for the US position and a win for countries wishing to protect their domestic cultural industries. As the implementation process of the Convention proceeds, it remains to be seen how its various consequences will work themselves out. In particular, interest will focus on whether cultural diversity itself, the key element permeating the entire process, will indeed be strengthened by the Convention's existence, and if so, whether the benefits expected to flow from it will in fact be realised.

## 6 Conclusions

This chapter has considered cultural diversity as a distinctive component of cultural policy that has a number of interactions with economic policy at national and international level. Our discussion has been couched in terms of the framework provided by the UNESCO Cultural Diversity Convention. As we have seen, the treaty specifies the rights of countries to formulate cultural policies to foster creative expression and to promote the positive aspects of cultural diversity within a context of respect for fundamental human rights and freedoms. It pays particular attention to the need for sustainable cultural and economic development, and proposes mechanisms for international cooperation and solidarity. It deals with threats to cultural diversity, however they might arise, by affirming the right of countries to take protective action if vulnerable forms of cultural expression are in danger of extinction or serious curtailment.

The Convention has the implicit objective of using culture to promote peace and goodwill. Is it likely that the contemporary state of the world will be receptive to exhortations that we all have to live together in harmony if humankind is to have a future? At a time when fundamentalists of many different kinds are becoming more strident in their assertions that they are right and everyone else is wrong, and are seeking more and more strongly to persuade or coerce others to their way of thinking, even the neutral virtue of tolerance seems a long way off. In these circumstances the utopian vision of the UNESCO treaty may seem an unrealisable dream. Yet human beings have always found that dreams are essential to seeing the way forward. Perhaps we can draw some hope from the fact that the best dreamers are artists – writers, painters, musicians, clowns and storytellers, those who engage the creative life and who rescue the poetry of civilisation for us all to see and hear. They are the ones, wherever they come from, who can teach us not just to accept difference, but to celebrate it as a rich and positive feature of the human condition.

*Notes*

1 Extract is from the poem entitled 'Snow', published in the collected poems of Louis MacNeice; see Dodds (1966: 30).
2 A discussion of measurement issues in relation to valuing cultural diversity can be found in Benhamou and Peltier (2007); see also reference to cultural diversity statistics in Chapter 14.
3 See Stenou (2007).
4 See Obuljen (2006: 22).
5 See respectively WCCD (1995); UNESCO (1998a; 2000).
6 See UNESCO (1998b).
7 A reference to the 'Huntington thesis'; see Huntington (1996).
8 See UNESCO (2002: 6–7).
9 Following the change of national government in November 2007, Australia moved to reverse its former position and ratified the Convention in September 2009.
10 See our earlier discussion of the arts in urban life (Chapter 7); on the role of public funding in this respect, see Rushton (2003).

# 11 | *Arts education*

EVELYN: ... my task here tonight is to unveil my semester's work, explain it and then smile and shake hands, leaving a few of you to examine it, grade it, etc. in essence, be at your mercy, which is fine, ... my graduate advisor gave me this advice five months ago ... 'strive to make art, but change the world.' pretty wise words, i thought, at the time, and so, being a good little student, that's what i set out to do ...

(Neil LaBute, *The Shape of Things*, 2001[1])

## 1 Introduction

Education and culture are so fundamentally interconnected that educational policy and cultural policy could in some respects be regarded as almost synonymous. Both formal and informal educational processes play a major role in forming cultural values, opening up cultural experience and stimulating cultural activity from the earliest pre-school years onwards. It is because of these strong links between education and culture that in some countries the administration of the cultural responsibilities of government is placed within the ministry of education.

Although the all-pervasive interrelationships between education and culture are acknowledged, we will confine our attention in this chapter to three main areas where a specific role for cultural policy can be identified: arts education in schools; the education and training of artists; and education as a factor determining demand for artistic goods and services. First, however, we outline briefly how economics is applied to the analysis of educational supply, demand and financing.

## 2 Economic analysis of education

The basic concept used by economists in analysing education is that of human capital. From the time of Adam Smith up until the middle

181

of the twentieth century, the interpretation of production in the economy relied on categorising three resources or inputs – land, labour and capital, where the last-mentioned related to *physical capital* in the form of buildings, machines, equipment, and so on. Then, in the 1960s, the economists Theodore Schultz and Gary Becker at the University of Chicago developed the theory of *human capital*, based on the proposition that the capacities and skills of human beings comprised a form of capital that, like physical capital, is productive in generating output in the economy.[2] It followed that if people's brains, so to speak, were a capital asset, education could be seen as a process of investment in this capital asset. Schultz and Becker argued that just as investment in physical capital yields greater productivity for the economy over time, so also is the productivity of human beings improved by investment in human capital via education.

The concept of human capital has implications for analysing the demand for education at both individual and social levels. From an economic viewpoint, the effect of education on an individual can be observed in the increased productivity that the person displays as a result of acquiring new ideas and skills that are useful in the workplace. Such enhanced productivity is likely to be rewarded by higher earnings than would be achieved by a similar but uneducated worker. If deciding whether to study for a particular qualification is voluntary, as it is for post-school education, the individual's decision can be portrayed as a problem in cost-benefit analysis, where the initial investment is the capital cost and the payoff to the investment is the discounted net value of the increase in life-time earnings that the education will be expected to generate.

Similar benefits accrue to society as a whole as a result of *public* investment in education – the increased productivity of an educated over an uneducated workforce is readily apparent, and the resulting effects on output and growth are well documented. But the social benefits from education are much wider than are simply measured by the achievements of a more productive labour force. In addition to the private benefits that education gives rise to, it also yields significant external and public-good effects enjoyed by the community at large. In particular, a strong educational system is the means towards a high level of literacy and numeracy amongst the population. Such a society displays a number of socially and economically desirable attributes, including:

- increased social cohesion;
- less crime and violence;
- better functioning of political processes;
- lower welfare costs;
- more efficient markets;
- improved communications;
- higher-quality media; and
- a stronger basis for intergenerational transfers.

In addition, education is an important vehicle for the redistribution of income, particularly through the effects of compulsory schooling on the capacity of succeeding generations to break out of life-cycle poverty. In virtually all countries around the world, education of children at least to primary level is mandatory and publicly-provided, and the latter characteristic makes it a significant avenue for income redistribution in kind.

Because of the indisputable social and economic benefits that education yields, some degree of financing for education is universally regarded as a government responsibility. However, private contributions, for example from student fees, may also be forthcoming. In practice, the mix of public and private funding of educational supply varies markedly between countries and between educational levels. As we have just observed, all countries mandate school education to a certain level because of the overwhelming public benefit derived from such expenditure. By contrast, the financing of post-school educational programmes such as university degrees ranges from a fully privately funded system in some countries to free provision in others, with many variations in between. As a general principle, public investment in education is (or should be) guided by a broad cost-benefit assessment, where the rate of return on investment is interpreted to cover both the direct economic effects and the wider social benefits that education brings. In turn, the mix of public and private sources of finance, at least at the post-school level, should roughly reflect the balance of the public and private benefits that accrue. In reality, however, the balance between public and private funding of education at all levels is everywhere determined more by political than by economic considerations.

All of the above concepts and analytical approaches can be applied to the specific issues of education in the arts and culture, to which we now turn.

## 3  Arts education in schools

Just as education in general brings benefits to the individual and to society, so also does education specifically in the arts. These benefits form the basis for government policy towards providing support for teaching the creative arts in schools, the educational arena where public financing is at its most essential. Yet it appears that sometimes the individual and social benefits flowing from exposing young children to music, drama, dance, literature and visual art at an early age remain insufficiently recognised. As a result the arts can become marginalised in school curricula, regarded as a luxury rather than a necessity.

There has been a great deal of fundamental and applied research on the role of the creative arts in the education of children, from kindergarten through to the teenage years.[3] The range of benefits to the individual child that have been identified include the following:

- simple enjoyment of creative and expressive activity; freedom for uninhibited self-expression; self discovery; skill development for its own sake, such as learning to play a musical instrument;
- inculcation of creative and innovative modes of thinking that spill over to improve performance in other subject areas such as mathematics and science;
- improved social interaction, greater tolerance and understanding of others, enhanced capacity for cooperation and working in groups, all of which are facilitated by creative activity in different artforms; and
- laying down of foundations for richer and more wide-ranging artistic and cultural experiences in later life; encouragement of aesthetic sensibilities; development of a sense of the importance of the arts and culture in human existence.

All of these benefits can be seen as part of a well-rounded education for the citizens of tomorrow. The public interest in ensuring that these benefits are realised provides a direct incentive for this aspect of cultural policy.

The main benefits flowing from arts education in schools that are enjoyed as public goods by society as a whole are derived from the following considerations:

- The fostering of creativity and the development of creative skills in children has an economic payoff both directly, through raising productivity in the future creative workforce, and indirectly, via the diffusion of creativity through the economy.
- Arts education contributes in many specific ways to virtually all of the social benefits of education in general that we listed above. For example, the arts fulfil an important role as a locus for social criticism, a role that is enhanced by arts education which instills in students an appreciation of the many ways in which art holds up a mirror to our society.
- Arts education yields long-term benefits for future generations. For example, building an appreciation of the arts among young people now is likely to increase demand for the arts in the future.

It is one thing to identify the existence of public-good benefits arising from arts education in the above terms, it is quite another to measure them. Yet as we have already seen, economists have made considerable progress in recent years in measuring demand for public goods, using survey methods to gauge the community's willingness to pay for the benefits involved. It is thus quite feasible to design a contingent-valuation study to assess how much value the population places on the public-good benefits obtained from education in the arts; in this way, the apparently intangible community or public benefits arising from arts education could, in principle at least, be measured in economic terms as a basis for policy guidance. Furthermore, it goes without saying that the purely cultural benefits of education, especially those that may not be fully reflected in willingness to pay, should be accounted for in such an assessment.[4]

What might policy interventions entail? There are many avenues by which government policy towards arts education for children of school age can be delivered, including the following:

- incorporation of the creative arts in state-mandated curricula at all levels from kindergarten to senior secondary;
- provision of resources for schools such as visual art materials, musical instruments, etc., and infrastructure facilities for arts teaching such as spaces for performance, etc.;
- teacher training in the arts to ensure an adequate supply of well-equipped teachers with attractive career-path prospects;[5]

- funding of artist-in-schools programmes to bring professional artists across all artforms into schools for various periods of time;
- partnerships with public and private cultural organisations to facilitate school visits, for example to galleries, museums, theatre performances, artists' studios, etc.;[6]
- vacation programmes for children such as music camps or cultural touring; and
- out-of-school programmes that use the arts to educate children in health matters and other awareness issues.[7]

Delivery of these sorts of policy strategies will generally involve cross-ministerial responsibilities, with funding provision expected to come from both culture and education budgets, and supplemented by private financial initiatives wherever appropriate.

## 4 Education and training of artists

Again we can distinguish between two levels of analysis here: that of the individual artist – Should I set out on an artistic career? How much formal training should I undertake? – and that of the economy or society as a whole – How much public funding should be devoted to training artists? Are we turning out more artists than the professional labour markets can absorb? Let us look at each in turn.

The individual decision as to whether to embark on an artistic career could, in economic terms, be cast as one of investment in human capital, just as described above. The prospective artist would need to consider the individual capital costs that he or she would incur in undergoing training, including not only tuition fees but also the opportunity costs of being out of the workforce during the training period, and associated expenses such as the purchase of materials (for a painter), equipment (for a potter) or an instrument (for a musician). The economic payoff would be measured by the expected time-stream of financial benefits into the future, as earnings from the artistic practice started to accrue in excess of what the individual's income would have been otherwise. So the cost-benefit analysis calculation could be applied to work out whether the financial return would warrant the initial cost.

Application of this sort of calculation is fraught with practical difficulties in any situation, but it is not hard to see that there are particular problems with this approach when it is applied to artists. Two difficulties are especially acute. Firstly, artists' expected earnings are likely to be both relatively small and highly unpredictable. Secondly, non-pecuniary motives are in any case likely to be much more important than any expectation of financial reward in propelling artists towards an artistic career. It could be concluded, therefore, that if cost-benefit analysis in strictly financial terms were universally applied by those contemplating an artistic career, most would be likely to be persuaded instead to become a doctor, a lawyer or a merchant banker. To put it another way, it would seem prima facie that the human capital model is unlikely to provide a particularly robust way of explaining artists' career-choice decisions.[8]

Nevertheless, the human capital model does have some relevance in analysing the economic consequences of artistic education. For example, we can ask: What effect does initial training as an artist actually have on future artistic income? In looking specifically at the effects of arts education and training on the earnings of artists, it is important to distinguish between 'creative' income and 'arts-related' income. *Creative income* is that derived from the core artistic practice of creating original works of art or original performances. *Arts-related income* is earned from professional work within an artist's artform but not deriving from core creative work; the most common example of such 'arts-related' work is teaching – a painter conducting classes in art school, a musician taking private pupils, and so on. Analysis of survey data on artists' income has suggested that arts education (i.e., training in the artist's artform) has a much stronger effect on arts-related income than on creative income. However, training is positively associated with the quality of creative output. It has also been found that on-the-job learning can be a significant contributor to artists' earning capacity, especially amongst those artists who have had no formal training at all.[9]

We turn now to the other aspect of the education of artists, the pay-offs to society and the economy at large from professional arts training. Let us focus on just one particular aspect of this question: the role of creativity. As noted earlier, creativity is increasingly being recognised as a key resource for the new economy. If it is true that artists are a primary source of creative ideas, then the support of training for professional artists could have eventual economic payoff, via the contribution their creativity makes to the economy. Such a proposition can be interpreted in the context of the concentric circles model of the cultural industries, introduced in Chapters 2 and 5 above. If artists

are indeed important 'content providers' for the new economy, and
if the skills inculcated in the creative workforce originate strongly in
the area of artistic education and training, then a further rationale for
this aspect of cultural policy is provided.

The evolution of the creative economy over recent years, together
with structural changes in labour markets across the board, have had
a combined impact on the patterns of artistic careers. No longer are
career paths of artists linear, from training through to established
practice. Rather, we see more fluid employment and self-employment
arrangements amongst practitioners across the whole spectrum of
artistic activity. In particular, there are increasing examples of artists
taking time out from their primary creative practice (sometimes by
choice, sometimes for reasons of economic necessity) to apply their
skills in other industries – visual artists designing corporate websites,
for example, or actors running workshops in human resource management programmes, or craftspeople working on new industrial
applications of ceramics or glass. Moreover, many artists return to
the education system at various times during their careers to refresh,
consolidate or enhance their skills and knowledge base.

A question often asked about arts training is: Why are we producing more artists across all artforms when there is already an over-
supply and labour markets in most areas cannot absorb any more
entrants? The answer usually given is that a qualification in the creative arts does not necessarily lead to a career as a practising artist.
Instead, the training can be seen as developing skills that are capable
of a wide range of application across the economy. Thus the graduates
of creative arts training programmes at universities, colleges, conservatoria, drama schools, and so on, spread themselves out through the
creative workforce and deploy their training not just in the core arts
areas but in the wider cultural industries and beyond.[10]

## 5  Education as a determinant of arts consumption

A considerable amount of research and effort in cultural economics
has been devoted to trying to understand demand for cultural goods
and services. Propositions that the arts – whether music, poetry, theatre, opera or visual art – are an acquired taste immediately raise the
question of how such taste-acquisition occurs. There is much support for the idea that family background and inherited traditions of

cultural consumption can be important in developing a person's taste for the arts; in addition, a substantial causal factor is education.[11] Early formal studies of the composition of audiences for the performing arts, such as Baumol and Bowen's (1966), showed that better-educated groups were strongly represented, a finding that has been replicated countless times since.

Nevertheless, it is well known that education is strongly correlated with income, such that demand studies in the arts have to grapple with a serious multicollinearity problem in trying to disentangle the relative effects on demand of education and income independently of each other. In an exhaustive appraisal of the empirical evidence on this question, Bruce Seaman finds conflicting results from different studies, some showing education to be more important than income, others the reverse.[12] What is not in dispute, however, is that education in the arts has a significant influence on taste formation that will affect artistic-consumption patterns in fundamental ways. From a cultural policy viewpoint this fact has implications for the ways in which arts support is delivered, reinforcing the sorts of arts education strategies noted above, and indicating an extension of arts education measures to cater for the general adult population as well.

## 6 Conclusions

The various ways in which education and the arts intersect comprise a significant area of interest for cultural policy that has important economic implications. In this chapter we have pointed to the economic and social benefits from arts education that accrue to students as individuals and to society as a whole, whether the education is delivered to schoolchildren to awaken their creative energies and to develop their creative skills, or to senior students seeking a professional training that might perhaps lead to an artistic career. Evaluation of the benefits and costs of arts education programmes using the investment appraisal methods of economic analysis can provide a useful input into policy formulation in these areas.

At the same time, arts education at every level delivers substantial cultural benefits that are valuable in their own terms, without reference to any economic justification. As always this brings us back to the need to distinguish between economic value and cultural value in considering the delivery of cultural policy. Arts education generates significant and varied types of cultural value that are vitally important in their own right in arguing the case for arts education in all its different aspects. By understanding the relationships between economic value and cultural value as arising from education and training in the arts, a more complete and balanced picture of the whole field can be gained and policy-making can hopefully become more enlightened.

## Notes

1  Quote is from LaBute (2001: 117–118).
2  Their original contributions are Schultz (1961); Becker (1964).
3  For a wide-ranging collection of papers on arts educational research, see Bresler (2007).
4  Valuing the arts for their intrinsic qualities may have to be reconciled with pressure to justify arts education in terms of its instrumental ability to improve students' mathematical skills, and so on; see a discussion in Gee (2007).
5  This may include programmes to take existing teachers out of school to allow them to train as practising artists. On return to the school environment, their capacities as arts teachers are likely to be significantly enhanced. See an assessment of one such scheme in Adams (2003).
6  As we noted in Chapter 6, most large cultural institutions, such as public museums and galleries, list education as one of their primary objectives, and most commit a significant volume of resources to educational programmes; for discussion of how to evaluate such programmes, see Ross (2003); Burnaford (2007).
7  An example is the use of drama and theatre-based activities as a means of spreading awareness amongst children of social and health issues such as HIV/AIDS; see, for example, Dalrymple (2006).
8  For a more extensive discussion of the application of human capital theory to artists, see Towse (2006).
9  See further in Throsby (1992, 1996); for an overview of empirical work on artists' incomes and careers, see Alper and Wassall (2006).
10  For a case study example, see Oakley, et al. (2008). See also Aston (1999); Harvey and Blackwell (1999); Bennett (2007).
11  The question of whether education could be considered a substitute for subsidies to arts consumption is discussed in Champarnaud, et al. (2008).
12  See Seaman (2006: 439–441).

# 12 | *Culture in economic development*

We must ... vigorously develop the cultural industry, launch major projects to lead the industry as a whole, speed up the development of cultural industry bases and clusters of cultural industries with regional features, nurture key enterprises and strategic investors, create a thriving cultural market and enhance the industry's international competitiveness.

(Hu Jintao, 2007[1])

## 1 Introduction

There is a sense in which culture is closer to the surface in the developing world than it is in industrialised countries. No doubt the idealised vision of the agrarian economy peopled by happy peasants living and working in harmony with the land and their culture is and always has been far removed from the grim realities of subsistence survival in poorer countries. Yet one cannot spend any time in a developing country without becoming aware of the extent to which cultural traditions and inherited knowledge, practices and values permeate the conduct of domestic, social and commercial life in the countryside and in towns and villages, if not also in at least some parts of the larger cities. In these environments the pervasive presence of culture in its various manifestations is taken for granted, is part of everyday existence and is not in any direct sense a matter of policy concern. Indeed, up until now, cultural policy as an explicit aspect of government action has been virtually non-existent in many parts of the Third World; perhaps there has been some concern for protecting cultural heritage, or some support for traditional arts practice, or some effort to promote the arts in education, but rarely much more than that.

However, things are changing. The breakdown of barriers to flows of capital and labour between countries, the rise of the internet, the growing internationalisation of markets – in short, globalisation – have all had profound effects on countries in the Third World. Indeed,

191

as we saw in Chapter 10, it was disquiet about the cultural impacts
of globalisation that was a key factor in prompting developing countries to push for the Cultural Diversity Convention and to accept the
cultural policy recommendations contained therein. In addition, there
are positive signs of a heightened public-sector awareness in some
developing countries of the value of arts and cultural activity in contributing to community life and in celebrating distinctive cultural
identities, leading to a stronger recognition of a possible role for government in supporting such activity. In all these circumstances a number of poorer countries are beginning to recognise cultural policy as
an important area of government concern.[2]

   In this chapter we consider the role of culture in economic development and its policy implications, drawing together and carrying forward some strands that have already been discussed regarding cultural
industries (Chapter 5), heritage (Chapter 6), and tourism (Chapter 7).
As in other aspects of the long-term relationships between culture and
the economy, we focus on sustainability and sustainable development
as providing the framework for our discussion.

## 2  Culture in development

During the 1980s, ideas about the centrality of economic growth in
development policy (increases in real GDP per head) that had permeated development thinking over the previous three decades or so,
were gradually being replaced by broader notions of development as a
human-centred rather than a commodity-centred process. Indicators
regarded as relevant for assessing levels of development in different
countries were expanded from those measuring only material gains
to those reflecting such aspects as nutritional levels of the population, health status, literacy levels, educational access and the quality of the natural environment. This paradigm shift was accelerated
particularly by the UNDP's *Human Development Reports*, which
began publication in 1991, and also by the writings of the economist
Amartya Sen, who characterised development as 'human capability
expansion', i.e., enhancement of the capacities of people to lead the
sorts of lives they desire, including their access to cultural resources
and cultural participation.[3]

   The particular role of culture in this evolving scenario was brought
into focus by the World Commission on Culture and Development,

referred to in Chapter 10 in relation to its 1995 report *Our Creative Diversity*. The Commission pointed to the essential cultural dimensions of a human-centred development paradigm, and proposed bringing culture in from the periphery of development thinking and placing it centre stage. UNESCO further elaborated these processes in the wide-ranging contents of the two editions of the *World Culture Report*, published in 1998 and 2000, and in the final communiqué from the International Conference on Cultural Policies for Development held in Stockholm in 1998, when the 150 governments represented agreed that they would take steps to integrate cultural policy into their development strategies.

The continuing consolidation of the concept of the creative or cultural industries in the early years of the third millennium has provided a new point of departure for cultural policy in the developing world. It is recognised that a wealth of creative talent exists in developing countries, as well as significant levels of both tangible and intangible cultural capital. Together these factors provide a pool of resources on which countries could draw in producing creative goods and services for domestic and international markets. An approach to interpreting the role of culture in economic development by reference to the cultural industries could be seen as opening up the possibility that cultural and economic development can proceed hand in hand, with each contributing beneficially to the other.[4]

Two significant contributions to our understanding of the role of the cultural industries in economic development have been the *Jodhpur Initiatives* put forward in 2004 by the Culture Unit in UNESCO's Bangkok office, and UNCTAD's *Creative Economy Report* of 2008. Both see traditional knowledge and distinctive cultural practices as fundamental resources on which these industries depend. This knowledge and these practices – the songs, the dances, the poetry, the stories, the images and symbols that are the unique heritage of the land and its people – are kept alive by written, oral, musical and pictorial transmission of cultural traditions from one generation to the next. They do not stay still, but are constantly interpreted, reinterpreted, added to, and adapted to new formats. They are accessed by the people in many different ways, serving as a rich cultural resource from which can be derived a wide variety of creative expressions. Some of these are routine and everyday in nature, such as traditional styles and patterns of clothing; other cultural expressions are created and interpreted by artists, using both traditional and modern skills to produce music, artworks, literature, performances, craft objects, and so on.

The transformation of traditional knowledge into creative goods and services reflects something significant about the cultural values of the country and its people. At the same time, the goods and services are also likely to have economic potential; they may be demanded by local consumers or they may enter international marketing channels to satisfy demands from consumers in other countries. The essential feature of the creative industries that links the traditional knowledge at one end of the chain to the ultimate consumer at the other end is their capacity to serve both cultural and economic objectives in the development process. In this regard the creative industries can be seen as consistent with the sustainable development paradigm for policy formulation in the developing world, because these industries bring together economic and cultural dimensions of development within a holistic policy framework. We turn to the question of culture in sustainable development in the next section.

## 3 Culture and sustainability

The concept of 'sustainable development' originated in the 1970s with the debate that was prompted at that time by the report of the Club of Rome, which drew attention to the environmental consequences of rapid economic growth.[5] But the concept did not take more substantial shape until the publication in 1987 of *Our Common Future*, the report of the World Commission on Environment and Development ('the Brundtland Commission'), which defined sustainable development as 'development that meets the needs of the present without compromising the ability of future generations to meet their own needs'.[6] Although this interpretation of sustainability was acknowledged by the World Commission on Culture and Development, the Commission refrained from committing itself to a specific concept of sustainable development in cultural terms. Yet the importance of taking a long-term view of the integration of culture into the development process persisted, becoming a fundamental element in the discussions and negotiations leading to the Cultural Diversity Convention. The Convention recognises the sustainable development of culture explicitly in two of its Articles:

*Article 2, para, 6 – Principle of sustainable development*: Cultural diversity is a rich asset for individuals and societies. The protection, promotion and maintenance of cultural diversity are an essential requirement for sustainable development for the benefit of present and future generations.

*Article 13 – Integration of culture in sustainable development*: Parties shall endeavour to integrate culture in their development policies at all levels for the creation of conditions conducive to sustainable development and, within this framework, foster aspects relating to the protection and promotion of the diversity of cultural expressions.

How are these provisions of the Convention to be interpreted? In our earlier discussions of sustainability we have argued that the concept is best represented as a set of principles identifying the main elements of the sustainability paradigm. Adapting these principles to define *culturally sustainable development*, we can suggest the following propositions:

- *Intergenerational equity*: Development must take a long-term view and not be such as to compromise the capacities of future generations to access cultural resources and meet their cultural needs; meeting this requirement will entail particular concern for protecting and enhancing a nation's tangible and intangible cultural capital.
- *Intragenerational equity*: Development must provide equity in access to cultural production, participation and enjoyment to all members of the community on a fair and non-discriminatory basis; in particular, attention must be paid to the poorest members of society to ensure that development is consistent with the objectives of poverty alleviation.
- *Importance of diversity*: Just as sustainable development requires the protection of biodiversity, so also should account be taken of the value of cultural diversity to the processes of economic, social and cultural development.
- *Precautionary principle*: When facing decisions with irreversible consequences, such as the destruction of cultural heritage or the extinction of valued cultural practices, a risk-averse position must be adopted.
- *Interconnectedness*: Economic, social, cultural and environmental systems should not be seen in isolation; rather, a holistic approach is required, i.e., one that recognises interconnectedness, especially between economic and cultural development.

These principles can be seen as a checklist against which particular policy measures can be judged in order to ensure their cultural sustainability.

## 4 Policy implications

We have argued that an appropriate way to approach the formulation of cultural policy in developing countries is within a broad-ranging cultural industries and sustainable development framework. The reasons for arguing in this way are essentially pragmatic. Development policy in both the developed and the developing world is generally framed in economic terms, articulated through the various means by which governments deliver economic policy, which we discussed in Chapter 2. As we have already pointed out, economists who control the purse strings in treasuries and ministries of finance tend sometimes to be unimpressed with propositions for expenditure that are based solely on the virtues of culture. Under these circumstances it can be suggested that the best hope for introducing culture into the development policy agenda is by demonstrating how the cultural industries can contribute to sustainable development, through the contribution that artistic and cultural production, dissemination, participation and consumption make to economic empowerment, cultural enrichment and social cohesion in the community.

In this area, as elsewhere, such an approach does not imply that economic objectives should take precedence over cultural ones. Indeed, achievement of sustainability in the development of cultural industries across the board requires careful nurturing of core artistic activity, an essential foundation upon which the wider industries are built. The proposition that a healthy and flourishing environment for creative artists and arts organisations is necessary to support the more commercial operations of the cultural sector is just as valid in the developing-country context as it is in any other part of the world.

We can draw the above considerations together into a set of practical guidelines for policy formulation aimed at integrating culture into sustainable development. The following guidelines are suggested:

• No single policy prescription or instrument will deliver culturally sustainable development; rather, a package of policy measures will be required, the components of which will differ in emphasis in different countries depending on particular needs.

- For this reason policy formulation will not be the responsibility of a single ministry, but will require collaboration and cooperation across a range of government instrumentalities and agencies concerned with economic, social and cultural development.
- Recognising the economic potential of the cultural industries provides a practical way for introducing culture into a broader economic development agenda. At the same time, the need for policy to deliver cultural as well as economic benefits must be recognised; this requires a clear distinction to be maintained between economic value and cultural value in the deliverables from the cultural sector of the economy.
- In line with the previous requirement, an essential element of any culturally sustainable development policy, regardless of the national context, will be attention to the needs of creative artists and arts organisations and a strong policy stance in regard to the conservation of tangible and intangible cultural heritage.
- Attention should be paid to long-term investment in infrastructure, including: *physical* infrastructure to support cultural production, distribution and consumption; *institutional* infrastructure such as public cultural instrumentalities and agencies; *legal* and *regulatory* infrastructure such as an effective copyright regime; and *financial* infrastructure to provide a sound basis for provision of financial services.
- Given that the processes of culturally sustainable development are ultimately played out within communities, it is important that long-term capacity-building at local level be undertaken, so that decision-making and resource allocation for culture can be devolved as far as possible to local communities.
- Any package of policy measures put together in accordance with these guidelines should be assessed against the principles for culturally sustainable development specified above, in order to ensure the essential requirements for sustainability are met.

## 5 Conclusions

The United Nations has laid down a series of Millennium Development Goals, with targets to be achieved by 2015. The goals cover poverty eradication, education, gender equality, sustainability, and so on. Culture is implicated in one way or another in all of them. In particular, the primary objective of poverty alleviation can be seen to be served by the sorts of policy strategies discussed in this chapter. The cultural industries in developing countries are built around small-to-medium enterprises, often family businesses operating at local level. As such these industries are especially well suited to community redevelopment that is consistent with cultural traditions. They often provide flexible opportunities for income and employment generation that can be reconciled with family and community obligations and with the informal economy. In short, they can be a direct vehicle for targeted policy measures that will make an immediate contribution to poverty alleviation.

Yet it must also be recognised that there are still a number of obstacles to be overcome in many parts of the developing world in advancing the sorts of cultural policies we have been discussing. Capital rationing remains a constraint, which is being vigorously addressed by micro-finance initiatives in some countries. Lack of entrepreneurial skills often holds back small-business development, indicating a need for specific training programmes that are adapted to the circumstances of artistic and cultural production. Policy can also contribute through improvements in public infrastructure. One element of the regulatory environment that needs particular attention in many instances is the copyright regime, a matter to which we turn in the next chapter.

*Notes*

1 Quote is an extract from a speech given by Hu Jintao, President of China, on the Opening of the 17th Congress of the Chinese Communist Party, in Beijing, on 15 October 2007.
2 For some illustrations from developing countries in the Commonwealth, see Commonwealth Foundation (2008).
3 See, for example, Sen (1990).
4 For a comprehensive discussion of these issues, with many practical illustrations, see the collection assembled in Barrowclough and Kozul-Wright (2008); see also papers collected in Matarasso (2001).
5 See Meadows, et al. (1972).
6 WCED, (1987: 43).

# 13 | *Intellectual property*

Man was made at the end of the week's work, when God was tired. Only one thing is impossible for God: to find any sense in any copyright law on the planet. Whenever a copyright law is to be made or altered, then the idiots assemble.

(Mark Twain, 1903[1])

## 1 Introduction

The field of intellectual property covers copyright, patents and trademarks. Of these it is copyright that has the most relevance for cultural policy. Copyright exists to protect creators of original artistic work from unauthorised use of their creations. It does not cover ideas, but rather the form in which those ideas are expressed or 'fixed'. The ideas may be expressed in literary, artistic, dramatic or musical form, as well as in the form of films, videos, sound recordings, television broadcasts, and so on. Protection is provided by means of the legal system, and intellectual property law, of which copyright law is a part, has grown to become a major branch of legal theory and practice.

In order to understand the implications of copyright for cultural policy, it is necessary to comprehend the economic rationale for the provision of protection and the basic economics of copyright administration. In the first sections of this chapter we consider these issues, with particular reference to the use of creators' collecting societies as a means for securing and distributing copyright revenues. The chapter then goes on to discuss the emergence of new digital technologies which have transformed the ways in which unauthorised use of copyright material can occur. Next we look at the international regulation of copyright and the role of intellectual property in developing countries. The chapter concludes with some policy considerations.

## 2  The economic basis for copyright

When an author publishes a novel or a composer releases a song, the artistic work involved becomes a public good, with all the non-rival and non-excludable properties that we have noted in earlier chapters as the public-good characteristics attributable to cultural phenomena. A work of literature or music is non-rival because one person's enjoyment of the work does not diminish the amount of it available for consumption by others, and it is non-excludable because once the work has been publicly exposed it is difficult or impossible to prevent any individual from consuming or otherwise making use of it.

As with other public goods these characteristics lead to a form of market failure, since the creator of the artistic work has no means of charging consumers for their access to the work. The most common remedy for market failure caused by public goods is collective action, usually in the form of government intervention through direct public-sector production of the good or through public financing of its production by the private sector. But there is an alternative avenue for government action to rectify market failure that is available in some situations, namely to establish property rights over the good, enabling a market to be set up where none existed before. There are three necessary conditions which must be met before such action can be considered feasible:

• the owners of the property rights must be able to be easily identified;
• the costs of negotiating contracts for exchange or use of rights must not be unreasonably high; and
• cases of infringement of rights must be able to be detected and pursued.

All these characteristics obtain in the case of intellectual property. Thus, in economic terms, the appropriate remedy for market failure when creative work is produced is the establishment of rights for producers over the public-good element of their output. It is important to note that the conferring of a negotiable right on creators does not change the fundamental nature of intellectual property as a public good.[2]

It is well established that market failure leads to inefficiency and loss of economic welfare. Thus, the economic benefits arising from a system of copyright are derived from the improvements in allocative efficiency within the economy that are brought about by the establishment of a market in these rights. On the supply side, copyright provides a means for payment for existing work and conveys an incentive to the continuation and expansion of production; on the demand side, copyright enables users to purchase the creative work they require and assures them access to a range of new work over time. The overall social benefit is seen in the elimination of the welfare loss due to the underproduction of cultural goods which would arise in a free market if property rights in such goods were non-existent.

The right conferred on a creator by the copyright system is a *monopoly* right, for two reasons. Firstly, the public-good characteristic of rights in intellectual property dictates that the rightsowner must be granted sole or monopoly rights over the work in question in order that the full value of the work will accrue to that person and to no one else. Secondly, original artistic works such as musical compositions are unique; artistic works are an extreme case of a *non-homogeneous good*. Thus the right held in a work by, say, a composer, is a monopoly right by virtue of the fact that there is in principle no substitute for that particular work. In practice, of course, there is some substitution possible between artistic works, since some works are less distinguished than others in terms, for instance, of popular recognition.[3] But such substitutability is quite limited and does not greatly weaken the essential monopoly characteristic of copyright deriving from this source.

It is important to understand that, in economic terms, the monopoly right of creators derives not from some deliberate act of anti-competitive behaviour by the rightsowner or from the assertion of market power in the sense frowned upon by trade practices legislation; rather, the monopoly characteristic of the right arises simply from the public-good nature of the commodity in question and from the intrinsic qualities of artistic works.[4] These features have implications for the administration of artists' rights, as we shall see further below.

The administration of rights in intellectual property is a matter of law. Copyright laws:

- provide the means by which the rights of creators can be recognised;
- set up markets upon which these rights can be exchanged; and

- put in place machinery to ensure the enforcement of rights and to deal with infringements.

Laws differ between countries in regard to matters such as the duration or term over which copyright in a particular work extends. But irrespective of detail, the effect of a copyright regime is to establish a market in the rights to use artistic works where previously no market existed.

There are several exceptions to the universal coverage of copyright in an artistic work. The most important is that labelled 'fair use' or 'fair dealing'. In some circumstances the amount of copying of a work is so small – for example, a few lines of text from a book – that charging for use is inefficient. In other cases, free use may be justified on grounds of non-commercial research, critical review, etc. Other exceptions may be granted by the creator if she believes that exploitation of the work may be beneficial in publicity or marketing terms; for example, a visual artist may sanction free use of a work on a calendar or greetings card if it is thought that the resulting exposure will add to her reputation. A somewhat grey area is that of appropriation, i.e., use of one artist's work by another as a basis for further creative output; for example, a composer may incorporate quotations from another person's composition in his or her own work. Whether such use comprises plagiarism or a 'homage' from one artist to another is a matter of opinion that could end up being tested in court.[5]

The right vested in the original creator of an artistic work is a primary right, which artists may exercise themselves, or which they may assign or sell to someone else. An exception is when the creative work is undertaken by an employee; in such a case of 'work-for-hire', the employer rather than the original creator is generally the legal owner of the right. In addition to the primary exploitation of copyright material there may also be secondary rights, such as those relating to photocopying or re-broadcasting. 'Neighbouring rights' may also be specified, being those rights in a work derived from and related to copyright, such as performers' rights whereby a musician, dancer or actor (or a group of performing artists) may assert rights over their interpretive creation of a musical, dramatic or dance performance.

A right relating specifically to works of visual art such as paintings is the resale royalty or *droit de suite*. This right, which exists in some jurisdictions and not in others, entitles an artist or assignee to a percentage of the increase in value of a work over its original price when the work is resold. The rationale for such a right is that the original creator is entitled to share in the capital appreciation in his or her work caused by a rising market. The resale royalty is often described as benefiting artists who sold works cheaply early in their careers when they were unknown, only to see the value of their works increase many times over when they become established and famous.

Copyright is classified as an economic right because it relates to payment and remuneration, in contrast to *moral rights*, which are concerned with the integrity and authenticity of works. Moral rights, which are especially important in France (the *droit moral*) and other European countries, provide creators with the right to assert their authorship of a work, and protect works from unauthorised alteration, abridgement or destruction. The codification of moral rights varies amongst the countries which recognise them – in some cases they are associated with the copyright in a work, in other cases they are independent of copyright. Several celebrated examples of moral rights infringement have occurred over the years, such as the *Tilted Arc* case in the US in which Richard Serra challenged the removal of his site-specific sculpture from the plaza in New York City where it had originally been placed.[6]

Cultural policy in the area of intellectual property is not only of concern to creators. Publishers of literary and musical works, record companies, broadcasters, filmmakers and other stakeholders in the cultural industries have significant interests in the maintenance of an efficient and effective copyright system. Consumers, too, are implicated, since copyright law affects the prices of the artistic works they wish to buy or copy. Indeed, in the end, copyright policy becomes an exercise in balancing the legitimate rights of creators, publishers and others to a reasonable reward for their labours, against the equally legitimate rights of users of copyright material for fair and reasonably priced access to copyright works.

## 3  Administration of artists' rights: the economic rationale for collecting societies

It is one thing to be granted a right over intellectual property, it is another thing to be able to exercise that right effectively and economically. The non-excludable nature of the commodity to which the right refers means that monitoring usage is far more difficult than controlling usage of a private good. For an individual artist acting unilaterally to administer her right in her creative work, she has to incur a number of costs, including:

- the *search costs* of discovering potential users;
- the *transactions costs* of negotiating contracts with users once they are located;
- the *collection costs* of obtaining payment for use; and
- the *enforcement costs* of taking action if the right is infringed.

The sum total of these costs for an individual exercising her right alone is likely to be prohibitive, or at least is likely to be greater than if she exercised her right jointly with others. The reason is that administration of rights incurs high fixed costs, so that spreading the costs over a larger number of units means that the average cost per unit (e.g., per individual right administered) falls sharply as the number of units increases. Hence collective rather than individual administration of rights is likely to be cost-effective. Typically this is effected through not-for-profit membership-based collecting societies.

In addition, there is an economic rationale for collective copyright administration arising from the demand side. Users also incur search costs in seeking out the owners of rights to works they wish to use. In the absence of a collecting society, these costs may in many cases be prohibitive, and would greatly restrict the range of works to which users would have access. Search costs to users are substantially reduced by the existence of a collecting society or societies commanding a repertoire covering the full range of works they are likely to require. Furthermore, users are likely to benefit from the pooling of transactions costs that is possible through collective administration.

Collecting societies in most artforms and in most countries around the world have tended to become monopolies, for two main reasons. The first is where the monopoly power has been formally sanctioned by government, for example when a society is declared by government to be the collecting society appointed to administer a statutory licence. In these circumstances the reasons for appointment of a single society have to do largely with administrative efficiency and convenience as far as the government is concerned; the society acts, as it were, on behalf of government, doing so under a form of regulation that ensures that it behaves in the manner of a public instrumentality.

The second reason derives from the costs of delivery of administrative services. As noted above, the average administrative cost per unit of output of a given collecting society (e.g., per input licence administered) will fall as the number of units expands. If there were several competing societies, the lowest per unit administrative costs would probably be incurred by the society with the largest number of members; in these circumstances, the lowest overall unit cost will be achievable by a single society covering the entire membership. This is essentially the *natural monopoly* reason for emergence of a single supplier; where scale economies are such that production of a given level of output by one firm incurs significantly lower overall costs than production of the same aggregate output by two or more firms, a monopoly will tend to eventuate.

Furthermore, such a monopoly is likely to remain protected from competition. The cost efficiency of a strong natural monopoly in any market provides an effective barrier against the entry of new firms, since a new entrant is unlikely to be able to achieve the same scale economies as those enjoyed by the incumbent firm. This is not to say that entry is impossible, since a new entrant might endeavour to compete on other grounds, such as the quality of service offered. Nevertheless, it is clear that the economic position of natural monopolies is likely to be reasonably secure; once established, they tend to last, as has been the case with collecting societies.

In economic terms there are both benefits and potential costs attaching to the emergence of monopoly collecting societies. Looking first at the *benefit* side, we can identify three major ways in which economic efficiency and/or equity may be improved as a result of there being only one collecting society in a particular market. The first potential benefit will arise if producers and consumers can gain from the increased efficiency possible deriving from the collective's natural-monopoly characteristics. Such gains would be reflected in the passing on of lower unit costs to users in the form of lower charges, and the passing back of a larger share of revenues to rightsholders. For these benefits to accrue, the collecting society must not use its monopoly position to raise prices to the sorts of levels that an unconstrained profit-maximising monopolist might set.

The second potential benefit from having a monopoly collecting society relates to the distribution of bargaining strength in the marketplace. In any market, efficiency and welfare losses may occur if market power is unequally distributed between the supply and demand sides of the market. In some such circumstances the assertion of a 'countervailing power' by or on behalf of the initially weaker side may be warranted as happens, for example, through consumer protection and other measures that governments take to assert the rights of consumers in the face of significant market power amongst producers. In the area of intellectual property it tends to be the producers who are in the initially weak bargaining position. Virtually all the costs of production of existing creative work are in the nature of sunk costs. Hence users are in a position to extract a low price from individual producers since they know there is no alternative use for the resources that have been committed to production. In these circumstances, rightsholders may be unable to negotiate a price that covers the full cost of production (including a normal profit or rate of return on capital). This problem is exacerbated if sellers face a monopsony (a single buyer) or a high degree of buyer concentration (only a few buyers, with substantial market power) on the demand side of the market. In the case of broadcast music, for example, there are only relatively few buyers but numerous composers and publishers; in these circumstances, a monopoly or near-monopoly position for a collecting society may be seen as a justifiable assertion of countervailing power. In the extreme case of bilateral monopoly (a single buyer facing a single seller), economic theory suggests that, if market power is distributed approximately evenly between the two players, negotiated pricing will be efficient.[7]

The third potential economic benefit from the existence of a single collection agency accrues to users. If consumers of a product can be satisfied that a monopoly supplier is not charging exploitative prices, they may find it simpler, cheaper and more convenient to obtain all their requirements for that commodity from a single source. This potential benefit may be particularly relevant to users of creative work, where the prospect of a 'one-stop-shop' to obtain licences covering all their needs may bring substantial time and cost savings.

Notwithstanding these benefits, there are also potential costs attached to the existence of a monopoly collecting society. In particular, the society might use its protected position to take an unreasonably large share of collections for its own purposes before distributing returns to its members. These 'administration' costs may go towards providing excessive salaries or benefits to executive staff, board members, etc.

Nevertheless, there are pressures acting to contain the administrative component of the society's cost structure. These pressures will arise partly through the scrutiny of members, whose interest lies in forcing management to keep administrative expenditures as low as possible, and partly through the fact that, although competitive entry by another firm may be unlikely, there is at least a threat that a new management or a new firm could appear on the scene which could take over the entire membership of a society if the existing management were to allow administrative expenses to become wasteful or inefficient.[8]

Alternatively, a monopoly collecting society could use its market power to extract what might be regarded as unreasonable prices from its licensees in order to maximise the returns to its members. Users, having no alternative source of supply, would be forced to pay the higher prices or go without. Since the possibility of such behaviour by a monopoly collecting society cannot be ruled out, the question becomes one of determining an appropriate policy instrument to deter or prevent exploitative pricing in the market. The most obvious means is through direct price oversight or regulation. In the economy at large, regulatory measures are occasionally used to ensure that prices are set such as to provide a reasonable rate of return to producers, for example, when an average-cost (or cost-plus-reasonable-rate-of-return-on-capital) pricing rule is imposed on regulated natural monopolies. In the case of copyright, this sort of regulation can be provided through the oversight of a regulatory board or tribunal; such an approach is in fact used in a number of countries. It can be shown that surveillance of a monopoly collective by such a tribunal may result in an outcome where lower tariffs prevail and more users avail themselves of the repertoire.[9]

To summarise, it can be seen that in economic terms the existence of a monopoly collecting society in a particular area is by no means inconsistent with achievement of the social objectives of an efficient and equitable copyright system, provided a means exists for monitoring the pricing behaviour of the collective. Competition does not emerge as an appropriate means for controlling prices in this field; encouraging the entry of new firms is not likely to be in the interests of either producers or consumers, because it will raise costs, will not provide sufficient return to producers, and will tend to reduce the flow of new creative work. Rather, price regulation or oversight by an independent tribunal would appear to offer a more appropriate alternative.

## 4 The effect of new technologies

The advent of the digital age has had a profound effect on copy-right.[10] Artistic works expressed in sound, text and image which can be fixed in digital form are capable of infinite reproduction at zero cost. They can be copied and transmitted from one person to many others, regardless of location. These characteristics open up endless possibilities for unauthorised use of copyright material without the knowledge of the rightsholder. In the music industry such infringing use is referred to as 'piracy', a phenomenon that has been known at least since illegal taping of broadcast music began, but far more wide-spread and difficult to detect since the advent of the internet.

Agencies, business firms and individual artists with interests in copyright protection have reacted to these developments in vari-ous ways. One obvious way has been to strengthen the processes of detecting illegal copying including, in particular, peer-to-peer file-sharing of audio-visual material over the internet. Some success has been achieved in closing down file-sharing networks and bringing prosecutions, but as soon as one source is eliminated, others spring up. Another approach has been to adopt a strategy of 'if you can't beat them, join them'. Thus film production houses, music publishers, record companies, and so on, have moved to embrace the digital age by promoting access to the legal purchase of material in digital form from their own websites. It is argued that if such material is made available at prices that are attractive to consumers and that provide a reasonable return to rightsholders, users will prefer to acquire their copyright works in this way rather than by breaking the law and risk-ing prosecution. Another strategy is to look to the technology itself to provide mechanisms to prevent piracy, for example via encryption or watermarking of digitised material such that only authorised copying is technically possible.[11]

Indeed the latter possibility could provide a means towards a uni-versalised administration of copyright. If creators of digitised artistic works were themselves able uniquely to identify their product and make it available for electronic distribution, and if they also possessed the means to command immediate payment for the downloading of their works via direct funds transfer to their bank account on a no-payment-no-sale basis, the transaction becomes one between original supplier and final consumer, eliminating the need for intermediaries.

Since the product is effectively transformed into a private good, no particular copyright protection would be needed to regulate such transactions, at least as far as primary rights are concerned. Even if artists themselves are not able to pursue such a strategy, downstream distributors of digitised cultural product, such as record companies, are already implementing new business models along these lines. Notwithstanding such developments, however, there remain many ways in which the rights in creative material will still have to be protected, so it is probably too early to predict a future 'world without copyright'.[12]

## 5 International regulation of copyright

Copyright originated in the early eighteenth century in England with the Statute of Anne, which for the first time gave authors, as distinct from printers, the right to benefit from the copying of their work.[13] The concept of authors' rights gradually took hold, and became codified and internationalised in the late nineteenth century with the conclusion of the Berne Convention for the Protection of Literary and Artistic Works. This Convention, revised and expanded in scope over the years, remains the world's major international copyright instrument, with a membership today of 164 countries. The Convention establishes common rules for copyright protection and enshrines the 'principle of national treatment', whereby member states agree to extend to creators in other member countries the same protection as they do to creators in their own country.

Further conventions affecting copyright came into force during the second half of the twentieth century. In 1952 the Universal Copyright Convention was signed, providing a lower level of protection especially for countries not yet ready to accede to the Berne Convention. Subsequently the Rome Convention was introduced in 1961 to apply the principle of national treatment specifically to the protection of performers, record producers and broadcasting organisations. In the mid-1980s, with the continuing growth in international trade in services, negotiations began on the GATS agreement, which we discussed in Chapter 9. As noted there, most countries have shied away from making commitments under GATS in respect of their trade in copyright material such as audio-visual product, in order to avoid having to extend national treatment to foreign providers of creative output, and to allow themselves to continue pursuing cultural policies such as local content quotas and domestic production subsidies.

An outcome of the Uruguay Round of trade negotiations was the TRIPs agreement concluded in 1994, which deals with trade-related aspects of intellectual property rights.[14] This agreement represents a major development in international copyright protection. It establishes minimum standards of protection for creators, performers, producers and broadcasters in WTO member countries, even if they are not parties to other copyright conventions. It also contains significant provisions for the enforcement of intellectual property rights and for the settlement of disputes between countries relating to rights implementation.

Nevertheless, despite these various efforts to provide an efficient and effective regime for copyright protection at an international level, gaps still remain. Piracy continues to rob rightsholders of significant amounts of revenue to which they are entitled, a problem that, as we have noted above, has been greatly exacerbated by the advent of the World Wide Web. Some countries still have inadequate national copyright laws and some have still not acceded to international copyright conventions. Given the importance of intellectual property rights in market arrangements for all types of cultural products, it is apparent that improving the global administration of copyright must remain an important and ongoing objective of international cultural policy.

## 6 Copyright in development

In the previous chapter we discussed the role of the cultural industries in promoting growth in output, employment and exports in developing countries. But the opportunities to realise the full potential of the creative sector in these countries are seriously jeopardised if the institutional and political support for protection of intellectual property rights is weak or non-existent. Without such protection the economic rewards to creative producers are reduced and the incentives to continue in production are diminished. Policy measures designed to assist the establishment and growth of small- to medium-sized creative enterprises cannot be fully effective if producers cannot rely on stable income flows from their output, particularly if the potential revenue from their creative work is stolen by unauthorised users.

Thus in developing countries where existing copyright protection is inadequate, the development of legislation that is relevant to local conditions and keyed to the wider framework of international protection for intellectual property rights needs to be a priority in cultural policy agendas. Indeed, policy strategies in this area should look beyond legislation to the broader infrastructure needed to support a copyright system, including monitoring agencies and collecting societies that can ensure proper distribution of copyright earnings to rightsholders once effective laws are in place.

International organisations concerned with culture, cultural trade and intellectual property rights administration have been unanimous in advocating improvements to copyright protection in the developing world. For example, recommendations along these lines are contained in the Development Agenda adopted by the General Assembly of the World Intellectual Property Organisation (WIPO) in 2004. The proposals for action put forward in this Agenda cover areas such as technical assistance and capacity-building, norm-setting, technology transfer, governance, and so on. WIPO is also actively concerned with intellectual property issues surrounding the exploitation of developing countries' genetic resources, traditional knowledge and folklore. These resources provide a potential source of economic wealth for many countries and the codification of property rights in them is seen as a step towards protecting them from exploitation by profit-seeking entities elsewhere, such as transnational companies. Nevertheless, it can be argued that the creation of proprietary rights in traditional knowledge, based on concepts of commodification and trade, may be a less appropriate means of protection than alternative or complementary approaches, which situate such knowledge within the sphere of cultural diversity and provide protection under, for example, human rights law.[15]

## 7 Conclusions

One of the three properties of cultural goods and services that enable them to be defined as a distinct category in economic terms is, as we noted in Chapter 2, the fact that at least potentially they have some intellectual property content. The content is produced as a result of the original work of artists and other creators and is protected by intellectual property legislation, in particular through laws relating to copyright. Thus it is apparent that there must be close relationships between cultural policy and the broad field of copyright administration.

This chapter has pointed to the importance of understanding the economics of copyright as a means of getting to grips with copyright policy and its connections with cultural policy. The matter of incentives to the continued production of creative works is a persistent theme through these discussions and indeed provides the basis for arguing that copyright should be seen as an essential part of cultural policy. As Ruth Towse has stated:

Copyright policy, by which is meant government policy on changing copyright law, should be considered part of cultural policy because copyright law influences the supply of creative work by artists and by the cultural industries which use their services.[16]

Towse points out that in the UK copyright is still divorced administratively from cultural policy. In fact, administrative arrangements for formulating, implementing and monitoring copyright law vary markedly around the world; copyright administration in some countries is handled by ministries of culture, but in others this responsibility rests in departments of justice, legal affairs, trade and industry, information, education, and more.[17]

We have also stressed the importance of a strong and effective copyright regime as a prerequisite for growth in the creative economies of developing countries. At a global level and in the interests of all countries regardless of their stage of development, continued efforts to improve the coverage of copyright law, especially in the face of challenges posed by new information technologies, will remain at the forefront of the international intellectual property agenda. For maximum effectiveness these efforts need to be fully integrated with national level cultural policy-making.

*Notes*

1 Quote is from Mark Twain's Notebook of May 23, 1903; see Paine (1972: 381–382).

2 Contributions to the literature on the economics of copyright include Hurt and Schuchman (1966); Landes and Posner (1989); and Besen and Raskind (1991). Updated overviews are contained in Landes (2003) and Landes and Levine (2006).

3 For an elaboration of this point, see Burrows (1994: 104–105).

4 The fact that the monopoly held by a creator derives from the inherent nature of the right may explain why, as Michael O'Hare notes, 'most people tend to regard the concept and the realisations of a transferable monopoly right in (intellectual) property as intrinsic elements of an organised society rather than as products of considered ... policy decisions' (O'Hare, 1985: 407).

5 See Landes (2000); for a discussion of this issue in the context of US law, see Scafidi (2005). See also some case studies documented in McKenna and Antonia (1994) and Cahir (2004).

6 See further in Senie (2001).

7 Furthermore, efficient negotiation between a monopoly collective and user groups may eliminate any incentive for competitive entry by new firms; see Besen, et al. (1992: 398–401).

8 For a more detailed analysis of competition between copyright collectives, see Besen, et al. (1992: 402–405).

9 See Alexander (1994); on the efficiency of collecting societies in Europe, see Rochelandet (2003).

10 For a discussion of the challenges for copyright arising from the digital economy, see contributions to Chantepie, et al. (2008); see also Liebowitz (2003); Farchy (2003).

11 For a discussion of these trends in the music industry, see Kretschmer, et al. (1999).

12 See Varian (2005: 134–136).

13 One of the first authors to take advantage of the new law was Alexander Pope, in 1741; see Rose (1994).

14 For a comprehensive account of the TRIPs provisions, see Sterling (2000).

15 See further in the collection of essays in MacMillan and Bowery (2006), especially the chapter contributed by Johanna Gibson.

16 See Towse (2001: 166).

17 See summary table in Andersen, et al. (2000: 19); for a complete list, see WIPO's *Directory of Intellectual Property Offices*, available at www.wipo.int/directory.

# 14 | *Cultural statistics*

> Culture is smitten with counting and measuring; it feels out
> of place and uncomfortable with the innumerable; its efforts
> tend, on the contrary, to limit the numbers in all domains; it
> tries to count on its fingers.
>
> (Jean Dubuffet, *Asphyxiating Culture*, 1986[1])

## 1 Introduction

Sound policy-making in any area of public administration needs to
be based on comprehensive and reliable data. This is especially true
in the cultural policy arena, where the intricate structure and diverse
operations of the cultural sector make data demands particularly
complex. Statistics covering the volume and value of cultural output,
levels of employment, cultural consumption and participation, public
and private funding, and so on, are required for purposes such as:

- describing the size of the cultural sector, its place in the economy
  and society, and the nature and extent of its functioning;
- underpinning evidence-based policy formation, which depends
  both on raw data and on relevant analysis of those data;
- monitoring and evaluation of the success or otherwise of cultural
  policies and programmes while they are being implemented or after
  they have been completed; and
- comparing various items of data using intra- or internationally
  comparable statistics to assist, for example, in the benchmarking of
  performance standards.

Cultural statistics that are useful for these purposes can be derived
from three sources. Firstly, official government statistical agencies
that routinely gather and publish data on the economy and society are
a major source of information about the arts and culture. The data
they provide may occur as a subset of more general statistical collections, such as censuses, national accounts or workforce surveys, or

214

they may be put together specifically for the arts and culture sector, perhaps by specialised units devoted to cultural statistics. Secondly, a number of independent bodies collect data of various kinds that may be relevant for policy purposes; for example, cultural observatories, university research institutes and private consultants carry out surveys, whilst industry bodies and NGOs gather data from their members. Thirdly, a number of international organisations publish data of relevance to the arts and culture, most notably the UNESCO Institute of Statistics (UIS), which has a primary responsibility to collate and publish cultural statistics from the member states of its parent body.

The range of data types covered by the overarching term 'cultural statistics' is very wide. This chapter discusses these various data types, paying particular attention to matters of definition and classification. The chapter also considers some special-purpose statistics that are designed for particular policy purposes, including cultural indicators, measures of diversity and creativity, and efforts to construct satellite accounts for culture. In many areas where national-level statistics are collected, international comparisons are hindered by a lack of comparability in the classification systems used in different countries. Cultural statistics are no exception, and so the chapter concludes by discussing the internationally coordinated effort to put together a new basis for classifying cultural statistics, which provides a common framework that national statistical agencies can refer to in setting up or revising their own classification systems.

## 2 Types of cultural statistics

### Cultural industries

Statistical compilations for the cultural industries face two problems. The first is the definitional problem, discussed in earlier chapters, which raises questions such as: Are they 'creative' or 'cultural' industries? Which industries are included? What product classifications are used?, and so on. Most countries base their industrial and product classifications on international standards such as the ISIC (International Standard Industrial Classification) and the CPC (Central Product Classification). These systems are related in turn to national or regional classifications such as the NACE (the Classification of Economic Activities in the European Community), the NAICS (the

North American Industrial Classification System), and the ANZSIC (the Australia and New Zealand Standard Industrial Classification). The specific industries regarded as either cultural or creative that are identified within national systems vary between countries, depending on the definition of the cultural or creative industries that is applied. Because of this it can readily be seen that international comparisons of, for example, the cultural industries' contribution to GDP can be problematical.

The second problem to be dealt with in specifying statistics for the cultural industries is to define the data series of interest for policy or other purposes. Conventional economic data that are routinely collected for all industries include gross value of production, contribution to GDP or GNP, value added, fixed capital formation, wholesale and retail prices, and so on, as well as trade and employment statistics (to be considered further below). Again, data on these variables for the cultural industries can be extracted from the economy-wide statistics by imposing whatever cultural industry classification scheme is in use.

## International trade in cultural goods and services

Statistics on cultural trade have to rely on a workable *product* classification system rather than on industrial or other classifications, since the concern is with the actual movement of identifiable goods and services across national borders. Data on flows of goods are generally compiled using the so-called Harmonised System, which provides a standard description and coding system for physical commodities. Data on the flows of services are generally classified using the EBOPS (Extended Balance of Payments Services Classification). But neither of these classification systems displays *cultural* goods or services as separate categories. Hence compilation of statistics on cultural trade has to rely on extracting the relevant numbers according to the particular definitions of cultural goods and services in use, as was also the case with the industry data discussed above.[2]

The audio-visual industries give rise to a particular difficulty in measuring cultural trade. Previously, international transactions relating to films or music, for example, could be readily observed, since they involved the export and import of physical commodities – reels of film, cassette tapes, compact discs, etc. With the advent of the internet, however, trade in audio-visual product now increasingly takes place on the World Wide Web – the material is transmitted in electronic form and so also is payment for rights, royalties, etc. Systematic tracking of these flows by statistical agencies is generally not possible, so estimates of the volume and value of such trade have to be assembled from other sources, for example from data provided by collecting societies that are responsible for the collection and distribution of copyright revenues. These data vary in their quality and coverage. Thus, compiling a fully comprehensive and accurate statistical picture of cultural trade in all its various forms is well nigh impossible.

## Cultural employment

Once again, issues of definition are raised when labour force statistics for the cultural sector are being derived. Questions arise such as: What is a cultural occupation? and How is the creative workforce to be delineated? The answers to these questions are not as straightforward as it may appear. For example, a *cultural worker* could be defined as someone who works in a cultural industry, whether the work that person does is 'cultural' (producing cultural output such as writing poetry or acting) or 'non-cultural' (such as selling tickets for a theatre company). But a *cultural occupation* has to be defined by reference not to the industry of employment but to the specifically cultural nature of the work that occupation entails. In this case it may make for clearer definition to identify *creative occupations* instead, since this terminology is related to an easily recognisable input (creativity) rather than to a less easily observed output (culture). Even so, the designation of a set of creative occupations from ISCO (the overall International Standard Classification of Occupations) is not a simple matter, since it depends on how far the adjective 'creative' is deemed to extend. As a result, different countries use different approaches to measuring cultural employment, the creative workforce, etc. Nevertheless, whatever classification system is used, most assessments which look at employment by industry find that significant numbers of creative or cultural workers actually work in non-cultural industries.[3]

Given the importance of arts policy as a component of cultural policy, an aspect of cultural employment of particular interest from a policy viewpoint is the working conditions of artists. Identifying the artistic workforce presents some difficulties. Many people in the community are engaged in artistic activity; thus as a first step in data collection it is necessary to distinguish between professional and amateur practice. This distinction is important for several reasons. In an economic context, it would be expected that the labour market behaviour of amateurs and professionals would be different, making it necessary to identify which is which for purposes of empirical analysis. Similarly in any larger model of the cultural sector incorporating variables such as the output of cultural goods, value added, employment levels, prices and other economic quantities, attention usually needs to focus on purposeful workers as distinct from leisure-makers. Finally, in a purely artistic sense the association of high artistic standards with professionalism suggests that it will be professional artists who will contribute most towards producing work of lasting artistic value and influence; this is one reason why public policy towards the arts has generally pursued its goals of excellence and innovation via support for professional and not for amateur practice.

How, then, is the distinction between professional and amateur to be codified? The use of a financial criterion is inadequate as a sole discriminator, because of multiple job-holding amongst artists and because some professional artists may receive little or no remuneration over significant time periods in their working lives. Rather, as several writers have shown, professionalism in the arts subsists in a complex set of attributes, none of which on its own is a sufficient condition for professional status, but not all of which are necessary conditions. Significant amongst these characteristics is a commitment to, and achievement of, a standard of work judged as acceptable by some appropriate peer-review process.[4]

Data about artists can be derived from two main sources. Firstly, a population or labour force census provides the most accurate information available on the size and characteristics of the population of workers within specific occupational categories. Given that in most countries' censuses, standard occupational classifications are adopted that include various identifiable types of artists, in some cases down to quite a fine level of occupational disaggregation, these statistics have been useful in studying the extent and nature of the artistic workforce. However, they suffer from several important drawbacks. Firstly, in most cases the allocation of an individual respondent to a job category is based on their main job at the time of the census or survey; it is well understood that this procedure will overlook many genuine artists who are forced to take other work as a means of supporting their artistic practice, and who are therefore working at some other 'main job' at the time of the data collection. Secondly, the categorisation of artist in such statistical collections does not distinguish professional from amateur; whilst it may be reasonable to assume professional status attaches to someone who declares their 'main job' as artist, there is no way of knowing if such individuals would meet more refined criteria for professionalism as discussed above. Thirdly, there may be problems in understanding what 'artist' means as a job category when the data collection is based on self-evaluation. Finally, the descriptive data collected via censuses may be very limited in their capacity to enable analysis of the sorts of issues of interest to economic and sociological researchers. For example, economists are usually concerned to identify time allocation and corresponding earnings from arts work and from non-arts work, and indeed even this two-way classification does not go far enough for many purposes.[5] Income data for artists derived from census returns is thus problematical for economic analysis, and researchers who use census data to analyse the income position of artists are inevitably limited in the conclusions they can draw.[6]

The second main data source is special-purpose surveys. Targeted surveys of artists can pick up part-time as well as full-time workers, including those temporarily not working, and hence more accurate estimates of the size of artist populations can be obtained than are usually possible from a general census. If the category of interest in a particular study is professional artists, filters can be used to screen out amateurs from the sample or, in a broader study aimed at covering a range of types of practice, appropriate questions can be included to establish precisely the occupational status of respondents. The definition of 'artist' is controllable by the researcher instead of being provided exogenously by census requirements. Finally, and of course most significantly, the quality and extent of data obtainable can be expected to be much richer in a specially targeted survey than in a general data collection, since the data collection is custom-designed to answer the precise questions of interest to the researcher.

Nevertheless, there are some problems with sample surveys. They are generally costly to administer. Furthermore, the usefulness of their results for purposes of inference depends critically on the researcher's capacity to identify the artist population of interest and to draw a statistically valid random sample from it. For some occupations, iden- tifying the artist population may be relatively straightforward. For example, in many countries actors or musicians are highly unionised; in such cases, with the cooperation of the union concerned, a researcher may be able to obtain a reasonably complete list of professional prac- titioners, together with contact details, from which to draw a sample. In most other artistic occupations, however, no such centralised lists exist. For artists such as writers, painters, sculptors and craftspeople, for example, a researcher will generally have to rely in the first instance on the assumption that most professional artists will appear on some list somewhere: an association membership list, a directory, a list of grant applicants, an agency register, even the *Yellow Pages*. Population lists may then be laboriously compiled by putting together lists from various sources and eliminating duplication. Inference from a sam- ple drawn from such an aggregated list will generally be based on an assumption that those artists not caught by the population list will be distributed with regard to the principal characteristics of the group in the same ways as those in the list. Nevertheless, it may still be difficult to establish the overall size of the relevant artist population by these means, since the extent of those not included in the population list may not be readily estimable. In these circumstances, the use of techniques such as network sampling or respondent-driven sampling may enable extension of the sample to capture those groups not on the original list; by these means it is possible both to test the validity of the above- mentioned assumption and to assess more accurately the size of the overall population from which the sample is being drawn.[7]

## Cultural consumption

At the end of the cultural value chain are consumers of the final prod- uct. Their demands and behaviours are represented in the following three types of cultural statistics.

(i) Demand for cultural goods
The volume and value of purchases of tangible cultural commodities are recorded in a variety of ways. They may be accessed via household expenditure data (see below) or collected for specific categories of

goods by commercial firms or by trade or industry associations, etc. Examples of the latter include:

- art market data collected and made available (usually at a price) by sales monitoring organisations; for instance, a wealth of data is available on the prices of artworks sold at auction by the major auction houses;
- record industry data on sales of music in various formats collected by the International Federation of the Phonographic Industry (IFPI); these data include estimates of levels of piracy (sales of illegally copied music) in various countries; and
- data collected by publishers' associations in various countries on the numbers and prices of different categories of books, magazines and newspapers sold.

In some cases, special-purpose surveys of cultural consumption are undertaken by statistical agencies, which provide a wide range of statistics on the artistic and cultural goods purchased by consumers.

(ii)  Consumer expenditure
Cultural consumption can be tracked via household expenditure surveys, either carried out across all types of expenditure, of which cultural spending is a part, or focussed specifically on consumption of the arts and culture. Either way, such surveys – a standard means of regular data collection employed by most official statistical agencies – can yield a rich source of information about individual and household spending on culture in all its forms. However, international comparisons of such statistics may be problematical; whilst data for particular items of expenditure may be compared, aggregate concepts such as 'total cultural spending', etc., will depend on the classification schemes for cultural goods and services, which may or may not be comparable between countries.

(iii)  Attendance and participation
The generic terms 'participation' or 'involvement' of people in the arts and culture cover a range of activities, from passive attendance as an audience at a concert or a theatrical performance to active engagement in acting, dancing, creative writing, musical performance, filmmaking, etc. In surveys concerned with these latter activities, it is assumed they are undertaken voluntarily and on a non-professional

basis for pleasure rather than reward. Despite the apparent clarity of a definition of participation along these lines, it remains a concept of some fuzziness, especially if international comparisons are involved. Nevertheless, sidestepping questions such as 'How "active" are apparently "passive" cultural pursuits like reading or going to the opera?', we can draw a pragmatic distinction between

• *attendance* as measured by surveys of cultural institutions or tabulated by the institutions themselves;
• *readership* as indicated by surveys of book, magazine and newspaper purchases, library borrowings, etc.;
• *viewing* and *listening* as assessed by television and radio ratings, etc.;
• *access* to on-line cultural consumption either streamed or downloaded and consumed subsequently, as measured by internet tracking and other services; and
• *creative involvement* in active artistic and cultural activities of any type, such as writing a novel, singing in a choir, or painting landscapes, as documented in special-purpose surveys.

All of these types of data and more can be gathered together under the generic heading of participation studies, of which there are many in existence.[8]

## Asset valuation

A neglected area of cultural statistics is that of valuation of cultural assets. In Chapter 6 a distinction was drawn between the stock of cultural capital, both tangible and intangible, and the flow of services it produces. The asset valuation issue relates to the former, and can have both micro and macro dimensions.

At the micro level the issue arises in attempts to value the cultural capital held, for example, by art museums in the form of their collections of artworks. This matter has practical relevance to an institution's accounting processes, raising issues such as what value for the asset holdings to include in the organisation's balance sheet, how to determine capital depreciation or appreciation, how to set replacement values for insurance purposes, and so on.[9] The difficulty is, of course, that market valuations of artworks may be uncertain, unstable, and contingent on a variety of circumstances – for example, the market price of a work sold on its own might be vastly different from what it would be likely to fetch if a gallery's entire collection was up for sale. Moreover, it could be argued that a full estimate of the asset value of an art collection should contain at least some indication of its cultural value. The value of heritage buildings and sites is likewise subject to the same sorts of problems. These difficulties are compounded when it comes to intangible heritage, since no readily comprehensible basis exists for assigning either a monetary or a cultural value to such assets.

Turning to the macro level, we note that in most countries, collections of aggregate financial statistics contain some reference to the value of the nation's physical capital stocks, amongst which might be included the purely physical-capital component of cultural assets such as museums, historic buildings, and so on. But from the viewpoint of cultural statistics, something more is needed. The totality of a country's cultural capital contains a wide variety of elements, including heritage architecture, public and privately held art collections, historic sites, not to mention items of intangible cultural capital. Measuring the aggregate value of such an extensive and heterogeneous stock of assets would be a daunting task for any cultural statistician to undertake, even if the scope of the exercise were limited to economic value. If an assessment of the cultural value of the capital stock were introduced into the picture, it is not difficult to see that the task is likely to be an impossible one.

## Cultural funding

Finally, one of the most important areas of cultural statistics from the viewpoint of cultural policy is that of the public sector's financial involvement with the arts and culture. As we have noted throughout this volume, the implementation of cultural policy in all its many guises entails direct and indirect expenditure by government, the levels of which are reported in various ways in national accounting data. Although standardised formats exist according to which national governments present their accounts, there are many variations in detail between countries as to what is counted as 'cultural', if indeed that adjective is used at all.

Moreover, it is not just at the national level that public funding of the arts and culture is important. Sub-national levels of government (states, counties, municipalities, cities, etc.) also provide funds to support the arts and culture through subsidies, grants, capital and operating allocations to cultural institutions, investment allowances, tax breaks, and so on. The formality and rigour with which these expenditures are recorded and published differ widely between jurisdictions, such that in some countries it is difficult or even impossible to aggregate cultural funding statistics across all tiers of government to obtain a comprehensive national picture.

These variations both within and between countries make international comparisons of cultural funding extremely hazardous.[10] Yet comparing the level of cultural funding per head is a favourite pastime in many quarters, even to the extent of constructing 'league tables' of countries ranked in order of their apparent commitment to arts and cultural support. Such comparative statistics suffer from three main problems. Firstly, as noted repeatedly in this chapter, different countries use different classification systems to assemble their data. Secondly, comparative statistics generally fail to account for the cost to the public purse of indirect support measures such as tax concessions. Finally, in concentrating on public-sector outlays these statistics neglect to account for direct private support for the arts and culture, which is necessary to complete the picture.[11]

## 3  Some special-purpose statistics

In this section we consider some examples of particular types of cultural statistics that are relevant to cultural policy analysis. They are: cultural indicators; cultural diversity statistics; measures of creativity; and satellite accounts for culture.

### *Cultural indicators*

Indicators are statistics that go beyond simply describing some phenomenon; they are intended to imply something more – for example, to be used in conjunction with other data to monitor or evaluate some circumstance or process. As such they occupy an intermediate position between raw data on the one hand and analysis on the other, in other words between the supply of information in the form of primary statistics and the demand for information for purposes of analysis and policy-making. Indicators can be either quantitative or qualitative in nature.

A cultural indicator can be defined as 'a statistic that can be used to make sense of, monitor or evaluate some aspect of culture, such as the arts, or cultural policies, programmes and activities'.[12] Examples include:

- a suite of statistics gathered together to indicate levels of cultural participation or enjoyment;
- performance indicators for cultural institutions to indicate their success or otherwise in achieving certain designated goals;
- 'quality of life' indicators to demonstrate the artistic or cultural ambience of a city or region, or the cultural vitality of communities;[13]
- various data that can be taken as indicators of cultural development in a developing country; and
- indicators of cultural value for some artistic or cultural phenomenon, to be used when direct measures of cultural value are not available.

Much effort has gone into devising workable procedures for constructing and utilising indicators of various sorts, including cultural indicators.[14] There is general agreement that good indicators should be firmly grounded in theory, linked to policy practice, and relevant, unambiguous, measurable and easily understood.

## *Measuring cultural diversity*

The increase in interest in the concept of cultural diversity as a key aspect of cultural policy, which has been given added impetus by the conclusion of the Cultural Diversity Convention (discussed in Chapter 10), raises the issue of measurement. How is the diversity of cultural expressions to be assessed and evaluated? This is another area where the use of indicators is clearly appropriate. The very nature of diversity is such that multiple datasets will be required, since diversity exists in identifying the differences and variations between and across datasets relating to a variety of cultural phenomena.

In a paper prepared for UNESCO, Renato Flôres proposes that a framework of statistics to address cultural diversity would need to cover the following areas:

- data relating to personal characteristics of individuals, such as age, ethnicity, nationality, religion, etc., including participation statistics;

- data relating to the range of outputs produced by the cultural industries;
- data based on cultural institutions and providers;
- data on particular types of cultural expressions that may be defined in locational or geographical terms, such as local festivals, handicrafts, etc.; and
- data on public and private funding sources.[15]

It may be tempting to try to combine various items of data into one or more 'diversity indexes' as a basis for policy development; however, such an exercise is fraught with theoretical, methodological and practical difficulties.

## Measuring creativity

Given the centrality of creativity to the cultural economy and hence to cultural policy, it is not surprising that various efforts have been made to provide measures of the importance of creativity in particular contexts. Two examples suffice to illustrate such efforts. Firstly, the Centre for Cultural Policy Research in Hong Kong has developed a 'creativity index' which purports to measure the social capital – expressed in terms of trust, reciprocity, cooperation and rich social networks – that forms an essential part of the infrastructure for a creative society.[16] Secondly, the Washington State Arts Commission and the Office of Arts and Cultural Affairs in the City of Seattle have proposed a 'creative vitality index' to provide an assessment of the health of the state's arts-related creative economy. The index combines measures of arts participation in the community with data on per capita concentrations of arts-related employment to produce an indicator of the contribution that creativity makes to the local economy. Its primary purpose has been one of advocacy.[17]

## Satellite accounts for culture

Satellite accounts provide a representation of national accounting data for a particular field that is more detailed than that available from the usual national accounts. Essentially, these accounts expand the System of National Accounts (SNA) that is used as a basis in most countries for the construction of statistics measuring aggregate economic activity such as national income and GDP. Since their construction entails data, expertise and resources that are not generally available, such accounts are relatively rare; to date the main areas where they are available in some countries are for tourism and the environment.[18]

Following these leads it is possible to imagine developing procedures for identifying satellite accounts for culture. If so, they could provide information on a range of macroeconomic data for the cultural sector with greater product and industry specificity than would otherwise be available. In addition, a system of cultural satellite accounts would be expected to cover various social and cultural dimensions of the operations of the cultural sector. At present, however, the development of satellite accounts for culture is in its infancy. Only two systematic efforts have been made to date in this direction, one in Colombia under the auspices of the Convenio Andrés Bello, the other by Statistics Finland. These two initiatives seem certain to illuminate the path towards a wider development of this form of cultural statistics in the future.

## 4 Towards a new framework for cultural statistics

As noted above, there are a number of international standard classifications which provide individual countries with a template for the design of their own classification systems for statistics covering a range of economic variables, including industry, occupation and commodity classifications. In the specialised field of cultural statistics, a framework was put forward in 1986 by UNESCO that was intended to provide some consistency across jurisdictions in national statistical collections for the arts and culture. The framework has guided the development of cultural statistics collections in many countries over the intervening years. However, the social, economic and technological changes that have occurred since the 1980s have rendered the original framework increasingly out of date, prompting the initiation of a process designed to produce a new framework for cultural statistics by the end of the first decade of the new millennium.[19]

The task confronting the framework revision has been one of establishing a conceptual foundation that captures the full range of cultural expressions, including new forms of production and consumption, and cultural practices not previously accounted for. In its final form the framework has been built around the concept of cultural 'domains', meaning areas in which specific cultural industries and cultural activities are located. Six domains are identified:

• cultural and natural heritage;
• performance and celebration;
• visual arts and crafts;
• books and press;
• audio-visual and interactive media; and
• design and creative services.

In addition, two 'related' domains are specified:

• tourism and
• recreation.

Cutting across all eight of the above domains are four transverse domains which are relevant to a greater or lesser extent across all the industries and activities identified. These transverse domains are:

• intangible cultural heritage;
• education and training;
• archiving and preservation; and
• equipment and support materials.

The framework provides a basis for classifying the cultural industries that can be integrated with broader standard industrial classifications both internationally and at the national or sub-national level. It also allows the specification of an updated system for classifying cultural occupations and for measuring cultural participation.

The revised Framework for Cultural Statistics is not intended to be a blueprint that every country will follow, since different features of cultural statistics are of different importance in different countries. Rather it provides a coherent and consistent basis on which national systems of cultural statistics can be developed. To the extent that the framework is utilised in different jurisdictions, we can hope in future that stronger, more reliable and more internationally comparable cultural statistics will result. If so, the benefits for the entire cultural policy process, from policy formulation through to monitoring and evaluation, will be substantial.

## 5 Conclusions

Statistics describing the cultural sector are an essential adjunct to the making and implementation of cultural policy. They are also necessary for effective monitoring of policy strategies so that the success or otherwise that such strategies have achieved can be evaluated. Some countries have taken the matter of cultural data collection seriously. The official statistical bureaux in Canada and Australia, for example, have longstanding interests in this area that have provided policy-makers and policy analysts with a rich source of data on the arts and cultural sectors in those countries. Other countries, however, have lagged behind in the development of their cultural statistics capability, and their cultural policy processes must inevitably have suffered as a result. The new Framework for Cultural Statistics discussed in the previous section will hopefully stimulate a stronger interest in cultural statistics in data collection agencies around the world.

At the same time it must be borne in mind that statistics are not collected just for their own sake, but to inform discussion and to enable analysis of the size, structure, interrelationships, causal connections, and so on, that characterise the cultural sector. The validity of such discussions and the strength of such analyses will depend critically on the quality of the data on which they are based, imposing a major responsibility on collection agencies to provide consistent, comprehensive and reliable statistics for the variety of users that they serve.

*Notes*

1 Quote is from Dubuffet (1988: 14).
2 For a recent re-assessment and compilation of physical trade statistics for cultural goods, see UNCTAD (2008: 101–137 and 225–331).
3 These workers have been referred to as 'embedded'; see, for example, Higgs, et al. (2008).
4 For a discussion in the context of the visual arts, see Jeffri and Throsby (1994); for criteria for identifying professional artists in different art-forms, see Throsby and Hollister (2003).
5 A three-way classification of artists' work, into creative work, arts-related work such as teaching art, music, etc., and non-arts work is now widely accepted; see Throsby (1996).

6  An example is Randall Filer who used census data to question the existence of the 'starving artist' phenomenon in the US, but whose results may be questioned on the grounds discussed; see Filer (1986).
7  See Heckathorn and Jeffri (2001); Salganik and Heckathorn (2004).
8  For a thorough account of the pitfalls and potential of participation studies, see Schuster (2007).
9  See Carnegie and Wolnizer (1995); Carman (1996).
10 See, for example, McCaughey (2005).
11 See a discussion of cross-country comparisons in Madden (2005b).
12 See Madden (2005a: 221).
13 A major project devising indicators of community cultural vitality is reported in Jackson, et al. (2006).
14 See, for example, Schuster (1996, 2002a, 2003); Pattanaik (1998); McKinley (1998); Fukuda-Parr (2001); Pignatoro (2003); for some earlier literature on this subject, see references in Schuster (2001: 19–20).
15 See Flôres (2009); see also Liikkanen (2007).
16 See Hui, et al. (2005).
17 See Irby and Hebert (2005).
18 See Chapter 8 above for reference to tourism satellite accounts.
19 See UNESCO Institute for Statistics (2009).

# 15 | *Conclusions*

And in the streets: the children screamed
The lovers cried, and the poets dreamed.
But not a word was spoken;
The church bells all were broken.
And the three men I admire most:
The father, son, and the holy ghost
They caught the last train for the coast
The day the music died.

(Don McLean, 'American Pie', 1971)

In 1999 Larry Rothfield published a paper whose title needs to be spoken aloud rather than read.[1] 'Cultural policy studies?' he asked, repeating the question three times, each time with a different word emphasised. Can there be policy studies about *culture*? Can studies of culture have any relevance to *policy*? And finally, accepting that there is such an animal as cultural policy, what is there about it that can be *studied*? The last of these questions is the relevant one for our purposes here. That cultural policy exists is clear enough; we defined its scope and coverage in Chapter 1. But how the analysis of cultural policy is to be approached, and what sort of advice for policy-makers might flow from cultural policy studies, remains a contested issue.

If 'cultural policy studies' exists at all as an identifiable area for scholarly research and empirical analysis, one of its principal points of origin can be traced to the cultural studies discipline, a loose assembly of scholars and writers concerned with the fundamental nature of culture and how it evolves as a sphere of influence for the state. Jim McGuigan notes that cultural studies has since its inception been concerned with emancipatory politics, constructing the role of culture as a political resource to be used by the state to govern and regulate its citizens.[2] Nevertheless, the extent to which cultural studies should engage with the policy process or try to do things that might be useful to policy-makers has been a matter of debate – a debate that has reached no obvious resolution, as a quick stroll through some of the writings in the field will indicate.[3] Yet some contributors to the cultural policy literature from the cultural studies tradition do see an important role for engagement in the policy process. For example, Toby Miller and George Yudice argue for a radical recontextualisation of cultural policy from a historical counter-cultural position, suggesting that 'getting to know cultural policy and intervening in it is an important part of participating in culture'.[4] As Adrienne Scullion and Beatriz Garcia put it, in commenting on Miller and Yudice's proposition:

The implied challenge is to strike a balance between the ideas, meaning and theories of cultural policy and their application – that is, between work that reflects back on the academisation of cultural policy [on the one hand] and applied research ... that feeds into policy formulation, implementation and evaluation [on the other].[5]

Indeed, researchers in the field of cultural policy studies as it has evolved over the last couple of decades extend well beyond those owing allegiance to the critical cultural studies tradition. For example, political scientists, economists and self-styled 'policy analysts' – of whom the late Mark Schuster was a paradigm case – have studied processes of cultural production and consumption, the collection and interpretation of cultural data, and the purposes and mechanics of government involvement with the arts and culture in order to draw theoretical and applied conclusions, both positive and normative, concerning the practical administration of cultural policy in the contemporary world. The work of such researchers might raise the ire of cultural theorists such as Frederic Jameson, who saw cooperation with the 'ideological state apparatuses' as a sinister form of anti-intellectualism, or Oliver Bennett, who described the cultural policy discourse inhabited by Schuster as being one from which 'history, values and meaning – in short, the distinctive contribution of both the humanities and a critical sociology – have been drained'.[6] Yet it can be argued that all work in the social sciences is carried out in a recognisable social and political context that informs the entire research process; just as economics cannot ultimately be described as a value-free science, neither can applied cultural policy studies be seen as necessarily lacking an understanding of the social, cultural and economic environment in which it is operating. Perhaps this is not as rich an interaction with theoretical traditions in cultural studies as some would like to see, but at least a pragmatic approach to cultural policy, if thoughtfully pursued, need not be entirely devoid of theoretical content. Indeed, if it should draw upon the intellectual foundations provided by the long history of economic thought, for example, its respect for values and meaning can be quite well established.

Nevertheless, such a self-satisfied assertion does not entirely dispel a lingering concern for the way that some applied cultural policy studies have dealt with, or have simply ignored, the effects of techno-capitalism and the dominance of the neoliberal economic paradigm in guiding national and international policy-making. These defining characteristics of the contemporary global economic system have had a profound impact on the public sphere – the arena within which policy is made – shifting the locus of power from public to private agents and diminishing the public sector's capacity to address serious issues to do with disadvantage, inequality, denial of rights, and so on. For applied cultural policy studies being undertaken in these circumstances, an acknowledgement of the social, economic and cultural environment within which they are being carried out, even if made explicit, may not be enough. Culture raises fundamental questions of value that demand to be recognised, and cultural policy studies should not take such value questions for granted.[7]

One area of cultural policy studies that is indeed concerned with the ways in which deeper issues of social and cultural justice can be addressed is that which connects them with an international agenda for cultural policy development. This area of policy engagement arises from three overarching motives:

- an appreciation of the values attaching to cultural diversity and of the pervasive importance of cultural diversity to economic, social and cultural life;
- a recognition of the increasing importance of intercultural dialogue as a means towards the reduction of cultural tensions and conflicts and towards a greater sense of understanding and respect both within and between nations; and
- an assertion of the fundamental role of human rights as a cornerstone of any cultural policy.

As is apparent, these issues follow closely upon the concerns of UNESCO's recently-adopted Cultural Diversity Convention, which we have discussed in earlier chapters. Indeed, as we have noted, the Convention provides a framework for formulating and implementing cultural policies in member states of UNESCO that is consistent with a central role for culture in national and international affairs. This arena for the emergence of a new internationally sanctioned approach to cultural policy formulation treads a curiously paradoxical path. On the one hand it has pragmatic credentials, connecting directly with the apparatus of actual policy administration at both the national level – through the direct participation of national governments in the implementation of the Convention's provisions within their own territories – and in the international sphere, through its reliance on a variety of standard-setting instruments of relevance to culture. On the other hand, however, the faith in intercultural dialogue and the promotion of the virtues of cultural diversity, which are essential features of the policy recommendations arising in this area, may seem somewhat utopian in a world marked by persistent tensions and seemingly intractable conflicts traceable to fundamental cultural differences.

So how do these various strands in the evolution of cultural policy studies relate to the project of the present volume? Where does economics 'fit' in this picture? It is true that there are plenty of economic studies analysing particular problems in cultural policy, but is there any rationale for a book that seeks to apply the methods of economic theory and analysis across the whole field covered by contemporary cultural policy? Should I have followed Rothfield's lead and appended a question mark to the book's title?

It is difficult to answer these questions without sounding like the sort of material that usually adorns the cover of a book like this one. Suffice it to say in summary terms that this book has endeavoured to show that applying economic theory and analysis to cultural policy can do three things. Firstly, it can draw on the rich intellectual heritage of economics to provide a framework for comprehending what policy-making is about and how its functioning can be analysed. In this regard, the economics to be invoked is not confined to the neoclassical school, with its limited interpretation of the scope of economic behaviour, but embraces the broader dimensions characteristic of classical political economy – in other words, an economics that is flexible, open-minded, and receptive to the intellectual influence of other disciplines in the social sciences and humanities.

The second aspect of the application of economic analysis to cultural policy that this book has tried to demonstrate is the necessity for the recognition of culture. Put simply, we have argued that the distinguishing feature of this area of policy-making is the fact that it is concerned with culture, with all the complexities that that concept entails. This might seem so self-evident as to make it unnecessary for it to be stated in these terms. However, the sort of economics that is conventionally applied to the analysis of cultural policy often seems to overlook this fact. Yet an essential concern of economics is with fundamental notions of value, and as we have argued throughout, a proper application of economics to any avenue of cultural policy concern needs to identify both the economic value and the cultural value involved.

Thirdly, and finally, we have stressed the fact that economics provides not only an intellectual framework for the analysis of cultural policy but also a variety of analytical tools that are capable of leading to practical policy recommendations. This book has ranged over a number of specific areas where public policy engages with the arts and culture, and has pointed to the sorts of pragmatic recommendations that this approach to cultural policy analysis can yield. If such recommendations are derived from analyses that also respect the first two points being made here, they may go some way towards meeting the concerns of the econo-sceptics who fear that the intrusion of economists into their domain will rob them of their distinctive voice.

Where to now? Perhaps it is overly alarmist to say that cultural policy studies is in a state of crisis. But there are certainly many forces at work pulling in different directions. There are at least half a dozen different interest groups, disciplinary factions, assemblages of policy wonks, coalitions of corporate or bureaucratic power, and gatherings of ivory-tower theorists that can be identified, all with their own agendas for the onward direction of the cultural policy caravan. Who will prevail? Will the techno-heads and economic-growth fetishists turn cultural policy into a mere servant of the digital economy? Will the arts establishment manage to retain its favoured status in the parliamentary corridors? Will the old-style revolutionaries, still awaiting the Marxist dawn, finally have their dreams realised? Will the management consultants and efficiency experts consign cultural policy to being just another case study for an MBA? Does anyone care?

Whatever happens in the policy arena, there seems little doubt that the trends in the external environment that affect cultural policy will continue to be felt, especially the processes that are the underlying causes of globalisation. Over the long term, further integration of the world economy is likely, and the technological change that has helped to bring this about will go on giving us new ways of interacting with the arts and culture. Patterns of production and consumption will continue to evolve in response to changes in technology and tastes. Internationally there seems only a faint hope of improvement in the global distribution of income and wealth. In all of these circumstances, governments will continue to have an inalienable responsibility to protect and advance the public interest. In the field of cultural policy this will require constant vigilance to ensure that the right balance is struck between fostering the economic potential of the cultural industries in all their various guises, promoting beneficial social change, and ensuring the long-term health and vitality of the art and culture that is the cornerstone of civilisation.

*Notes*

1 See Rothfield (1999).
2 See McGuigan (2001: 191).
3 As collected, for example, in Justin Lewis and Toby Miller's edited volume (Lewis and Miller, 2003).
4 See Miller and Yudice (2002: 34).
5 See Scullion and Garcia (2005: 117).
6 See respectively Jameson (1993: 29–30); Bennett (2004: 244).
7 For a more detailed discussion of these issues, see McGuigan (2004).

# References

Abrams, Burton A. and Schmitz, Mark D., 1978. 'The "crowding-out" effect of governmental transfers on private charitable contributions', *Public Choice*, **33**(1): 29–39

Acheson, Keith and Maule, Christopher, 2006. 'Culture in international trade', in Ginsburgh and Throsby (eds.) (2006), pp. 1141–1182

Adams, Jeff, 2003. 'The artist-teacher scheme as postgraduate professional development in higher education', *International Journal of Art and Design Education*, **22**(2): 183–194

Adler, Moshe, 2006. 'Stardom and talent', in Ginsburgh and Throsby (eds.) (2006), pp. 895–905

Adorno, Theodor and Horkheimer, Max, 1947. *Dialektik der Aufklärung: Philosophische Fragmente*, Amsterdam: Querido; English trans. by John Cumming, *Dialectic of Enlightenment*, London: Verso, 1979

Alexander, Judith A., 1994. 'Public goods and the public performance tariff: the experience of the Copyright Board of Canada', paper presented at the Economics of Intellectual Property Rights Conference, University of Venice, October 6–8

Allen Consulting Group, 2005. 'Valuing the Priceless: the Value of Historic Heritage in Australia', Research Report 2, Sydney: Heritage Chairs and Officials of Australia and New Zealand

Alper, Neil O. and Wassall, Gregory H., 2006. 'Artists' careers and their labor markets', in Ginsburgh and Throsby (eds.) (2006), pp. 813–864

Americans for the Arts, 2008. *Arts and Economic Prosperity III*, Washington, DC: Americans for the Arts

Andersen, Birgitte, Kozul-Wright, Zeljka and Kozul-Wright, Richard, 2000. 'Copyrights, Competition, and Development', UNCTAD Discussion Paper No. 145, January. Geneva: UNCTAD

Anderson, Maxwell L., 2004. 'Metrics of Success in Art Museums', paper commissioned by Getty Leadership Institute, Los Angeles: Getty Foundation

Appadurai, Arjun, 2006. 'The risks of dialogue' in UNESCO, *New Stakes for Intercultural Dialogue*, Paris: UNESCO, pp. 33–37

Arnold, Matthew, 1869. *Culture and Anarchy*, edited by J. Dover Wilson (1935), Cambridge: Cambridge University Press

Arrow, Kenneth, et al., 1993. 'Report of the NOAA Panel on Contingent Valuation', *Federal Register*, 58: 4601–4614

Arts Council of Great Britain, 1945–1946. *Annual Report*, London: Arts Council of Great Britain

Ashenfelter, Orley and Graddy, Kathryn, 2005. 'Anatomy of the rise and fall of a price-fixing conspiracy: auctions at Sotheby's and Christie's', *Journal of Competition Law and Economics*, 1(1): 3–20

Aston, Jane, 1999. 'Ambitions and destinations: the careers and retrospective views of art and design graduates and postgraduates', *Journal of Art and Design Education*, 18(2): 231–240

Australian Council for the Arts, 1973. *First Annual Report, January – December 1973*, North Sydney: Australian Council for the Arts

Bailey, Christopher, Miles, Steven and Stark, Peter, 2004. 'Culture-led urban regeneration and the revitalisation of identities in Newcastle, Gateshead and the North East of England', *International Journal of Cultural Policy*, 10(1): 47–65

Bakhshi, Hasan, McVittie, Eric and Simmie, James, 2008. *Creating Innovation: Do the Creative Industries Support Innovation in the Wider Economy?*, London: National Endowment for Science, Technology and the Arts

Balsas, Carlos J. L., 2004. 'City centre regeneration in the context of the 2001 European capital of culture in Porto, Portugal', *Local Economy*, 19(4): 396–410

Baniotopoulou, Evdoxia, 2001. 'Art for whose sake? Modern art museums and their role in transforming societies: the case of the Guggenheim Bilbao', *Journal of Conservation and Museum Studies*, 7(1): 1–15

Barrowclough, Diana and Kozul-Wright, Zeljka (eds.), 2008. *Creative Industries and Developing Countries: Voice, Choice and Economic Growth*, London: Routledge

Baumol, William J., 2002. *The Free-Market Innovation Machine: Analyzing the Growth Miracle of Capitalism*, Princeton, NJ: Princeton University Press

Baumol, William J. and Bowen, William G., 1966. *Performing Arts: The Economic Dilemma*, New York: Twentieth Century Fund

Becker, Gary S., 1964. *Human Capital: A Theoretical and Empirical Analysis, with Special Reference to Education*, New York: National Bureau of Economic Research

Bellamy, Carol and Weinberg, Adam, 2008. 'Educational and cultural exchanges to restore America's image', *Washington Quarterly*, 31(3): 55–68

Benhamou, Françoise, 2003. 'Heritage', in Towse (ed.) (2003), pp. 255–262

Benhamou, Françoise, 2006. *Les Dérèglements de l'Exception Culturelle*, Paris: Editions du Seuil

Benhamou, Françoise and Peltier, Stéphanie, 2007. 'How should cultural diversity be measured? An application using the French publishing industry', *Journal of Cultural Economics*, 31(2): 85–107

Bennett, Dawn, 2007. 'Utopia for music performance graduates. Is it achievable, and how should it be defined?', *British Journal of Music Education*, 24(02): 179–189

Bennett, Oliver, 2004. 'Review essay: the torn halves of cultural policy research', *International Journal of Cultural Policy*, 10(2): 237–248

Besen, Stanley M., Kirby, Sheila N. and Salop, Steven C., 1992. 'An economic analysis of copyright collectives', *Virginia Law Review*, 78(1): 383–411

Besen, Stanley M. and Raskind, Leo J., 1991. 'An introduction to the law and economics of intellectual property', *Journal of Economic Perspectives*, 5(1): 3–27

Bille, Trine and Schulze, Günther G., 2006. 'Culture in urban and regional development', in Ginsburgh and Throsby (eds.) (2006), pp. 1051–1100

Blake, Adam, et al., 2001. 'Modelling Tourism and Travel using Tourism Satellite Accounts and Tourism Policy and Forecasting Models', Christel DeHaan Tourism and Travel Research Institute Discussion Paper 2001/4. Nottingham: Nottingham University Business School

Bland, Roger, 2005. 'Rescuing our neglected heritage: the evolution of the Government's policy on portable antiquities in England and Wales', *Cultural Trends*, 14(4): 257–296

Bolton, Richard (ed.), 1992. *Culture Wars: Documents from the Recent Controversies in the Arts*, New York: New Press

Boorsma, Peter B., van Hemel, Annemoon and van der Wielen, Niki (eds.), 1998. *Privatisation and Culture: Experiences in the Arts, Heritage, and Cultural Industries in Europe*, Dordrecht: Kluwer Academic Publishers

Borgonovi, Francesca and O' Hare, Michael, 2004. 'The impact of the National Endowment for the Arts in the United States: institutional and sectoral effects on private funding', *Journal of Cultural Economics*, 28(1): 21–36

Boyle, Stephen, 2007. 'Ownership, Efficiency, and Identity: The Transition of Australia's Symphony Orchestras from Government Departments to Corporate Entities', unpublished PhD thesis. Department of Economics, Macquarie University, Sydney

Bresler, Liora (ed.), 2007. *International Handbook of Research in Arts Education*, Dordrecht: Springer

Brighton, Andrew, 2006. 'Consumed by the political: the ruination of the Arts Council', in Mirza (ed.) (2006), pp. 111–129

Briguglio, Lino, et al. (eds.), 1996. *Sustainable Tourism in Islands and Small States: Issues and Policies*, London: Pinter

British Broadcasting Corporation (BBC), 2004. *Building Public Value: Renewing the BBC for a Digital World*, London: BBC

Brooks, Arthur C., 2000. 'Public subsidies and charitable giving: crowding out, crowding in, or both?', *Journal of Policy Analysis and Management* 19(3): 451–464

Brooks, Arthur C., 2008. 'The public value of controversial art: the case of the *Sensation* exhibit', in Hutter and Throsby (eds.) (2008), pp. 270–282

Brown, Katrina, et al., 1995. 'Tourism and Sustainability in Environmentally Fragile Areas: Case Studies from the Maldives and Nepal', The Centre for Social and Economic Research on the Global Environment: Working Paper GEC-1995–30, University of East Anglia, Norwich, United Kingdom

Bryan, Jane, et al., 2000. 'Assessing the role of the arts and cultural industries in a local economy', *Environment and Planning A*, 32: 1391–1408

Bryant, William D. A. and Throsby, David, 2006. 'Creativity and the behavior of artists', in Ginsburgh and Throsby (eds.) (2006), pp. 507–529

Burnaford, Gail A., 2007. 'Moving toward a culture of evidence: documentation and action research in the practice of arts partnerships', *Arts Education Policy Review*, 108(3): 35–40

Burney, Fanny, 1782. *Cecilia: Or, Memoirs of an Heiress*, London: Virago, 1986

Burrows, Paul, 1994. 'Justice, efficiency and copyright in cultural goods', in Peacock and Rizzo (eds.) (1994), pp. 99–110

Bussell, Helen and Forbes, Deborah, 2006. 'Volunteer management in arts organisations: a case study and managerial implications', *International Journal of Arts Management*, 9(2): 16

Bustamante, Enrique, 2004. 'Cultural industries in the digital age: some provisional conclusions', *Media, Culture and Society*, 26(6): 803–820

Cahir, Linda C., 2004. 'Narratological parallels in Joseph Conrad's *Heart of Darkness* and Francis Ford Coppola's *Apocalypse Now*', in Gene M. Moore (ed.), *Joseph Conrad's Heart of Darkness: A Casebook*, Oxford: Oxford University Press, pp. 183–196

Canada Council for the Arts, 2008. *Moving Forward: Action Plan 2008–2011*, Ottawa: Canada Council for the Arts

Cannon-Brookes, Peter, 1996. 'Cultural-economic analyses of art museums: a British curator's viewpoint', in Ginsburgh and Menger (eds.) (1996), pp. 255–274

Carman, John, 1996. *Valuing Ancient Things: Archaeology and Law*, London: Leicester University Press

Carnegie, Garry D. and Wolnizer, Peter W., 1995. 'The financial value of cultural, heritage and scientific collections: an accounting fiction', *Australian Accounting Review*, 5(9): 31–47

Castells, Manuel, 2001. *The Internet Galaxy: Reflections on the Internet, Business and Society*, Oxford: Oxford University Press

Caves, Richard E., 2000. *Creative Industries: Contracts between Art and Commerce*, Cambridge, MA: Harvard University Press

Cernea, Michael, 2001. *Cultural Heritage and Development: A Framework for Action in the Middle East and North Africa*, Washington, D.C.: World Bank

Champarnaud, Luc, Ginsburgh, Victor and Michel, Philippe, 2008. 'Can public arts education replace arts subsidization?', *Journal of Cultural Economics*, 32(2): 109–126

Chan, Tak Wing and Goldthorpe, John H., 2005. 'The social stratification of theatre, dance and cinema attendance', *Cultural Trends*, 14(3): 193–212

Chantepie, Philippe, et al., 2008. Special issue on 'Culture and the Intangible Economy', *Communications and Strategies*, 71(3)

Cheng, Sao-Wen, 2006. 'Cultural goods production, cultural capital formation and the provision of cultural services', *Journal of Cultural Economics*, 30(4): 263–286

Choi, Andy S., Papandrea, Franco and Bennett, Jeff, 2007. 'Assessing cultural values: developing an attitudinal scale', *Journal of Cultural Economics*, 31(4): 311–335

Coase, Ronald H., 1960. 'The problem of social cost', *Journal of Law and Economics*, 3(1): 1–44

Commonwealth of Australia, 1994. *Creative Nation: Commonwealth Cultural Policy*, Canberra: Department of Communications and the Arts

Commonwealth Foundation, 2008. *Putting Culture First: Commonwealth Perspectives on Culture and Development*, London: Commonwealth Foundation

Connor, Steven, 1992. *Theory and Cultural Value*, Oxford: Blackwell

Costanza, Robert, 1992. *Ecological Economics: the Science and Management of Sustainability*, New York: Columbia University Press

Cowell, Ben, 2007. 'Measuring the impact of free admission', *Cultural Trends*, 16(3): 203–224

Cowen, Tyler, 2006. *Good and Plenty: The Creative Successes of American Arts Funding*, Princeton, NJ: Princeton University Press

Cowen, Tyler and Tabarrok, Anton, 2000. 'An economic theory of avant-garde and popular art, or high and low culture', *Southern Economic Journal*, **35**(2): 232–252

Cunningham, Stuart D., 2006. 'What Price a Creative Economy?', Platform Paper No. 8, Sydney: Currency House

Curran, James, Petley, Julian and Gaber, Ivor, 2005. *Culture Wars: the Media and the British Left*, Edinburgh: Edinburgh University Press

Dalrymple, Lynn, 2006. 'Has it made a difference? Understanding and measuring the impact of applied theatre with young people in the South African context', *Research in Drama Education*, **11**(2): 201–218

Delacroix, Jacques and Bornon, Julien, 2005. 'Can protectionism ever be respectable? A sceptic's case for the cultural exception, with special reference to French movies', *Independent Review,* **9**(3): 353–374

Deodhar, Vinita, 2007. 'Economic Valuation of the Benefits of Local Heritage Policy Programs', unpublished PhD thesis, Department of Economics, Macquarie University, Sydney

Département des Etudes de la Prospective et des Statistiques, 2006. *Aperçu statistique des industries culturelles No. 6*, Paris: Ministry of Culture and Communication

Department for Culture, Media and Sport (DCMS), 2006. 'Creative Industries Economic Estimates Statistical Bulletin'. No. 5, September, London: DCMS

Department for Culture, Media and Sport (DCMS), 2007a. *The Creative Economy Programme: A Summary of Projects Commissioned in 2006/7*, London: DCMS

Department for Culture, Media and Sport (DCMS), 2007b. *Export of Objects of Cultural Interest*, London: DCMS

DeVereaux, Constance, 2006. 'Any way the wind blows: changing dynamics in American arts policy', *Journal of Arts Management, Law and Society,* **36**(3): 168–180

Dodds, Eric R. (ed.), 1966. *The Collected Poems of Louis MacNeice*, London: Faber and Faber

Donegan, Mary and Lowe, Nicola, 2008. 'Inequality in the creative city: is there still a place for "old-fashioned" institutions?', *Economic Development Quarterly,* **22**(1): 46–62

Drew, Philip and Browell, Anthony, 2002. *Sydney Opera House: Joern Utzon*, London: Phaidon

Dubuffet, Jean, 1988. *Asphyxiating Culture and Other Writings*, trans. by Carol Volk, New York: Four Walls Eight Windows

Dwyer, Larry, et al., 2000. 'Economic impacts of inbound tourism under different assumptions regarding the macroeconomy', *Current Issues in Tourism,* **3**(4): 325–363

Dwyer, Larry, Forsyth, Peter and Spurr, Ray, 2004. 'Evaluating tourism's economic effects: new and old approaches', *Tourism Management*, 25(3): 307–317

Edwards-Jones, Gareth, Davies, Ben and Hussain, Salman, 2000. *Ecological Economics: An Introduction*, Oxford: Blackwell

Ellis, Adrian, 2003. *Valuing Culture*, London: AEA Consulting, mimeograph

Engelsman, Steven, 2006. 'Privatization of museums in the Netherlands: twelve years later', *Museum International*, 58(4): 37–42

ERICarts, 2008. *Sharing Diversity: National Approaches to Intercultural Dialogue in Europe. A Study for the European Commission*, Bonn: ERICarts.

Farchy, Joëlle, 1999. *La Fin de l'Exception Culturelle?*, Paris: CNRS Éditions

Farchy, Joëlle, 2003. *Internet et le droit d'auteur*, Paris: CNRS Éditions

Feld, Alan L., O' Hare, Michael and Schuster, J. Mark, 1983. *Patrons Despite Themselves: Taxpayers and Arts Policy*, New York: New York University Press

Filer, Randall K., 1986. 'The "starving artist" – myth or reality? Earnings of artists in the United States', *Journal of Political Economy*, 94(1): 56–75; reprinted in Towse (ed.) (1997), II, pp. 227–246

Fisher, David, 2003. 'Tourism and change in local economic behaviour', in David Harrison (ed.) (2003), pp. 58–68

Flew, Terry, 2002. 'Beyond ad hocery: defining creative industries'. Paper presented at the Cultural Sites, Cultural Theory, Cultural Policy: Second International Conference on Cultural Policy Research, Wellington, New Zealand, 23–26 January

Flôres, Renato G. Jr., 2009. 'A Preliminary Inventory of Data Sources and Indicators on Measuring the Diversity of Cultural Expressions', Report prepared for UNESCO Institute for Statistics, Montréal: UIS

Florida, Richard, 2002. *The Rise of the Creative Class: and How it's Transforming Work, Leisure, Community and Everyday Life*, New York: Basic Books

Florida, Richard, 2008. *Who's Your City?: How the Creative Economy is Making Where You Live the Most Important Decision of Your Life*, New York: Basic Books

Frey, Bruno S., 2003. 'Public support', in Towse (ed.) (2003), pp. 389–398

Frey, Bruno S., 2008. 'What values should count in the arts? The tension between economic effects and cultural value', in Hutter and Throsby (eds.) (2008), pp. 261–269

Frey, Bruno S. and Jegen, Reto, 2001. 'Motivation crowding theory: a survey of empirical evidence', *Journal of Economic Surveys*, 15(5): 589–611

Frey, Bruno S. and Meier, Stephan, 2006. 'The economics of museums', in
Ginsburgh and Throsby (eds.) (2006), pp. 1017–1047

Frey, Bruno S. and Oberholzer-Gee, Felix, 1998. 'Public choice, cost-benefit analysis, and the evaluation of cultural heritage', in Peacock (ed.)
(1998), pp. 27–53

Fukuda-Parr, Sakiko, 2001. 'In search of indicators of culture and development: review of progress and proposals for next steps', paper presented at the Second Global Forum on Human Development, Rio de
Janeiro, Brazil, 9–10 October

Galloway, Susan, 2008. 'Cultural industries or creative industries: a crit-
ical approach', paper presented at the 3es Journées d'Economie de la
Culture: Nouvelles frontières de l'économie de la culture, Paris, 2–3
October

Galloway, Susan and Dunlop, Stewart, 2007. 'A critique of definitions of
the cultural and creative industries in public policy', *International
Journal of Cultural Policy,* 13(1): 17–31

Galt, Frederick S., 2004. 'The life, death, and rebirth of the Cultural
Exception in the multilateral trading system: an evolutionary analysis of cultural protection and intervention in the face of American
pop culture's hegemony', *Washington University Global Studies Law
Review,* 3(3): 909–935

Garnham, Nicholas, 1990. *Capitalism and Communication: Global
Culture and the Economics of Information,* London: Sage

Garnham, Nicholas, 2001. 'Afterword: the cultural commodity and cultural policy', in Selwood (ed.) (2001), pp. 445–458

Garnham, Nicholas, 2005. 'From cultural to creative industries',
*International Journal of Cultural Policy,* 11(1): 15–29

Geber, Kati, 2006. 'Participatory digital cultural content', *Museum
International,* 58(1–2): 121–122

Gee, Constance Bumgarner, 2007. 'Valuing the arts on their own terms?
(Ceci n'est pas une pipe)', *Arts Education Policy Review,* 108(3): 3–12

Gibson, Chris and Klocker, Natascha, 2004. 'Academic publishing as "creative" industry, and recent discourses of "creative economies": some
critical reflections', *Area,* 36(4): 423–434

Gibson, Chris, Murphy, Peter and Freestone, Robert, 2002. 'Employment
and socio-spatial relations in Australia's cultural economy', *Australian
Geographer,* 33(2): 173–189

Gilmore, Audrey, Carson, David and Ascenção, Mário, 2007. 'Sustainable
tourism marketing at a World Heritage site', *Journal of Strategic
Marketing,* 15(2): 253–264

Ginsburgh, Victor and Menger, Pierre-Michel (eds.), 1996. *Economics of
the Arts: Selected Essays,* Amsterdam: North Holland

Ginsburgh, Victor and Throsby, David (eds.), 2006. *Handbook of the Economics of Art and Culture*, vol. i, Amsterdam: Elsevier

Ginsburgh, Victor A., Legros, Patrick and Sahuguet, Nicolas, 2005. 'How to Win Twice at an Auction. On the Incidence of Commissions in Auction Markets', CEPR Discussion Papers 4876, London: Centre for Economic Policy Research

Glass, Aaron, 2004. 'Return to sender: on the politics of cultural property and the proper address of art', *Journal of Material Culture*, 9(2): 115–139

Gordon, Wendy J. and Watt, Richard (eds.), 2003. *The Economics of Copyright: Developments in Research and Analysis*, Cheltenham: Edward Elgar

Graber, Christoph B., 2006. 'The new UNESCO Convention on Cultural Diversity: a counterbalance to the WTO?', *Journal of International Economic Law*, 9(3): 553–574

Grant, Peter S. and Wood, Chris, 2005. *Blockbusters and Trade Wars: Popular Culture in a Globalized World*, Vancouver: Douglas & McIntyre

Gratton, Chris and Taylor, Peter, 1995. 'Impacts of festival events: a case study of Edinburgh', in Gregory J. Ashworth and A.G.J. Dietvorst (eds.), *Tourism and Spatial Transformations: Implications for Policy and Planning*, Wallingford: CAB International, pp. 225–238

Green, Michael and Wilding, Michael, 1970. *Cultural Policy in Great Britain*, Paris: UNESCO

Greenfield, Jeanette, 2007. *The Return of Cultural Treasures*, 3rd edn., Cambridge: Cambridge University Press

Grenier, Robert, Nutley, David and Cochran, Ian (eds.), 2006. *Underwater Cultural Heritage at Risk: Managing Natural and Human Impacts*, Paris: International Council on Monuments and Sites

Gumucio, Mariano B., 1978. *Cultural Policy in Bolivia*, Paris: UNESCO

Hahn, Michael, 2006. 'A clash of cultures? The UNESCO Diversity Convention and international trade law', *Journal of International Economic Law*, 9(3): 515–552

Hall, Peter, 1998. *Cities in Civilisation: Culture, Innovation and Urban Order*, London: Weidenfeld & Nicolson

Harmon, David, 2007. 'A bridge over the chasm: finding ways to achieve integrated natural and cultural heritage conservation', *International Journal of Heritage Studies*, 13(4): 380–392

Harrison, David (ed.), 2003. *Pacific Island Tourism*, New York: Cognizant Communication Corporation

Hartley, John (ed.), 2005. *Creative Industries*, Oxford: Blackwell

Harvey, Lee and Blackwell, Alison, 1999. *Destinations and Reflections: Careers of British Art, Craft and Design Graduates*,

Birmingham: Centre for Research into Quality, University of Central England in Birmingham

Hayes, Nicky and Stratton, Peter, 2003. *A Student's Dictionary of Psychology*, New York: Hodder Arnold

Hearn, Greg, Roodhouse, Simon and Blakey, Julie, 2007. 'From value chain to value creating ecology', *International Journal of Cultural Policy*, 13(4): 419–436

Heckathorn, Douglas D. and Jeffri, Joan, 2001. 'Finding the beat: using respondent-driven sampling to study jazz musicians', *Poetics*, 28(4): 307–329

Heilbrun, James, 2003. 'Baumol's cost disease', in Towse (ed.) (2003), pp. 91–101

Hesmondhalgh, David, 2007. *The Cultural Industries*, 2nd edn., London: Sage

Hesmondhalgh, David and Pratt, Andy C., 2005. 'Cultural industries and cultural policy', *International Journal of Cultural Policy*, 11(1): 1–13

Higgs, Peter, Cunningham, Stuart and Bakhshi, Hasan, 2008. *Beyond the Creative Industries: Mapping the Creative Economy in the United Kingdom*, London: National Endowment for Science, Technology and the Arts

Hodur, Nancy M. and Leistritz, F. Larry, 2007. 'Estimating the economic impact of event tourism', *Journal of Convention and Event Tourism*, 8(4): 63–79

Hoffman, Barbara T. (ed.), 2006. *Art and Cultural Heritage: Law, Policy and Practice*, New York: Cambridge University Press

Holden, John, 2004. *Capturing Cultural Value: How Culture has Become a Tool of Government Policy*, London: Demos

Holden, John, 2008. *Democratic Culture: Opening Up the Arts to Everyone*, London: Demos

Howkins, John, 2001. *The Creative Economy: How People Make Money from Ideas*, London: Penguin

Hughes, Howard L., 1998. 'Theatre in London and the inter-relationship with tourism', *Tourism Management*, 19(5): 445–452

Hughes, Howard L., 2000. *Arts, Entertainment and Tourism*, Oxford: Butterworth Heinemann

Hughes, Patricia N. and Luksetich, William A., 1999. 'The relationship among funding sources for art and history museums', *Nonprofit Management and Leadership*, 10(1): 21–37

Hui, Desmond, et al., 2005. *A Study on Creativity Index*, Hong Kong: Centre for Cultural Policy Research, University of Hong Kong, and Home Affairs Bureau, HKSAR Government

Huntington, Samuel P., 1996. *The Clash of Civilizations and the Remaking of World Order*, New York: Simon and Schuster

Hurt, Robert M. and Schuchman, Robert M., 1966. 'The economic rationale of copyright', *American Economic Review,* 56(1/2): 421–432

Hutter, Michael and Rizzo, Ilde (eds.), 1997. *Economic Perspectives on Cultural Heritage*, London: Macmillan

Hutter, Michael and Throsby, David (eds.), 2008. *Beyond Price: Value in Culture, Economics and the Arts,* New York: Cambridge University Press

Irby, Paul and Hebert, Jim, 2005. *Creative Vitality Index*, Seattle, WA: Washington State Arts Commission and the Office of Arts and Cultural Affairs

Ivey, Bill, 2008. *Arts, Inc.: How Greed and Neglect Have Destroyed our Cultural Rights*, Berkeley, CA: University of California Press

Izushi, Hiro and Aoyama, Yuko, 2006. 'Industry evolution and cross-sectoral skill transfers: a comparative analysis of the video game industry in Japan, the United States and the United Kingdom', *Environment and Planning A,* 38(10): 1843–1861

Jackson, Maria R., Kabwasa-Green, Florence and Herranz, Joaquin, 2006. *Cultural Vitality in Communities: Interpretation and Indicators*, Washington, DC: The Urban Institute

Jacobs, Jane, 1970. *The Economy of Cities*, London: Cape

Jameson, Fredric, 1993. 'On "cultural studies"', *Social Text,* 34: 17–52

Jansson, AnnMari, et al. (eds.), 1994. *Investing in Natural Capital: the Ecological Economics Approach to Sustainability*, Washington, DC: Island Press

Jeffri, Joan and Throsby, David, 1994. 'Professionalism and the visual artist', *European Journal of Cultural Policy,* 1: 99–108

Jelin, Elizabeth, 1998. 'Cities, culture and globalization', in UNESCO (1998a), pp. 105–124

Jennings, Simon, 2005. *The New Artist's Manual: the Complete Guide to Painting and Drawing*, San Francisco: Chronicle Books

Johnston, Alison M, 2006. *Is the Sacred for Sale? Tourism and Indigenous Peoples*, London: Earthscan

Jones, Calvin, Munday, Max and Roberts, Annette, 2003. 'Regional tourism satellite accounts: a useful policy tool?', *Urban Studies,* 40(13): 2777–2794

Jowell, Tessa, 2004. *Government and the Value of Culture*, London: Department for Culture, Media and Sport

KEA European Affairs, 2006. *Economy of Culture in Europe*, Brussels: European Commission, Directorate-General for Education and Culture

Keaney, Emily, 2006. *Public Value and the Arts: Literature Review*, London: Arts Council of England

Keeble, David and Cavanagh, Richard, 2008. 'Concepts in value chain analysis and their utility in understanding cultural industries', in Conference Board of Canada (ed.), *Compendium of Research Papers from the International Forum on the Creative Economy*, Ottawa: Conference Board of Canada, pp. 161–170

King, Karen and Blaug, Mark, 1976. 'Does the Arts Council know what it is doing?', in Mark Blaug (ed.), *The Economics of the Arts*, London: Martin Robinson, pp. 6–16

Kirshenblatt-Gimblett, Barbara, 2006. 'World heritage and cultural economics', in Ivan Karp, et al. (eds.), *Museum Frictions: Public Cultures/Global Transformations*, Durham, NC: Duke University Press, pp. 161–202

Klamer, Arjo and Zuidhof, Peter-Wim, 1999. 'The values of cultural heritage: merging economic and cultural appraisals', in Randall Mason (ed.), *Economics and Heritage Conservation*, Los Angeles: The Getty Conservation Institute, pp. 23–61

Kokkranikal, Jithendran, McLellan, Rory and Baum, Tom, 2003. 'Island tourism and sustainability: a case study of the Lakshadweep Islands', *Journal of Sustainable Tourism*, 11(5): 426–447

Kretschmer, Martin, Klimis, George M. and Wallis, Roger, 1999. 'The changing location of intellectual property rights in music: a study of music publishers, collecting societies and media conglomerates', *Prometheus*, 17(2): 163–186

LaBute, Neil, 2001. *The Shape of Things*, London: Faber and Faber

Lam, Peng E., 2007. 'Japan's quest for "soft power": attraction and limitation', *East Asia*, 24(4): 349–363

Landes, William M., 2000. 'Copyright, borrowed images and appropriation art: an economic approach', *George Mason Law Review*, 9: 1–24

Landes, William M., 2003. 'Copyright', in Towse (ed.) (2003), pp. 9–31

Landes, William M. and Levine, Daniel B., 2006. 'The economic analysis of art law', in Ginsburgh and Throsby (eds.) (2006), pp. 211–251

Landes, William M. and Posner, Richard A., 1989. 'The economic analysis of copyright law', *Journal of Legal Studies*, 18(2): 325–363

Landry, Charles, 2000. *The Creative City: A Toolkit for Urban Innovators*, London: Comedia/Earthscan

Lazzeretti, Luciana (ed.), 2004. *Art Cities, Cultural Districts and Museums: an Economic and Managerial Study of the Culture Sector in Florence*, Florence: Firenze University Press

Leask, Anna and Fyall, Alan (eds.), 2006. *Managing World Heritage Sites*, Amsterdam: Elsevier

Leichenko, Robin M., Coulson, N. Edward and Listokin, David, 2001. 'Historic preservation and residential property values: an analysis of Texas cities', *Urban Studies*, 38(11)

Lewis, Justin and Miller, Toby (eds.), 2003. *Critical Cultural Policy Studies: A Reader*, Oxford: Blackwell

Libreros, Marion, Massieu, Antonio and Meis, Scott, 2006. 'Progress in tourism satellite account implementation and development', *Journal of Travel Research*, 45(1): 83–91

Lichfield, Nathaniel (ed.), 1998. *Evaluation in Planning: Facing the Challenge of Complexity*, Boston: Kluwer Academic Publishers

Liebowitz, Stan, 2003. 'Back to the future: can copyright owners appropriate revenues in the face of new copying technologies?', in Gordon and Watt (eds.) (2003), pp. 1–25

Liikkanen, Mirja, 2007. 'Convention on the Protection and Promotion of the Diversity of Cultural Expressions: Possible Statistical Implications?', Report prepared for UNESCO, Paris: UNESCO

Lindberg, Kreg, 1999. *Sustainable Tourism and Cultural Heritage: A Review of Development Assistance and its Potential to Promote Sustainability*, Paris: World Heritage

Long, Veronica H. and Wall, Geoffrey, 1995. 'Small-scale tourism development in Bali', in Michael V. Conlin and Tom Baum (eds.), *Island Tourism: Management Principles and Practice*, Chichester: John Wiley & Sons, pp. 237–257

Lynn, Jonathan and Jay, Anthony, 1984. *The Complete Yes Minister: the Diaries of a Cabinet Minister by the Right Hon. James Hacker MP*, London: BBC Books

Macleod, Donald V. L., 2006. 'Power, resources and identity: the influence of tourism on indigenous communities', in Peter M. Burns and Marina Novelli (eds.), *Tourism and Social Identities: Global Frameworks and Local Realities*, Amsterdam: Elsevier, pp. 111–124

MacMillan, Fiona and Bowery, Kathy (eds.), 2006. *New Directions in Copyright Law*, vol. III, Cheltenham: Edward Elgar

Madden, Christopher, 2005a. 'Indicators for arts and cultural policy: a global perspective', *Cultural Trends*, 14(3): 217–247

Madden, Christopher, 2005b. 'Cross-country comparisons of cultural statistics: issues and good practice', *Cultural Trends*, 14(4): 299–316

Mann, Thomas, 1912. *Death in Venice*, trans. by Michael H. Hein, New York: Ecco/Harper Collins, 2005

Markusen, Ann, 2006. 'Urban development and the politics of a creative class: evidence from a study of artists', *Environment and Planning A*, 38(10): 1921–1940

Markusen, Ann, et al., 2008. 'Defining the creative economy: industry and occupational approaches', *Economic Development Quarterly*, 22(1): 24–45

Marquis, Alice G., 1995. *Art Lessons: Learning from the Rise and Fall of Public Arts Funding*, New York: Basic Books

Marshall, Alfred, 1890. *Principles of Economics*, London: MacMillan, 8th edn., 1930

Mason, Randall, 2005. *Economics of Historic Preservation: A Guide and Review of the Literature*, Washington, DC: Brookings Institution

Matarasso, François (ed.), 2001. *Recognising Culture: A Series of Briefing Papers on Culture and Development*, Stroud: Comedia, together with the Department of Canadian Heritage and UNESCO

Maurice, Clare and Turnor, Richard, 1992. 'Export licensing rules in the United Kingdom and the Waverley Criteria', *International Journal of Cultural Property*, 1(2): 273–296

McCain, Roger, 2006. 'Defining cultural and artistic products', in Ginsburgh and Throsby (eds.) (2006), pp. 147–167

McCarthy, Kevin F., et al., 2004. *Gifts of the Muse: Reframing the Debate about the Benefits of the Arts*, Santa Monica, CA: RAND Corporation

McCaughey, Claire, 2005. *Comparisons of Arts Funding in Selected Countries: Preliminary Findings*, Ottawa: Canada Council for the Arts

McGuigan, Jim, 2001. 'Problems of cultural analysis and policy in the information age', *Cultural Studies, Critical Methodologies*, 1(2): 190–219

McGuigan, Jim, 2004. *Rethinking Cultural Policy*, Buckingham: Open University Press

McKenna, Wayne and Antonia, Alexis, 1994. 'Intertextuality and Joyce's "Oxen of the Sun" episode in Ulysses: the relation between literary and computational evidence', *Extrait de la Revue Informatique et Statistique dans les Sciences Humaines*, 30(1–4): 75–90

McKercher, Bob and Du Cros, Hilary, 2002. *Cultural Tourism: The Partnership Between Tourism and Cultural Heritage Management*, New York: Haworth Hospitality Press

McKinley, Terry, 1998. 'Measuring the contribution of culture to human well-being: cultural indicators of development', in UNESCO (1998a), pp. 322–332

McMaster, Sir Brian, 2008. *Supporting Excellence in the Arts*, London: Department for Culture, Media and Sport

Meadows, Donella H., et al., 1972. *The Limits to Growth: A Report for the Club of Rome's Project on the Predicament of Mankind*, New York: Universe Books

Meier, Richard, 1997. *Building the Getty*, New York: Alfred Knopf

Menger, Pierre-Michel, 2006. 'Artists' labour markets: contingent work, excess supply and occupational risk management', in Ginsburgh and Throsby (eds.) (2006), pp. 765–811

Miles, Steven and Paddison, Ronan, 2005. 'Introduction: the rise and rise of culture-led urban regeneration', *Urban Studies*, 42(5): 833–839

Miller, Toby and Yúdice, George, 2002. *Cultural Policy*, London: Sage

Minghetti, Valeria, Moretti, Andrea and Micelli, Stefano, 2001. 'Reengineering the museum's role in the tourism value chain: towards an IT business model', *Journal of Information Technology and Tourism*, 4(1): 131–143

Mirza, Munira (ed.), 2006. *Culture Vultures: Is UK Arts Policy Damaging the Arts?*, London: Policy Exchange

Moore, Mark H., 1995. *Creating Public Value: Strategic Management in Government*, Cambridge, MA: Harvard University Press

Moore, Mark H. and Williams Moore, Gaylen., 2005. *Creating Public Value through State Arts Agencies*, Minneapolis, MN: Arts Midwest

Mumford, Lewis, 1958. *The Culture of Cities*, 3rd edn., London: Secker & Warburg

Murdoch, Iris, 1954. *Under the Net*, London: Chatto and Windus

Musgrave, Richard, 1990. 'Merit goods', in Geoffrey Brennan and Cliff Walsh (eds.), *Rationality, Individualism and Public Policy*, Canberra: Centre for Research on Federal Financial Relations, Australian National University, pp. 207–210

Myerscough, John, 1988. *The Economic Importance of the Arts in Britain*, London: Policy Studies Institute

National Endowment for the Arts (NEA), 2007. *How the United States Funds the Arts*, 2nd edn., Washington, DC: NEA

Navrud, Ståle and Ready, Richard C. (eds.), 2002. *Valuing Cultural Heritage: Applying Environmental Valuation Techniques to Historic Buildings, Monuments and Artifacts,* Cheltenham: Edward Elgar

Netzer, Dick, 2006. 'Cultural policy: an American view', in Ginsburgh and Throsby (eds.) (2006), pp. 1233–1251

Nijkamp, Peter, 1995. 'Quantity and quality: evaluation indicators for our cultural-architectural heritage', in Harry Coccossis and Peter Nijkamp (eds.), *Planning for Our Cultural Heritage*, Aldershot: Avebury, pp. 17–37

Noonan, Douglas S., 2003. 'Contingent valuation and cultural resources: a meta-analytic review of the literature', *Journal of Cultural Economics*, 27(3): 159–176

Nye Jr, Joseph S., 1990. 'Soft power', *Foreign Policy*, 80(3): 153–171

Nye Jr, Joseph S., 2004. 'Soft power and American foreign policy', *Political Science Quarterly*, 119(2): 255–270

O'Connor, Justin, 1999. *The Definition of 'Cultural Industries'*, Manchester Institute for Popular Culture, Manchester Metropolitan University, mimeograph

O'Connor, Justin, 2006. 'Art, popular culture and cultural policy: variations on a theme of John Carey', *Critical Quarterly*, 48(4): 49–104

O'Hare, Michael, 1985. 'Copyright: when is monopoly efficient?', *Journal of Policy Analysis and Management*, **4**(3): 407–418

Oakley, Kate, Sperry, Brooke and Pratt, Andy, 2008. *The Art of Innovation: How Fine Arts Graduates Contribute to Innovation*, London: National Endowment for Science, Technology and the Arts

Obuljen, Nina, 2006. 'From *Our Creative Diversity* to the Convention on Cultural Diversity: introduction to the debate', in Nina Obuljen and Joost Smiers (eds.), *UNESCO's Convention on the Protection and Promotion of the Diversity of Cultural Expressions: Making it Work*, Zagreb: Institute for International Relations, pp. 17–38

Paine, Albert Bigelow (ed.), 1972. *Mark Twain's Notebook,* New York: Cooper Square Publishers

Palazuelos, Manuel, 2005. 'Clusters: myth or realistic ambition for policy-makers?', *Local Economy*, **20**(2): 131–140

Papandrea, Franco, 2005. 'Trade and cultural diversity: an Australian perspective', *Prometheus*, **23**(2): 227–237

Pattanaik, Prasanta, 1998. 'Cultural indicators of well-being, some conceptual issues', in UNESCO (1998a), pp. 333–340

Peacock, Alan (ed.), 1998. *Does the Past Have a Future? The Political Economy of Heritage*, London: Institute of Economic Affairs

Peacock, Alan and Rizzo, Ilde (eds.), 1994. *Cultural Economics and Cultural Policies*, Dordrecht: Kluwer

Peck, Jamie, 2005. 'Struggling with the creative class', *International Journal of Urban and Regional Research*, **29**(4): 740–770

Peterson, Richard A., 1992. 'Understanding audience segmentation: from elite and mass to omnivore and univore', *Poetics*, **21**(4): 243–258

Pignatoro, Giacomo, 2003. 'Performance indicators', in Towse (ed.) (2003), pp. 366–372

Plaza, Beatriz, 2000. 'Evaluating the influence of a large cultural artifact in the attraction of tourism: the Guggenheim Museum Bilbao case', *Urban Affairs Review*, **36**(2): 264–274

Porter, Michael E., 1998. *On Competition*, Cambridge, MA: Harvard Business School Press

Porter, Michael E., 2000. 'Localisation, competition and economic development: local clusters in a global economy', *Economic Development Quarterly*, **14**(1): 15–31

Potts, Jason, et al., 2008. 'Social network markets: a new definition of the creative industries', *Journal of Cultural Economics*, **32**(3): 167–185

Pratt, Andy C., 2005. 'Cultural industries and public policy: an oxymoron?', *International Journal of Cultural Policy*, **11**(1): 31–44

Prevots, Naima and Foner, Eric, 2001. *Dance for Export: Cultural Diplomacy and the Cold War*, Middletown, CT: Wesleyan University Press

Productivity Commission (Australia), 2006. 'Conservation of Australia's Historic Heritage Places', PC Inquiry Report No. 37, Canberra: Productivity Commission

Provins, Allan, et al., 2008. 'Valuation of the historic environment: the scope for using economic valuation evidence in the appraisal of heritage-related projects', *Progress in Planning*, 69(4): 131–175

Quinn, Bernadette, 2005. 'Arts festivals and the city', *Urban Studies*, 42(5/6): 927–943

Rahel, Shafie, 1978. *Cultural Policy in Afghanistan*, Paris: UNESCO

Rausch, Stephen and Negrey, Cynthia, 2006. 'Does the creative engine run? A consideration of the effect of creative class on economic strength and growth', *Journal of Urban Affairs*, 28(5): 473–489

Rayward, W. Boyd and Twidale, Michael B., 1999. 'From docent to cyberdocent: education and guidance in the virtual museum', *Archives and Museum Informatics*, 13(1): 23–53

Richards, Greg and Wilson, Julie, 2004. 'The impact of cultural events on city image: Rotterdam, cultural capital of Europe 2001', *Urban Studies*, 41(10): 1931–1951

Richmond, Yale, 2003. *Cultural Exchange and the Cold War: Raising the Iron Curtain*, University Park, IL: Pennsylvania State University Press

Richmond, Yale, 2005. 'Cultural exchange and the Cold War: how the arts influenced policy', *Journal of Arts Management, Law and Society*, 35(3): 239–245

Rizzo, Ilde and Throsby, David, 2006. 'Cultural heritage: economic analysis and public policy', in Ginsburgh and Throsby (eds.) (2006), pp. 983–1016

Rizzo, Ilde and Towse, Ruth (eds.), 2002. *The Economics of Heritage: A Study of the Political Economy of Culture in Sicily*, Cheltenham: Edward Elgar

Robertson, Iain, 2005. *Understanding International Art Markets and Management*, London: Routledge

Robinson, Michael D. and Montgomery, Sarah S., 2000. 'The time allocation and earnings of artists', *Industrial Relations*, 39(3): 525–534

Rocchi, Cesare, et al., 2004. 'The museum visit: generating seamless personalized presentations on multiple devices', in Nuno J. Nunes and Charles Rich (eds.), *Proceedings of the 9th International Conference on Intelligent User Interfaces*, Madeira, Portugal, 2004, pp. 316–318

Rochelandet, Fabrice, 2003. 'Are copyright collecting societies efficient organisations? An evaluation of collective administration of copyright in Europe', in Gordon and Watt (eds.) (2003), pp. 176–197

Rose, Mark, 1994. 'The author in court: Pope v. Curll', in Martha Woodmansee and Jaszi Peter (eds.), *The Construction of Authorship: Textual*

*Appropriation in Law and Literature*, Durham, NC: Duke University Press, pp. 211–229

Rosen, Sherwin, 1981. 'The economics of superstars', *American Economic Review*, 71(5): 845–858

Ross, Malcolm, 2003. 'Evaluating education programmes in arts organisations', *Music Education Research*, 5(1): 69–79

Rothfield, Lawrence, 1999. 'Cultural *Policy* Studies?! *Cultural* Policy Studies?! Cultural Policy *Studies*?! A Guide for Perplexed Humanists', Working Paper, Cultural Policy Center, University of Chicago

Rothfield, Lawrence (ed.), 2001. *Unsettling 'Sensation': Arts-Policy Lessons from the Brooklyn Museum of Art Controversy*, New Brunswick, NJ: Rutgers University Press

Rushton, Michael, 2000. 'Public funding of controversial art', *Journal of Cultural Economics*, 24(4): 267–282

Rushton, Michael, 2003. 'Cultural diversity and public funding of the arts: a view from cultural economics', *Journal of Arts Management, Law and Society*, 33(2): 85–97

Ryan, Chris and Aicken, Michelle (eds.), 2005. *Indigenous Tourism: the Commodification and Management of Culture*, Amsterdam: Elsevier

Salganik, Matthew J. and Heckathorn, Douglas D., 2004. 'Sampling and estimation in hidden populations using respondent-driven sampling', *Sociological Methodology*, 34: 193–239

Santagata, Walter, 2002. 'Cultural districts, property rights and sustainable economic growth', *International Journal of Urban and Regional Research*, 26(1): 9–23

Santagata, Walter, 2006. 'Cultural districts and their role in developed and developing countries', in Ginsburgh and Throsby (eds.) (2006), pp. 1101–1119

Sasaki, Masayuki, 2004. 'The role of culture in urban regeneration'. Paper presented at the Fòrum Universal de les Cultures, Barcelona, 9 May–26 September

Scafidi, Susan, 2005. *Who Owns Culture?: Appropriation and Authenticity in American Law*, New Brunswick, NJ: Rutgers University Press

Schultz, Theodore W., 1961. 'Investment in human capital', *American Economic Review*, 51(1): 1–17

Schuster, J. Mark, 1996. 'The performance of performance indicators in the arts', *Nonprofit Management and Leadership*, 7(3): 253–269

Schuster, J. Mark, 2001. 'Policy and Planning with a Purpose or the Art of Making Choices in Arts Funding', Working Paper, Cultural Policy Center, University of Chicago

Schuster, J. Mark, 2002a. *Informing Cultural Policy: The Research and Information Infrastructure*, Newark, NJ: Center for Urban Policy Research, Rutgers University

Schuster, J. Mark, 2002b. 'Sub-national cultural policy – where the action is: mapping state cultural policy in the United States', *International Journal of Cultural Policy*, 8(2): 181–196

Schuster, J. Mark, 2003. 'Informing cultural policy – data, statistics and meaning', in Serge Bernier and Denise Lievesley (eds.), *Proceedings of the International Symposium on Culture Statistics: Montréal, 21 to 23 October 2002*, Montréal: Government of Québec, pp. 41–61

Schuster, J. Mark, 2006. 'Tax incentives in cultural policy', in Ginsburgh and Throsby (eds.) (2006), pp. 1253–1298

Schuster, J. Mark, 2007. 'Participation studies and cross-national comparison: proliferation, prudence, and possibility', *Cultural Trends*, 16(2): 99–196

Schuster, J. Mark, de Monchaux, John and Riley, Charles A. (eds.), 1997. *Preserving the Built Heritage: Tools for Implementation*, Hanover, NH: University Press of New England

Scott, Allen J., 2005. *On Hollywood: The Place, The Industry*, Princeton, NJ: Princeton University Press

Scott, Carol, 2006. 'Museums: impact and value', *Cultural Trends*, 15(1): 45–75

Scottish Arts Council, 2007. *Corporate Plan 2007–2009*, Edinburgh: Scottish Arts Council

Scullion, Adrienne and García, Beatriz, 2005. 'What is cultural policy research?', *International Journal of Cultural Policy*, 11(2): 113–127

Seaman, Bruce A., 1987. 'Arts impact studies: a fashionable excess', in *Economic Impact of the Arts: A Sourcebook, National Conference of State Legislatures*, pp. 43–75; reprinted in Towse (ed.) (1997), II, pp. 723–755

Seaman, Bruce A., 2004. 'Competition and the non-profit arts: the lost industrial organisation agenda', *Journal of Cultural Economics*, 28(3): 167–193

Seaman, Bruce A., 2006. 'Empirical studies of the demand for the performing arts', in Ginsburgh and Throsby (eds.) (2006), pp. 415–472

Segers, Katia and Huijgh, Ellen, 2006. 'Clarifying the Complexity and Ambivalence of the Cultural Industries', Working Paper No. 8: Centre for Media Sociology, Free University of Brussels.

Selwood, Sara (ed.), 2001. *The UK Cultural Sector: Profile and Policy Issues*, London: Policy Studies Institute

Selwood, Sara, 2006. 'Unreliable evidence: the rhetorics of data collection in the cultural sector', in Mirza (ed.) (2006), pp. 38–52

Sen, Amartya, 1990. 'Development as capacity expansion', in Keith Griffin and John Knight (eds.), *Human Development and the International Development Strategy for the 1990s*, London: Macmillan, pp. 41–58

Senie, Harriet F., 2001. *The Tilted Arc Controversy: Dangerous Precedent?*, Minneapolis, MN: University of Minnesota Press

Shim, Doobo, 2006. 'Hybridity and the rise of Korean popular culture in Asia', *Media, Culture and Society,* **28**(1): 25–44

Shipley, Robert, 2000. 'Heritage designation and property values: is there an effect?', *International Journal of Heritage Studies,* **6**(1): 83–100

Shockley, Gordon E., 2004. 'Government investment in cultural capital: a methodology for comparing direct government support for the arts in the US and the UK', *Public Finance and Management,* **4**(1): 75–102

Sigala, Marianna, 2005. 'New media and technologies: trends and management issues for cultural tourism', in Marianna Sigala and Leslie David (eds.), *International Cultural Tourism: Management, Implications and Cases,* Amsterdam: Elsevier, pp. 181–200

Smeral, Egon, 2006. 'Tourism satellite accounts: a critical assessment', *Journal of Travel Research,* **45**(1): 92–98

Smith, Laurajane and Akagawa, Natsuko (eds.), 2009. *Intangible Heritage,* London: Routledge

Stenou, Katérina (ed.), 2007. *UNESCO and the Issue of Cultural Diversity: Review and Strategy, 1946–2007,* Paris: UNESCO

Sterling, J. Adrian, 2000. *TRIPs Agreement: Copyright and Related Rights,* Luxembourg: Office for Official Publication of European Communities

Strati, Anastasia, 1995. *The Protection of the Underwater Cultural Heritage: An Emerging Objective of the Contemporary Law of the Sea,* The Hague: Martinus Nijhoff Publishers

Strom, Elizabeth, 1999. 'Let's put on a show! Performing arts and urban revitalization in Newark, New Jersey', *Journal of Urban Affairs,* **21**(4): 423–435

The Work Foundation, 2007. *Staying Ahead: the Economic Performance of the UK's Creative Industries,* London: Department for Culture, Media and Sport

Throsby, David, 1992. 'Artists as workers', in Ruth Towse and Abdul Khakee (eds.), *Cultural Economics,* Heidelberg: Springer-Verlag, pp. 201–208

Throsby, David, 1994. 'A work-preference model of artist behaviour', in Peacock and Rizzo (eds.) (1994), pp. 69–80

Throsby, David, 1996. 'Disaggregated earnings functions for artists', in Ginsburgh and Menger (eds.) (1996), pp. 331–346

Throsby, David, 1997a. 'Seven questions in the economics of cultural heritage', in Hutter and Rizzo (eds.) (1997), pp. 12–30

Throsby, David, 1997b. 'Making preservation happen: the pros and cons of regulation', in Schuster, de Monchaux and Riley (eds.) (1997), pp. 32–48

Throsby, David, 1999. 'Cultural capital', *Journal of Cultural Economics,* **23**(1): 3–12

Throsby, David, 2001. *Economics and Culture,* Cambridge: Cambridge University Press

Throsby, David, 2004. 'Assessing the impacts of a cultural industry', *Journal of Arts Management, Law and Society,* **34**(3): 188–204

Throsby, David, 2006. 'Introduction and overview', in Ginsburgh and Throsby (eds.) (2006), pp. 3–22

Throsby, David, 2008a. 'Modelling the cultural industries', *International Journal of Cultural Policy,* **14**(3): 217–232

Throsby, David, 2008b. 'The concentric circles model of the cultural industries', *Cultural Trends,* **17**(3): 147–164

Throsby, David and Hollister, Virginia, 2003. *Don't Give Up Your Day Job: An Economic Study of Professional Artists in Australia,* Sydney: Australia Council

Throsby, David and Zednik, Anita, 2008. 'The Value of Arts and Cultural Activities in Australia: Survey Results', Macquarie Economics Research Paper 2/2008, Sydney: Macquarie University

Thurow, Lester C., 1971. 'The income distribution as a pure public good', *Quarterly Journal of Economics,* **85**(2): 327–336

Tisdell, Clem, 2003. *Ecological and Environmental Economics: Selected Issues and Policy Responses,* Cheltenham: Edward Elgar

Tisdell, Clem and McKee, David L., 2001. 'Tourism as an industry for the economic expansion of archipelagos and small island states', in Clem Tisdell (ed.), *Tourism Economics, the Environment and Development: Analysis and Policy,* Cheltenham: Edward Elgar, pp. 181–189

Tisdell, Clem and Wilson, Clevo, 2002. 'World heritage listing of Australian natural sites: tourism stimulus and its economic value', *Economic Analysis and Policy,* **32**(2): 27–50

Toepler, Stefan, 2006. 'The role and changing face of non-market provision of culture in the United States', *Museum International,* **58**(4): 55–63

Tohmo, Timo, 2005. 'Economic impacts of cultural events on local economies: an input-output analysis of the Kaustinen Folk Music Festival', *Tourism Economics,* **11**(3): 431–451

Towse, Ruth (ed.), 1997. *Cultural Economics: the Arts, the Heritage and the Media Industries,* 2 Vols., Cheltenham: Edward Elgar

Towse, Ruth, 2001. *Creativity, Incentive and Reward: An Economic Analysis of Copyright and Culture in the Information Age,* Cheltenham: Edward Elgar

Towse, Ruth (ed.), 2003. *Handbook of Cultural Economics,* Cheltenham: Edward Elgar

Towse, Ruth, 2006. 'Human capital and artists' labour markets', in Ginsburgh and Throsby (eds.) (2006), pp. 865–894

Tyrrell, Timothy J. and Johnston, Robert J., 2001. 'A framework for assessing direct economic impacts of tourist events: distinguishing origins, destinations, and causes of expenditures', *Journal of Travel Research*, 40(1): 94–100

Ulibarri, Carlos A., 2000. 'Rational philanthropy and cultural capital', *Journal of Cultural Economics*, 24(2): 135–146

UNCTAD, 2008. *Creative Economy Report 2008*, Geneva: United Nations

UNESCO, 1969. *Cultural Policy: A Preliminary Study*, Paris: UNESCO

UNESCO, 1998a. *World Culture Report: Culture, Creativity and Markets*, Paris: UNESCO

UNESCO, 1998b. *Final Report of Intergovernmental Conference on Cultural Policies for Development: The Power of Culture, Stockholm, 30 March–2 April*, Paris: UNESCO

UNESCO, 2000. *World Culture Report No. 2: Cultural Diversity, Conflict and Pluralism*, Paris: UNESCO

UNESCO, 2002. *Universal Declaration on Cultural Diversity*, Paris: UNESCO

UNESCO, 2003. *Convention for the Safeguarding of the Intangible Cultural Heritage*, Paris: UNESCO

UNESCO Institute of Statistics (UIS), 2009. *The 2009 UNESCO Framework for Cultural Statistics*, Montreal: UIS

Upton, Andrew, 2008. *Riflemind*, London: Faber and Faber

van Bruggen, Coosje, 1997. *Frank O. Gehry: Guggenheim Museum Bilbao*, New York: Guggenheim Museum Publications

van der Ploeg, Frederick, 2006. 'The making of cultural policy: a European perspective', in Ginsburgh and Throsby (eds.) (2006), pp. 1183–1222

Varian, Hal R., 2005. 'Copying and copyright', *Journal of Economic Perspectives*, 19(2): 121–138

Vickery, Jonathan, 2007. 'The Emergence of Culture-led Regeneration: A Policy Concept and its Discontents', Centre for Cultural Policy Studies Research Papers No. 9, Coventry: University of Warwick

Young, Greg, 2008. *Reshaping Planning with Culture*, Aldershot: Ashgate

Wall, Geoffrey, 1999. 'Partnerships involving indigenous peoples in the management of heritage sites', in Mike Robinson and Priscilla Boniface (eds.), *Tourism and Cultural Conflicts*, Wallingford: CABI Publishing, pp. 269–286

Weil, Stephen E., 2000. 'Transformed from a cemetery of bric-a-brac', in Institute of Museum and Library Services, *Perspectives on Outcome Based Evaluation for Libraries and Museums*, Washington DC: IMLS, pp. 4–15

West, Edwin G., 1986. 'Arts vouchers to replace grants', *Economic Affairs*, 6(3): 9–16; reprinted in Towse (ed.) (1997), II, pp. 665–668

Wiesand, Andreas and Söndermann, Michael, 2005. *The 'Creative Sector': An Engine for Diversity, Growth and Jobs in Europe: An*

*Overview of Research Findings and Debates prepared for the European Cultural Foundation*, Amsterdam: European Cultural Foundation

Winter, Tim, 2008. 'Post-conflict heritage and tourism in Cambodia: the burden of Angkor', *International Journal of Heritage Studies*, **14**(6): 524–539

World Bank, 2001. 'Tunisia: Cultural Heritage Project, Project Appraisal Document', Report no. 20413, Washington, DC: World Bank

World Bank, 2007. 'Jordan: Cultural Heritage, Tourism and Urban Development Project. Project Appraisal Document', Report no. 38162, Washington, DC: World Bank

World Commission Environment and Development (WCED), 1987. *Our Common Future*, Oxford: Oxford University Press

World Commission on Culture and Development (WCCD), 1995. *Our Creative Diversity*, Paris: UNESCO

World Intellectual Property Organisation (WIPO), 2003. *Guide on Surveying the Economic Contribution of the Copyright-Based Industries*, Geneva: WIPO

Zan, Luca, Baraldi, Sara B. and Gordon, Christopher, 2007. 'Cultural heritage between centralisation and decentralisation: insights from the Italian context', *International Journal of Cultural Policy*, **13**(1): 49–70

# Name index

# Subject index

Printed in Great Britain
by Amazon

66630565R00169